Dog Training

FOR

DUMMIES®

2ND EDITION

by Jack and Wendy Volhard

Wiley Publishing, Inc.

Dog Training For Dummies,® 2nd Edition

Published by
Wiley Publishing, Inc.
111 River St.
Hoboken, NJ 07030-5774
www.wiley.com

For general information on our other products and services, please contact our Customer Care Department within the U.S. at 800-762-2974, outside the U.S. at 317-572-3993, or fax 317-572-4002.

For technical support, please visit www.wiley.com/techsupport.

Wiley also publishes its books in a variety of electronic formats. Some content that appears in print may not be available in electronic books.

Library of Congress Control Number: 2005924073

ISBN: 978-0-7645-8418-3

Manufactured in the United States of America

10 9 8 7

2O/TR/QT/QY/IN

WILEY

About the Authors

Jack and Wendy Volhard share their home with two Labrador Retrievers, a Landseer Newfoundland, three Standard Wirehaired Dachshunds, and one cat. The dogs are more or less well-trained, depending on who you ask, and the cat does his own thing. All are allowed on the furniture, but do get off when told. The Volhards are true practitioners — they have obtained more than 50 conformation and performance titles with their dogs.

Through their classes, lectures, seminars and training camps in the United States, Canada, and England, the Volhards have taught countless owners how to communicate more effectively with their pets. Individuals from almost every state and 15 countries have attended their training camps. Veterinarians, breeders, trainers, and dog owners like you, regularly consult them on questions about behavior, heath, nutrition, and training. Internationally recognized as "trainers of trainers," they're also award-winning authors, and their books have been translated into three languages. This is their ninth book.

In addition to their work together, both Jack and Wendy are well recognized in the training community for their individual accomplishments.

Jack is the recipient of five awards from the Dog Writers' Association of America (DWAA) and an American Kennel Club obedience judge for 30 years. He's the author of more than 100 articles for various dog publications and senior author of *Teaching Dog Obedience Classes: The Manual for Instructors,* knows as "the bible" for trainers, and *Training Your Dog: The Step-by-Step Manual,* named Best Care and Training Book for 1983 by the DWAA.

Wendy is the recipient of four awards from the DWAA. She's the author of numerous articles, a regular columnist for the *American Kennel Gazette,* and co-author of five books, including the *Canine Good Citizen: Every Dog Can be One,* named Best Care and Training Book for 1995 by the DWAA, and *The Holistic Guide for a Healthy Dog,* now in its second edition.

Wendy, whose expertise extends to helping owners gain a better understanding of why their pets do what they do, developed the *Canine Personality Profile,* and her two-part series, "Drives — A New Look at an Old Concept," was named Best Article for 1991 in a Specialty Magazine by the DWAA. She also developed the most widely used system for evaluating and selecting puppies, and her film, *Puppy Aptitude Testing,* was named Best Film on Dogs for 1980 by the DWAA. Wendy specializes in behavior, nutrition, and alternative sources of healthcare for dogs, such as acupuncture and homeopathy, and has formulated a balanced homemade diet for dogs.

Dedication

This book is for those who like their dogs and who have them first and foremost as pets and companions.

Authors' Acknowledgments

All of us are the product of our life experiences. Our life experiences with dogs started in the 1960s, when we were exposed to many of the famous behaviorists of the day. Being avid readers, we absorbed as much information as we could from individuals such as Konrad Most, Konrad Lorenz, and Eberhard Trummler. We discovered why dogs do what they do and how to apply a behavioral approach to training, one that copies how dogs interact with each other. John Fuller's work at Bar Harbor, Maine, and Clarence Pfaffenberger's with Guide Dogs for the Blind, as well as the experiments done in Switzerland by Humphrey and Warner to indicate the working abilities of German Shepherds, all went into the mix that eventually became our *Motivational Method* of training.

Since the 1960s, we have had nine generations of dogs and all of them have been our teachers. We ran an obedience school for 25 years, and all the students and their dogs have been our teachers as well. We continue today with training, seminars, and camps, and we're fortunate to be presented with enough dog challenges to continue our quest for knowledge. So to all of you who have passed through our hands, we thank you and your dogs for providing us with the interest that still drives us today.

Our special thanks to those who contributed to this book and shared their insights: Betsy Blackford, Sheila Hamilton-Andrews, Jane Kelso and the beautiful Labradors of Mountain Run Kennel, Desmond and Lise O'Neill, Hilary Schenk, Danny and Pauline Scott, Gary Wilkes, and Mary Ann Zeigenfuse.

Finally, we thank our editors at Wiley Publishing — Acquisitions Editor Tracy Boggier, Tech Editor Michael Eldridge, Project Editor Natalie Harris, and Copy Editors Chad Sievers and Trisha Strietelmeier. They have demonstrated the two most important qualities of a good dog trainer — patience and persistence.

Publisher's Acknowledgments

We're proud of this book; please send us your comments through our Dummies online registration form located at www.dummies.com/register/.

Some of the people who helped bring this book to market include the following:

Acquisitions, Editorial, and Media Development

Project Editor: Natalie Harris

(Previous Edition: Michael Kelly)

Acquisitions Editor: Tracy Boggier

Copy Editors: Chad Sievers, Trisha Strietelmeier

Editorial Program Assistant: Courtney Allen

General Reviewer: Michael Eldridge

(Previous Edition: Mary Ann Zeigenfuse)

Senior Permissions Editor: Carmen Krikorian

Editorial Manager: Michelle Hacker

(Previous Edition: Pam Mourouzis)

Editorial Assistant: Hanna Scott, Melissa Bennett

Cover Photos: © Abbie Enneking/2005

Interior Photos: Jack and Wendy Volhard, except as indicated

Cartoons: Rich Tennant (www.the5thwave.com)

Composition Services

Project Coordinator: Shannon Schiller

Layout and Graphics: Carl Byers, Joyce Haughey, Heather Ryan, Julie Trippetti

Proofreaders: Leeann Harney, Jessica Kramer, Carl William Pierce, TECHBOOKS Production Services

Indexer: TECHBOOKS Production Services

Publishing and Editorial for Consumer Dummies

Diane Graves Steele, Vice President and Publisher, Consumer Dummies

Joyce Pepple, Acquisitions Director, Consumer Dummies

Kristin A. Cocks, Product Development Director, Consumer Dummies

Michael Spring, Vice President and Publisher, Travel

Kelly Regan, Editorial Director, Travel

Publishing for Technology Dummies

Andy Cummings, Vice President and Publisher, Dummies Technology/General User

Composition Services

Gerry Fahey, Vice President of Production Services

Debbie Stailey, Director of Composition Services

Contents at a Glance

Table of Contents

Part V: The Part of Tens *325*

Introduction

• •

*B*oth of us have had dogs of one kind or another since we were children. Although neither one of us was the primary caregiver, we did have the responsibility of walking the dog.

Children have entirely different expectations of their dogs than adults do. For one thing, children don't believe in leashes. And because both of us were brought up in a city, we had to train our respective dogs to stay close by during our walks. Neither one of us remembers exactly how we did that. No doubt our dogs were smarter than we were and viewed their daily outings as having to keep an eye on us rather than the other way around.

Not until 1968 did we get involved in a more structured way of training. We had a Landseer Newfoundland and were encouraged to join the local training club. Before we knew it, a pleasant pastime turned into a hobby and then an avocation. Before long, we were conducting seminars and five-day training camps, which have taken us to almost every state in the United States, and Canada and England.

More than 30 years later we're still sharing what we have learned along the way. Every one of our dogs has been more of a teacher than a pupil, and we have discovered much more from our dogs than we could ever have hoped to teach them. This book is our attempt to pass on to you what our dogs have taught us.

Without help, few people can become proficient, much less an expert, in a given field. We certainly have had plenty of help. A well-trained dog is the result of education, more yours than your dog's. You need to know what makes a dog a dog, how he thinks, how he reacts, how he grows, how he expresses himself, what his needs are, and most important, why he does what he does. When you understand your dog, you can achieve a mutually rewarding relationship. A dog isn't a homogenous commodity. Each one is a unique individual, and in their differences lies the challenge.

About This Book

We want this book to be a useful tool for you. And we don't want dog training to feel like a chore that you have to slog through step by step. So we've structured this book in such a way that you can jump in and out of the text as it interests you and applies to your situation. For instance, is your dog partially trained, but needs to learn a few things? Then go directly to the chapters you need.

Nor do we expect you to internalize every bit of information in this book. Throughout the text, we include reminders of key points and cross-references to more information about the topic at hand. Remember, dog training is fun! It isn't a series of tests that you have to pass, unless you and your dog enter the world of competitive events.

Conventions Used in This Book

We use the following conventions throughout the text to make everything consistent and easy to understand.

- ✔ All Web addresses appear in `monofont`.
- ✔ New terms appear in *italics* and are closely followed by a definition.
- ✔ **Bold** text indicates keywords in bulleted lists or highlights the action parts of numbered lists.
- ✔ When referring to a specific dog training command or signal, we capitalize it and place it quotation marks. For example, use the "Come" command.

  The same goes for giving commands. For example, if you want your dog, you say "Come."

- ✔ When referring to a position, we capitalize the term. For example, the Heel position.

- ✔ No matter what your dog's name is, in this book we refer to your dog as Buddy. And isn't he your best bud?

What You're Not to Read

We've written this book like any *For Dummies* book so you can easily find just the information that you need. For instance, you may have had a dog for years and you just want a few pointers to help with your training. No matter what your circumstance, chances are you don't have all the time to read every single word. In that case, we simplify it so you can identify "skippable" material. Although this information is interesting and related to the topic at hand, it's not essential for you to know:

- **Text in sidebars:** The sidebars are the shaded boxes you see here and there. They share fun facts and interesting stories, but nothing that's essential to the success of training your dog.

- **Anything with a Technical Stuff icon attached:** This information is interesting, but if you skip it, you still can train your dog successfully. (Check out "Icons Used in This Book" later in this Introduction for more about icons.)

- **The stuff on the copyright page:** Hey, you may find all these Library of Congress numbers and legal language enthralling, but feel free to skip over them if you want.

Foolish Assumptions

In writing this book, we assume a few things about you:

- You have a dog or plan to get one.
- You want your dog to be well behaved — for his sake as well as yours.
- You know little about training a dog, or have tried it on your own with limited success.

Even if you do have training experience, you'll find this book helpful. Through our many years of working with a wide variety of dog breeds and personalities, we have picked up many tricks that are sure to prove useful even to experienced dog trainers.

How This Book Is Organized

In structuring this book, we went from basic to intermediate and finally to advanced training. Each part contains the respective training progressions you need, plus some supplementary information to ensure success. You can apply all of it to your dog — or just the parts you want.

Part I: Training for You and Your Dog

This part helps you prepare yourself for the task of training your dog. In this part you find chapters on recognizing the importance of training, setting the stage for training, surviving the puppy period, housetraining, understanding your dog's mind, selecting training equipment such as collars and leashes, and training your dog in the basics — sitting, staying, coming when called, walking without pulling, and more.

Part II: Giving Your Dog's Training Its Best Shot

In this part, you find out about how you can ensure training success, from developing training savvy to dealing with the not-so-pleasant behaviors that your dog may exhibit from time to time. We also include your introduction to organized dog events — training your dog to become a Canine Good Citizen, the enormously popular American Kennel Club–administered program.

Part III: Training for Competition

In this part you get down to training your dog for competitive events held under the auspices of the American Kennel Club (AKC). Each chapter takes you through the various levels from basic control to advanced training.

Part IV: Beyond Training: Addressing Your Dog's Needs

Your dog's nutritional needs and his health contribute a great deal to his behavior, so this part talks about the importance of good nutrition and quality healthcare. We also include a chapter on when and where to get professional help.

Part V: The Part of Tens

Every *For Dummies* book has The Part of Tens. In this part, you find quick lists of ten items each — bits of handy information about dog training and other related topics that you can read through in a flash. For fun and games, check out the chapter on tricks.

Icons Used in This Book

To help you navigate your way through the text, we have included some highlights of important material, some hints, some cautions, and some true stories of success. This key information is marked with little pictures (or icons) in the margins. Here's what the icons tell you:

This icon draws your attention to ways to save time, money, energy, and your sanity.

This icon raises a red flag; your safety or your dog's may be at risk. It also tells you about the don'ts of dog training. Proceed at your own risk!

This icon directs you to information that's important to remember — key points that you'll want to focus on.

This icon highlights more in-depth information that isn't critical for you to know, but can enhance your knowledge of dog training and may make you a better teacher.

This icon points out dog training techniques and strategies that our clients and we have found to be successful.

Where to Go from Here

The important thing about dog training is to get started *today*. The sooner you train your dog to behave the way you want him to, the sooner the two of you can live in peace together, and the more problems you can prevent down the road. So turn the page (or use the Table of Contents or Index to get to the information you need the most) and get going! Your dog will thank you for it.

Part I
Training for You and Your Dog

The 5th Wave   By Rich Tennant

"We're still working on the basic commands. 'sit', 'stay', 'stop flushing daddy's neckties down the toilet'..."

In this part . . .

You can't expect a dog to do what you want him to do (or *don't* want him to do) unless you show him what your expectations are. And your dog won't learn properly or be willing to heed your commands unless you use effective training methods. In this part, we describe how to prepare yourself, the human part of the equation, for training: how to choose the right approach, how to adapt your methods to your particular dog, and how to establish yourself as pack leader.

If your dog is still a puppy, we explain what a puppy goes through to help you understand what he needs both physically and emotionally. You'll appreciate the chapter on housetraining, of critical importance to every dog owner. We also help you select the best leashes and collars for training and explain why bribery in the form of treats really works. Finally, we walk you through basic training maneuvers such as sitting, staying, and coming when called — the things that every well-behaved dog needs to know.

Chapter 1

Recognizing Why Dog Training Is Important

*O*ver the course of the last 30 years, dog training has undergone enormous changes. When we started training dogs in the late 1960s, dogs were hauled around on choke chains and jerked every which way without any clue of what was expected of them. They did get trained, but it wasn't pretty.

We felt that there was an inherent unfairness in "correcting" a dog that had no idea why he was being corrected. There had to be a fairer way — a way in which the dog is systematically taught a command without the use of sheer brute force.

At that time, the use of food in training was considered anathema, and when we introduced food in the teaching process, the dog training community promptly labeled us heretics. Today, the use of food in training is considered de rigueur. As a result, training has become user-friendlier for you and your dog.

As a gift to yourself and your dog, as well as your family and your friends and neighbors, train your dog. Doing so means sanity for you, safety for your dog, and compliments from people you meet. Make him an ambassador of good-will for all dogs. Your dog has a life expectancy of 8 to 16 years. Now is the time to ensure that these years are mutually rewarding for you and your dog. This book shows you how to teach him to be the well-trained dog you want him to be. Believe us, it's well worth the investment.

Identifying a Well-Trained Dog

A well-trained dog is a joy to have around. He is welcome almost anywhere because he behaves around people and around other dogs. He knows how to stay, and he comes when called. He's a pleasure to take for a walk, and he can be let loose for a romp in the park. He can be taken on trips and family outings. He is a member of the family in every sense of the word.

The most important benefit for your dog is your safety, the safety of others, and his own safety. A dog that listens and does what he's told rarely gets into trouble. Instead of being a slave to a leash or a line, a trained dog is truly a free dog — he can be trusted to stay when told, not to jump on people, to come when called, and not to chase a cat across the road.

For more than 30 years, we have taught dog training classes, seminars, and weeklong training camps. We listen carefully when our students tell us what a well-trained dog should be. First and foremost, they say, he has to be house-trained (see Chapter 4). After that, in order of importance, a well-trained dog is one who

- Doesn't jump on people
- Doesn't beg at the table
- Doesn't bother guests
- Comes when called
- Doesn't pull on the leash

Note that these requirements, with one exception, are expressed in the negative — that is, *dog, don't do that.* For purposes of training, you need to express these requirements in the positive so that you can teach your dog exactly what you expect from him. (See Chapter 10.) Here is what the new list of requirements for a well-trained dog looks like:

- Sit when I tell you.
- Go somewhere and chill out.

> ✔ Lie down when I tell you and stay there.
>
> ✔ Come when called.
>
> ✔ Walk on a loose leash.

The "Sit" and "Down-Stay" commands are the building blocks for a well-trained dog; if Buddy knows nothing else, you can live with him. Of course, your Buddy might have some additional wrinkles that need ironing out, some of which are more matters of management than training (see Chapter 10). He may enjoy *landscaping,* as do our Dachshunds, who delight in digging holes in the backyard and can do so with amazing speed and vigor. Unless you're willing to put up with what can become major excavation projects, the best defense is to expend this digging energy with plenty of exercise, training, and supervision. Another favorite pastime of some dogs is raiding the garbage. Prevention is the cure here: Put the garbage where your dog can't get to it.

One of our Dachshunds learned to open the refrigerator by yanking on the towel we kept draped through the door handle and to help himself to anything he could reach. Prevention was the answer. We removed the towel.

Identifying the Basic Five Commands

Every dog needs to know five basic commands: "Sit," "Go Lie Down," "Down," "Come," and "Easy." You can look at these as safety and sanity commands — your dog's safety and your sanity.

The "Sit" command

You use the "Sit" command (check out Chapter 7) to teach your dog to sit politely for petting instead of jumping on people, to sit at the door instead of barging ahead of you, to sit when you put his food dish on the floor instead of trying to grab it out of your hand, and anytime you need him to control himself. See Figure 1-1.

The "Go Lie Down" command

You use the "Go Lie Down" command (see Chapter 7) to send your dog to a particular place and stay there when you want to eat your meal in peace instead of having him beg at the table, or when you have company instead of having him pester your guests.

Figure 1-1:
Dogs and puppies sit naturally, but training them to do so on command helps keep them well behaved.

Photograph by Jane Kelso

The "Down" command

You use the "Down" command (see Chapters 7 and 16) when you want him to down in place and stay there until you release him.

The "Come" command

You need to teach your dog the "Come" command (see Chapters 8 and 14) so you can call him when you take him for a hike or when he wants to chase a squirrel, or whatever.

The "Easy" command

You want to teach your dog the "Easy" command (check out Chapter 8) so that you can walk him on leash without being pulled off your feet.

What is an untrained dog?

The untrained dog has few privileges. When guests come, he is locked away because he is too unruly. When the family sits down to eat, he's locked up or put outside because he begs at the table. He's never allowed off leash because he runs away and stays out for hours at a time. Nobody wants to take him for a walk because he pulls, and he never gets to go on family outings because he's a nuisance.

Dogs are social animals, and one of the cruelest forms of punishment is to deprive them of the opportunity to interact with family members on a regular basis. Isolating a dog from contact with humans is inhumane. Spending quality time with your dog by training him will make him the beloved pet he deserves to be.

Just Who Is Training Whom?

Training is a two-way street: Buddy is just as involved in training you as you are in trying to train him. The trouble is that Buddy is already a genius at training you, a skill with which he was born. Put another way, a dog comes into the world knowing what is to his advantage and what isn't, and he'll do whatever he can to get what he wants. You, on the other hand, have to discover the skills of training him, just as we had to. (See Chapter 2.)

One of these skills is figuring out how to recognize when you're inadvertently rewarding behaviors you may not want to reinforce. Begging at the dinner table is a good example. When Buddy begs at the table and you slip him some food, he is training you to feed him from the table. You need to ask yourself, "Is this a behavior I want to encourage?" If the answer is no, then stop doing it, no matter what. (And check out Chapter 7.)

Most dogs eventually ignore commands that don't lead to tangible consequences. When he responds to a command, reward him by praising him. If he chooses not to respond to a command he has been taught, correct him.

Now look at another situation: Buddy has taken himself for an unauthorized walk through the neighborhood. You're late for an appointment but don't want to leave with Buddy out on the streets. You frantically call and call. Finally, Buddy makes an appearance, happily sauntering up to you. You, on the other hand, are fit to be tied, and you let him know your displeasure in no uncertain terms by giving him a thorough scolding. You now need to ask yourself, "Is this the kind of greeting that will make Buddy want to come to me?" If the answer is no, then stop doing it, no matter what. (And check out Chapter 8.)

Here are two examples of how your dog is training you:

- ✔ Buddy drops his ball in your lap while you're watching television and you throw it for him.
- ✔ Buddy nudges or paws your elbow when you're sitting on the couch and you pet him.

Buddy has trained you well. Is there anything wrong with that? Not at all, *provided* you can tell him to go lie down when you don't feel like throwing the ball or petting him.

Understanding the YOU Factor

Several factors influence how successful you'll be in turning your pet into a well-trained dog. Some of these are under your direct control, and others come with your dog.

The factors that are under your direct control are

- ✔ Your expectations
- ✔ Your attitude
- ✔ Your dog's environment
- ✔ Your dog's social needs
- ✔ Your dog's emotional needs
- ✔ Your dog's physical needs
- ✔ Your dog's nutritional needs

There is a direct relationship between your awareness and understanding of these factors and your success as your dog's teacher. This section focuses on the first two factors: your expectations and your attitudes. We deal with the other factors in Chapter 9.

Knowing your expectations

Most people have varying ideas of what they expect from their companions. Some of these expectations are realistic; others aren't. You have heard people say, "My dog understands every word I say," and perhaps you think that your dog does. If it were as easy as that, you wouldn't need dog trainers or training books.

Sometimes your dog may seem to really understand what you say. However, if a dog understands every word his owner says, how come the dog doesn't do what he is told? Still, enough truth does exist to perpetuate the myth. Although dogs don't understand the words you use, they do understand tone of voice, and sometimes even your intent.

Are your expectations realistic?

Do you believe your dog obeys commands because he

- ✔ Loves you
- ✔ Wants to please you
- ✔ Is grateful
- ✔ Has a sense of duty
- ✔ Feels a moral obligation

We suspect that you answered, "yes" to the first and second questions, became unsure at the third question, and then realized that we were leading you down a primrose path.

If your approach to training is based on moral ideas regarding punishment, reward, obedience, duty, and the like, you're bound to handle the dog in the wrong way. No doubt your dog loves you, but he won't obey commands for that reason. Does he want to please you? Not exactly, but it sometimes seems like he does. What he is really doing is pleasing himself.

Moreover, Buddy doesn't have the least bit of gratitude for anything you do for him and won't obey commands for that reason either. He's interested in only one thing: What's in it for me right now? Buddy certainly has no sense of duty or feelings of moral obligation. The sooner you discard beliefs like that, the quicker you'll come to terms with how to approach his education.

Are your expectations too low?

Do you believe your dog doesn't obey commands because he

- ✔ Is stubborn
- ✔ Is hardheaded
- ✔ Is stupid
- ✔ Lies awake at night thinking of ways to aggravate you

If you answered "yes" to any of these, you're guilty of *anthropomorphizing,* that is, attributing human characteristics and attributes to an animal. Making this characterization is easy to do, but it doesn't help in your training.

Dogs aren't stubborn or hardheaded. To the contrary, they're quite smart when it comes to figuring out how to get their way. And they don't lie awake at night thinking of ways to aggravate you — they sleep, just like everybody else.

What should your expectations be?

So why does your dog obey your command? Usually for one of three reasons:

- ✔ He wants something.
- ✔ He thinks it's fun, like retrieving a ball.
- ✔ He has been trained to obey.

When he obeys for either the first or the second reason, he does it for himself; when he obeys for the third reason, he does it for you. This distinction is important because it deals with reliability and safety. Ask yourself this question: If Buddy obeys only because he wants something or because it's fun, will he obey when he doesn't want something or when it's no longer fun? The answer is obvious.

The well-trained dog obeys because he has been trained. This doesn't mean you and he can't have fun in the process, so long as the end result is clearly understood. When you say, "Come," there are no options, especially when the safety of others, or his own, is involved.

Knowing your attitude

One of the most important aspects of training is your attitude toward your dog. During training, you want to maintain a friendly and positive attitude. For many people, maintaining this attitude can be enormously difficult because frequently they don't start to think about training until Buddy has become an uncontrollable nuisance. He's no longer cute and cuddly, he has become incredibly rambunctious, everything he does is wrong, and he certainly doesn't listen.

Don't train your dog when you're irritable or tired. You want training to be a positive experience for your dog. If you ever get frustrated during training, stop and come back to it at another time. When you're frustrated, your communications consist of "no," "bad dog," "how could you do this," and "get out and stay out." You're unhappy and Buddy is unhappy because you're unhappy.

A better approach is to train him with firm kindness so both of you can be happy. An unfriendly or hostile approach doesn't gain you your dog's cooperation and will needlessly prolong the training process. When you become frustrated or angry, the dog becomes anxious and nervous, and is unable to learn (see Chapter 9). When you feel that you're becoming a little irritable, stop training and come back to it in a better frame of mind. You want training to be a positive experience for Buddy (and you).

Training and your dog's age

From birth until maturity, your dog goes through physical and mental developmental periods. What happens during these stages can, and often does, have a lasting effect on your dog. His outlook on life will be shaped during these periods, as will his behavior.

The age at which a puppy is separated from its mother and littermates has a profound influence on his behavior as an adult. Taking a pup away from the mother too soon may have a negative effect on his ability to handle training. For example, housetraining may be more difficult under these circumstances. A pup's ability to learn is important to becoming a well-trained dog. It will also affect his dealings with people and other dogs. So what is the ideal time for your puppy to make the transition to its new home? All the behavioral studies that have been done recommend the 49th day, give or take a day or two.

These studies have also shown that dogs begin to learn at 3 weeks of age. At 7 weeks old, their brains are neurologically complete, and all the circuits are wired. Their mind is a blank page, and all you have to do is fill it with the right information. They won't forget what they learn in the next few weeks. If you wait until your dog is older, he'll probably have picked up several bad habits, which means you have to erase the page and start all over, a much more tedious job than starting when he's a puppy.

Figuring Out How Your Dog Thinks

Does your dog think? Certainly. He just thinks like a dog, and to anyone who has been around dogs, sometimes it's uncanny! It's almost as though he can read your mind. But is it your mind he is reading, or has he simply memorized your behavior patterns?

Using your powers of observation, you too can discover what goes through Buddy's mind. The direction of his eyes, his body posture, his tail position, the position of his ears, up or down, and the direction of his whiskers, pointed forward or pulled close to his muzzle, are all indicators of what he is thinking at the moment. The more the two of you interact, the better you'll become at knowing what Buddy thinks.

"Reading" your dog

Just as your dog takes his cues from watching you, so can you figure out how to interpret what's on his mind by watching him. For instance, you know Buddy has the propensity to jump on the counter to see whether he can find any food to steal. Because he has done this a number of times before, you begin to recognize his intentions by the look on his face — for example, head and ears are up, whiskers pointed forward, intent stare — and the way he moves in the direction of the counter — with deliberate tail wagging.

What do you need to do? You interrupt Buddy's thought process by derailing the train. Say "just a minute, young man, not so fast," in a stern tone of voice. You can also whistle or clap your hands, anything to distract him. After that, tell him to go lie down and to forget about stealing the food.

What if he has already started the objectionable behavior? He has his paws firmly planted on the counter and is just about to snatch the steak. Use the same words to stop the thought process, physically remove him from the counter by his collar, and take him to his corner and tell him to lie down. For more on "reading" your dog, see Chapter 5.

When you don't read your dog in time

What should you do if your dog has already managed to achieve the objectionable behavior? Absolutely nothing! Discipline after the fact is useless and inhumane. Your dog can't make the connection. The time to intervene is when your dog is thinking about what you don't want him to do.

Don't attempt any discipline after the offending deed has been accomplished. Your dog can't make the connection between the discipline and his actions. Your dog may look guilty, but not because he understands what he has done; he looks guilty because he understands you're upset.

Visualize yourself preparing a piece of meat for dinner. You leave the counter to answer the phone and after you return, the meat is gone. You know Buddy ate it. Your first reaction is anger. Immediately, Buddy looks guilty, and you assume he's guilty because he knows he has done wrong. However, Buddy knows no such thing. He's reacting to your anger and wonders why you're mad and, perhaps based on prior experience, expects to be the target of your wrath.

Your dog is already an expert at reading you. With a little time and practice, you, too, will be able to tell what's on his mind and read him like a book. His behavior is just as predictable as yours.

Look at it from Buddy's viewpoint. He thoroughly enjoyed the meat. Unfortunately, it's gone, and you can't bring it back. Nor can you make him un-enjoy it. If you discipline Buddy now, he won't understand why because he can't make the connection between the discipline and the meat he just ate. He can only make the connection between your anger and being disciplined.

If you don't believe us, try this experiment. Without Buddy's seeing you, drop a crumpled up piece of paper on the floor. Call Buddy to you and point accusingly at the paper and say in your most blaming voice, "What have you done, bad dog!" He will reward you with his most guilty look without having a clue what it's all about.

Moral of the story: Don't leave your valued belongings such as shoes, socks, or anything else near and dear to your heart lying about, where your dog can destroy them. Look at it this way — if you weren't a neat freak before you got your dog, you will be now.

If you attribute human qualities and reasoning abilities to your dog, your dealings with him are doomed to failure. He certainly doesn't experience guilt. Blaming the dog because "he ought to know better," or "he shouldn't have done it," or "how could he do this to me" won't improve his behavior. He also doesn't "understand every word you say," and is only able to interpret your tone of voice and body language.

Tackling distractions

Training your dog to respond to you in your backyard, with you being the center of his attention, is fairly simple. But then, the level of difficulty increases in relationship to the distractions the dog encounters in real life, such as:

- Joggers and cyclists
- New locations
- Other dogs
- Other people
- People coming to your home
- Wildlife

The ultimate goal of training is to have your dog respond to you under any and all circumstances. Your dog's Personality Profile (check out Chapter 5) can tell you how you have to train him to reach that goal. Also see Chapters 8, 13, and 14 for training around distractions, and Chapter 10 for more on dealing with objectionable behaviors.

Exploring Advanced Training for Fun and Competition

Obedience competitions for companion dogs date back to the early 1930s, and the first obedience trial under American Kennel Club (AKC) rules took place in 1936. The purpose of obedience trials, as stated in the AKC Obedience Regulations, is to "demonstrate the dog's ability to follow specified routines in the obedience ring and emphasize the usefulness of the purebred dog as a companion of man." We touch on the main trials in this section.

The Novice, Open, and Utility classes

The three obedience classes, Novice, Open, and Utility, are designed so that dogs of any breed can participate. The level of difficulty increases with each class. The Novice class consists of basic control exercises, such as Heeling On and Off Leash, Coming When Called, and a Sit and Down-Stay (see Chapters 13 and 14). The Open class consists of Heeling Off Leash, Retrieving and Jumping, and a Sit and Down-Stay with the owner out of sight of the dog (see Chapters 15 and 16). In the Utility class the dog is expected to respond to signals to Heel, Sit, Stand and Down, and a more complex Retrieving exercise (see Chapter 17).

The Canine Good Citizen Certificate

In the early 1970s the AKC developed the popular Canine Good Citizen test, the only AKC-administered program for both purebred dogs and mixed breeds. The Canine Good Citizen test uses a series of exercises that demonstrate the dog's ability to behave in an acceptable manner in public. Its purpose is to show that the dog, as a companion for all people, can be a respected member of the community and can be trained and conditioned to always behave in the home, in public places, and in the presence of other dogs in a manner that reflects credit on the dog (see Chapter 12).

Agility, Rally Obedience, and more

Since the Canine Good Citizen was started, the AKC has added Agility competitions (see Chapter 21) and most recently, Rally Obedience (see Chapter 13). For different breed-specific competitive events, such as Field Trials and Hunting Tests, Earthdog Trials, and Lure Coursing, see Chapter 21.

More than Training: Understanding How Dogs Help People

Man and dog have been together for a long time. It didn't take man long to recognize the dog's potential as a valuable helper. Originally, the dog's main jobs were guarding, hauling, herding, and hunting. Over time, more jobs were added and now dogs perform an amazing variety of tasks. These tasks fall into four broad categories: service dogs, detection dogs, assistance dogs, and companion dogs. (See Chapter 21 for more information.)

Chapter 2

Setting the Stage for Training

●●

●●

*T*he term "training" is used to describe two separate and distinct concepts:

✔ **To teach Buddy to do something that you want him to do, but that he wouldn't do on his own.** For example, Buddy knows how to sit and sits on his own, but you want him to sit on command, something he doesn't do on his own without training.

This concept is called *action* training. *Action* training relies mainly on using pleasant experiences, such as inducing your dog to sit with a treat. Teaching Buddy the commands "Sit," "Down," "Stand," and "Come" are examples of action training.

✔ **To teach Buddy to stop doing something he would do on his own, which you don't want him to do.** For example, Buddy chases bicyclists, something he does on his own that you want him to stop.

This concept is called *abstention* training. *Abstention* training typically relies on unpleasant experiences. The dog learns to avoid the unpleasant experience by not chasing the bicyclist. For example, to teach Buddy not to pull on the leash, use a check. A *check* is a crisp snap on the leash with an immediate release of tension. In order to be effective, the leash must be loose before the check is made. Buddy can avoid the check by not pulling. Another example of an abstention exercise is the "Stay" command — don't move.

The Quasi training of Cece

For more than 30 years, we've had a multidog household and at least one cat, and have witnessed the abstention training phenomenon countless times. Our current menagerie consists of three Standard Wirehaired Dachshunds, ranging in age from 2 to 16, two Labrador Retrievers, 2 and 6, an 8-year old Landseer Newfoundland, and Quasi, an 18-year old male cat who was left on our door step when he was 6 weeks old. Quasi is an expert at *abstention* training.

When we got our youngest Dachshund, Cece, she was 8 weeks old. Naturally, she was quite respectful of the older dogs, but treated Quasi as though he was a stuffed toy. Quasi, who had brought up a number of puppies, was amazingly tolerant of Cece. When Cece got too rough with

him, he would growl and hiss, and hit her with his paw. When Cece didn't get the message, Quasi finally let her have it — he hauled off, all claws extended, and swiped her across the nose. Cece screamed and jumped back in horror, her nose dripping with blood.

Was Cece psychologically scarred for life? Did Cece take offense? Did she go away and sulk? Did she hold a grudge against Quasi? Nothing of the kind. Cece didn't hold any hard feelings; in fact, she gained a little more respect for Quasi. They still play together, and they sleep together. The only difference is that Cece discovered an important lesson — unacceptable behavior results in unpleasant experiences. Incidentally, all the other dogs received the same treatment at one point or another.

Dogs already know avoiding unpleasant experiences is to their advantage because that is how they deal with each other. The training begins with the mother dog. When the puppies reach about 6 weeks old, she begins the weaning process. At that point in time, the puppies have sharp little teeth, not very pleasant for the mother when she feeds them. She begins to growl at the puppies to communicate to them not to bite so hard. She snarls and snaps at those who ignore her growls until they stop. An offending puppy may scream to high heaven and roll over on its back, having learned its lesson. The mother dog usually follows the disagreeable experience by an agreeable one — by nuzzling the puppy.

This chapter focuses on the different models of dog training, from traditional training to operant conditioning and clicker training. Although the dog hasn't changed, the approach to training him has been refined. We take you on a brief tour of the major training theories, their terminologies, and how they fit together.

Selecting a Training Model

There are many ways to train a dog, ranging from rather primitive to fairly sophisticated. Even technology has had its impact on dog training. For example, rather than fenced yards, people now have invisible fences, which contain dogs within their confines by means of an electrical shock.

The method, or combination of methods, you ultimately choose depends on which one works best for you and your dog. Our purpose in this chapter is to provide you with options so you can select one that suits your personality and needs, as well as those of your dog. To make the decision which approach is best for your dog, check out Chapter 5.

Before you embark on your training program, consider what you want your dog to master and compare it to the task for which he was bred. Many people typically select their dogs based on appearance and without regard to breed-specific functions and behaviors. The results are frequently all too predictable — the cute little puppy becomes a grown dog and now no longer fits into the scheme of things.

Although most dogs can be trained to obey basic obedience commands, breed-specific traits determine the ease or difficulty. For example, both the Newfoundland and the Parson Russell Terrier can learn a "Down-Stay" command, but we suspect you'll need a great deal more determination, patience, and time to teach this exercise to the Parson Russell Terrier than you will to the Newfoundland.

According to the 2003 statistics of the American Kennel Club (AKC), the Labrador Retriever was first in registrations, with almost three times the number of registrations as the second most popular breed, the Golden Retriever — 144,934 to 52,530. We're not questioning that the Labrador is a fine breed — we have two ourselves. Labs tend to be healthy, are good with children, are easy to train, have an average protectiveness trait, and require little grooming. What prospective buyers frequently don't consider, however, are the Lab's activity level and exercise requirements, both of which are high. Moreover, as the name implies, a Labrador Retriever is a retriever, which means he likes to retrieve, anything and everything that isn't nailed down and doesn't necessarily belong to him.

An excellent resource for breed-specific behavior and traits is *The Roger Caras Dog Book: A Complete Guide to Every AKC Breed,* by Roger Caras and Alton Anderson (M. Evans & Co.), now in its third edition. For instance, the book shows how the Labrador is one of 24 breeds in the Sporting Group. For each breed, the book lists a scale from 1 to 10 of three characteristics: the amount of coat care required, the amount of exercise required, and the suitability for urban/apartment life. Thirteen breeds in this group are considered unsuitable for urban/apartment live. The remaining eleven breeds, which include the Labrador, are considered suitable, but *only* if the dog's exercise requirements are being met. Another excellent source is *Paws to Consider: Choosing the Right Dog for You and Your Family,* by Brian Kilcommons and Sarah Wilson (Warner Books).

Looking back at a brief history of dogs

Dogs were originally bred for specific functions, such as guarding, herding, hauling, hunting, and so on. Before 1945, most dogs worked for a living, and many still do. The popularity as a household pet is a relatively recent phenomenon, fueled in part by the heroic exploits of the dogs used in World War II, as well as the fictional Rin Tin Tin and Lassie. The upshot of this popularity has been a demand for the "family" dog — easy to train, good with children, a little bit protective, and relatively quiet.

Traditional training

We use the term "traditional training" to describe the most widely used training method for the last 100 years. The first comprehensive written record of traditional training is based on the principle that unacceptable behaviors result in unpleasant consequences and acceptable behaviors result in pleasant consequences. Konrad Most, a German service dog trainer, developed this method in the early 1900s; he also wrote *Training Dogs: A Manual.* (Dogwise Publishing has republished *Training Dogs: A Manual,* and it's available at www.dogwise.com.) His method was introduced in this country in the early 1920s, when several of Most's students immigrated to the United States and became the teachers of future dog training instructors.

Most explains that training a dog consists of *primary* inducements and *secondary* inducements. *Primary* inducements result in the behavior you want to elicit from the dog, and *secondary* inducements are commands and signals. By pairing the two, you can condition the dog to respond solely to commands and signals, the ultimate goal of any training.

Primary inducements can be a pleasant or an unpleasant experience for the dog. Pleasant experiences are called *rewards* and consist of an object the dog will actively work for, such as food, an inviting body posture, verbal praise, or physical affection, such as petting, to induce the desired behavior. A common example is the owner who encourages his puppy to come to him by squatting down and opening his arms in an inviting fashion. Another example is to use a treat to induce the dog to sit.

Unpleasant experiences are called *corrections* and can be a check on the leash, a harsh tone of voice, a threatening body posture, or throwing something at the dog. In order to extinguish the undesired behavior, the correction must be sufficiently unpleasant for the dog so that he wants to avoid it and change his behavior. Moreover, you must administer the correction immediately *before* or *during* the undesired behavior. What constitutes an unpleasant experience varies from dog to dog and depends on his Personality Profile (see Chapter 5). What is perceived as a sufficiently unpleasant experience to inhibit the unwanted behavior by one dog may be perceived as just an annoyance by another dog.

Classical conditioning

Classical conditioning is a type of learning that results from the association or pairing of two stimuli. The best-known example is Ivan Pavlov's experiment that involved ringing a bell before feeding his dogs. After a number of repetitions, the sound of the bell caused the dogs to salivate, even in the absence of food. By pairing the sound of the bell with the food, the dogs "learned" to salivate to the sound of the bell.

Every dog owner, in one way or another, has classically conditioned his dog. In our household, withdrawing a knife from the block causes several dogs to seemingly appear from nowhere. Based on prior experience, they know food is involved and that they have a good chance of getting a scrap or two. Although the dogs react to the knife, only the cat reacts to the sound of the electric can opener.

Operant conditioning

B.F. Skinner, the famous theoretical behaviorist, used the term *operant conditioning* to describe the effects of a trainer's particular action on the future occurrence of an animal's behavior. There are four quadrants to *operant conditioning,* and we show them in Table 2-1.

Table 2-1	The Four Quadrants to Operant Conditioning	
	Add Something	*Remove Something*
Pleasant	Quadrant 1) Positive reinforcement — following a behavior with something the dog perceives as pleasant will increase the behavior.	Quadrant 2) Negative punishment — following a behavior with removing something the dog perceives as pleasant will decrease the behavior.
Unpleasant	Quadrant 3) Positive punishment — following a behavior with something the dog perceives as unpleasant will decrease the behavior.	Quadrant 4) Negative reinforcement — following a behavior with removal of something the dog perceives as unpleasant will increase the behavior.

If these four quadrants sound confusing to you, you aren't alone. And, if you think that "negative punishment" is a redundancy and "positive punishment" is an oxymoron, you're also not alone. Moreover, we have always considered the word "punishment" singularly inappropriate in the context of dog training. The general understanding of the word is "a penalty for wrongdoing," but does a dog, untrained or trained, know he has done something wrong? An answer in the affirmative implies that a dog knows, in the moral sense, right from wrong, which is highly unlikely.

Having said all that, here are examples of the Four Quadrants:

- **Quadrant 1 — positive reinforcement:** When one of our Dachshunds, Diggy, was still quite young, she assumed the begging position by sitting up on her haunches. She did this spontaneously and on her own, without any coaxing on our part. Naturally, we thought it was cute, so we gave her a treat, which increased the behavior. We periodically reinforced the behavior with a treat, and now, 14 years later, she still offers this behavior in hopes of getting a treat.

- **Quadrant 2 — negative punishment:** You're watching TV and your dog drops his ball in your lap hoping you'll throw it. You get up and leave, which will decrease the behavior.

- **Quadrant 3 — positive punishment:** Your dog jumps on you to greet you and you spritz him with water, which will decrease the behavior.

- **Quadrant 4 — negative reinforcement:** You lift up on your dog's collar until he sits, and then you release the collar, which will increase the behavior of sitting.

The bottom line for following the classics

So, what is the bottom line in all this information about traditional training and operant conditioning? It's actually rather simple:

- Acceptable behaviors result in pleasant experiences.

- Unacceptable behaviors result in unpleasant experiences.

- All behaviors have consequences.

And just to help you keep all the training terminology straight, we provide Table 2-2 to combine it all into a neat, small package.

Table 2-2	How Dog Training Terminology Fits Together	
Vernacular	*Traditional Training*	*Operant Conditioning*
Correction	*Anything the dog perceives as unpleasant*, such as a check on the training collar, yelling "no," a harsh tone of voice, a threatening body posture, or throwing something at the dog.	An *aversive*, such as negative punishment or positive punishment. An *aversive* is anything the dog perceives as unpleasant, such as a check on the training collar, yelling "no," in a harsh tone of voice, a threatening body posture, or throwing something at the dog.
Reward	*Anything the dog perceives as pleasant*, such as anything the dog will actively work for, which can be a treat, a ball, a stick, praise, or physical affection in the form of petting.	*Positive reinforcement*, such as anything the dog will actively work for, which can be a treat, a ball, a stick, praise, or physical affection in the form of petting.

Clicker training

Keller and Marian Breland created the foundation of the modern clicker training movement. In the mid-1940s, the Brelands were the first to apply clicker training to train dogs. The movement didn't, however, become popular until the early 1990s when Karen Pryor and Gary Wilkes teamed up and began to give seminars on clicker training. Pryor is a retired dolphin trainer and author of *Don't Shoot the Dog: The New Art of Teaching and Training* (Bantam). Although *Don't Shoot the Dog* isn't a "how-to" training book, it provides some general rules based on the concepts of operant conditioning for influencing behavior. Meanwhile, Wilkes is an animal behaviorist and since 1987 the foremost practitioner and teacher of clicker training. (For more information about Wilkes and clicker training, go to www.clickandtreat.com.)

Clicker training is based on the concepts of operant conditioning (see the section earlier in this chapter). The dog is first trained to associate the clicker sound with getting a treat, a pleasant experience. After the dog associates the click with getting a treat, the trainer has two options:

- **Option 1:** The trainer can wait until the dog voluntarily offers the desired behavior on his own, such as sit. When the dog sits, the trainer clicks, marking the end of the behavior, and reinforces the behavior with a treat. This option works well with extroverted dogs that will offer a variety of behaviors in the hope that one of them will get them a treat. An introverted dog, on the other hand, may show little interest in the game. The "wait and see what happens" approach, depending on the dog, can be a lengthy process and extremely stressful for the dog — he may stop offering any behaviors and just lie down.

- **Option 2:** The trainer doesn't have the time or patience to wait for the desired behavior to happen, so he induces the behavior. Again, in the case of the Sit, the trainer uses a treat to get the dog to assume the sitting position, and when the dog sits, the trainer clicks, marking the end of the behavior, and gives the treat. Obviously, this approach is much more efficient than waiting for the dog to offer the desired behavior on his own.

After the dog consistently offers the behavior of sitting, for which he is rewarded with a click and a treat (Quadrant 1 — positive reinforcement), the trainer then adds a cue to the behavior, such as a command or signal, or both. The trainer waits until he thinks the dog is going to sit and says/signals "Sit." When the dog does, the trainer clicks and treats.

Now that the dog understands the cue of "Sit," the trainer eliminates the click and treat when the dog offers the behavior on his own (Quadrant 2 — negative punishment). If the trainer is looking for a different behavior, he may say "Wrong" or "Oops" to convey to the dog that he wants something else (Quadrant 3 — positive punishment, but actually a hybrid, meaning "Try again").

With a clicker the trainer can mark the end of the desired behavior with greater accuracy than he can with verbal praise, which means clearer communication with the dog. Although the dog does all the work, clicker training requires keen powers of observation and split-second timing to mark the end of the desired behavior and plenty of patience.

The ultimate object of any training is to have your dog respond reliably to your commands. Ideally, he responds to the first command. Telling your dog to do something and have him ignore you is frustrating. Think of Buddy's response in terms of choices. Do you want to teach Buddy to think he has a choice of responding to you? We don't think so. We think you want a dog that understands, after you have trained him, that he has to do what you tell him.

Establishing Trust with Your Dog

Picture Buddy chasing a cat across the road. Your heart is in your mouth because you're afraid he might get hit. When he finally returns, you're angry and soundly scold him for chasing the cat and giving you such a scare. How does Buddy look at this situation? First, he chased the cat, which was fun. Then he came back to you and was reprimanded, which was no fun at all. What you wanted to teach him was not to chase the cat. What you actually taught him was that returning to you is unpleasant.

One of the commands you want your dog to master is to come when called. To be successful, remember this principle: Whenever your dog comes to you, be nice to him. Don't do anything the *dog* perceives as unpleasant. If you want to give him a bath or a pill, don't just call him to you. Instead, go get him or call him, and then first give him a cookie before the bath or pill.

No matter what he may have done, be pleasant and greet him with a kind word, a pat on the head, and a smile. Teach your dog to trust you by being a safe place for him. When he's with you, follows you, or comes to you, make him feel wanted.

If you call him to you and then punish him, you undermine his trust in you. When your dog comes to you on his own and you punish him, he thinks he's being punished for coming to you. You may ask though, "How can I be nice to my dog when he brings me the remains of one of my brand-new shoes, or when he wants to jump on me with muddy paws, or when I just discovered an unwanted present on the carpet?"

We can certainly empathize with these questions, having experienced the same and similar scenarios on many occasions. We know how utterly frustrating a dog's behavior can be. What we have discovered and accepted is that at that moment in time the dog doesn't understand that he did anything wrong. He only understands your anger — but not the reason for it. As difficult as it may be, you have to grin and bear it, lest you undermine the very relationship of mutual trust you're trying to achieve through training. (Take a look at Chapter 5 for info on how to understand your dog's mind and check out Chapter 4 for info on housetraining.)

Punishment after the fact is cruel and inhumane. Even if the dog's behavior changes as a result of being punished, it changes in spite of it and not because of it. The answer lies in prevention and training. *Prevention* means providing the dog with plenty of outlets for his energies in the form of exercise, play, and training. It also means not putting the dog in a position where he can get at your brand-new pair of shoes. *Training* means teaching your dog to sit on command so that he doesn't jump on you (see Chapter 7 for training basics).

Being consistent with commands and tone of voice

If there is any magic to training your dog, it's consistency. Your dog can't understand "sometimes," "maybe," "perhaps," or "only on Sundays." He can and does understand "yes" and "no." For example, you confuse your dog when you encourage him to jump up on you while you're wearing old clothes but then get angry with him when he joyfully plants muddy paws on your best suit.

Here's another example: Bill loved to wrestle with Brandy, his Golden Retriever. Then one day, when Grandma came to visit, Brandy flattened her. Bill was angry, and Brandy was confused — she thought roughhousing was a wonderful way to show affection. After all, that's what Bill had taught her.

Sometimes dogs pick up consistent cues from unexpected sources. For example, before leaving for work, Wendy always put Heidi in her crate. It wasn't long before Heidi went into her crate on her own when Wendy was about to leave. "What a clever puppy," thought Wendy, "She knows that I'm going to work."

Dogs often give the appearance of being able to read your mind. What happens in actuality is that by observing you and studying your habits, they learn to anticipate your actions. Because they communicate with each other through body language, they quickly become experts at reading yours.

What Heidi observed was that immediately before leaving for work, Wendy invariably put on her makeup and then crated her. Heidi's cue to go into her crate was seeing Wendy putting on her makeup.

Then one evening, before dinner guests were to arrive, Wendy started "putting on her face." When Heidi immediately went into her crate, Wendy realized the dog hadn't been reading her mind, but had learned the routine through observation. (See Chapter 5.)

Consistency in training means handling your dog in a predictable and uniform manner. If more than one person is in the household, everyone needs to handle the dog in the same way. Otherwise, the dog becomes confused and unreliable in his responses.

So does this mean that you can never permit your puppy to jump up on you? Not at all. But you have to teach him that he may only do so when you tell him it's okay. But beware: Training a dog to make this distinction is more difficult than training him not to jump up at all. The more black and white you can make it, the easier it will be for Buddy to understand what you want.

Outlasting your dog — be persistent

Training your dog is a question of who is more persistent — you or your dog. Some things he can master quickly; others will take more time. If several tries don't bring success, be patient, remain calm, and try again.

How quickly your dog will learn a particular command depends on the extent to which the behavior you're trying to teach him is in harmony with the function for which he was bred. For example, a Labrador Retriever, bred to retrieve game birds on land and in the water, will readily learn how to fetch a stick or a ball on command. On the other hand, an Afghan Hound, bred as a coursing hound that pursues its quarry by sight, may take many repetitions before he understands the command to fetch and then responds to it each and every time. A Shetland Sheepdog, bred to herd and guard livestock, will learn to walk on a loose leash more quickly than a Beagle, bred to hunt hares.

Knowing to avoid "no"

As of right now, eliminate the word "no" from your training vocabulary. All too often, *no* is the only command a dog hears, and he's expected to figure out what it means. There is no exercise or command in training called "no." Avoid negative communications with your dog because they undermine the relationship you're trying to build. Don't use your dog's name as a reprimand. Don't nag your dog by repeatedly using his name without telling him what you want him to do.

At one of our training camps, one of the participants wore a T-shirt depicting a dog greeting another dog with "Hi. My name is 'No, No. Bad Dog.' What's yours?"

Begin to focus on the way in which you communicate with Buddy. Does he perceive the interaction as positive or negative, pleasant or unpleasant, friendly or unfriendly? How many times do you use the word "no," and how many times do you say "Good dog" when interacting with your dog? Our experience during more than 30 years of teaching has been that by the time we see the dogs, most have been no'ed to death. Everything the dog does brings forth a stern "Don't do this," "Don't do that," or "No, bad dog." Negative communications from you have a negative effect on your dog's motivation to work for you.

In dealing with your dog, ask yourself, "What exactly do I want Buddy to do or not to do?" Use a *do* command whenever possible so that you can praise your dog instead of reprimanding him. You'll notice a direct relationship between your dog's willingness to cooperate and your attitude. Get out of the blaming habit of assuming that Buddy's failure to respond is his fault. Your dog only does what comes naturally. More important, your dog's conduct is a direct reflection of your training. Train Buddy — in a positive way — what you expect from him, and more than likely he'll enthusiastically go along with the program.

Does this mean you can never use the "no" word? In an emergency, you do what you have to do. But, remember, only in dire need.

Repeating commands

In training, use your dog's name once *before* a command to get his attention, for example, "Buddy, come." The quickest way to teach your dog to ignore you is to use his name repeatedly and with changing inflections of your voice.

Get into the habit of giving a command once and in a normal tone of voice — a dog's hearing is 80 times better than yours. Repeating commands teaches your dog that he can ignore you, and changes in inflections from pleas to threats don't help, either. Our experience has been that most people are unaware of how many times they repeat a command. Give the command and if your dog doesn't respond, reinforce the command or show him exactly what it is you want him to do.

Taking charge

Dogs are pack animals, and a pack consists of followers and one leader. The leader is in charge and dictates what happens when.

From Buddy's perspective, a pack leader's Bill of Rights looks something like this:

- To eat first and to eat as much as he wants to
- To stand, sit, or lie down wherever he wants to
- To have access to the prime spots in the household, including the furniture and the beds
- To control entry to or from any room in the house

- ✔ To proceed through all narrow openings first
- ✔ To demand attention from subordinate pack members any time he wants to
- ✔ To ignore or actively discourage unwanted attention
- ✔ To restrict the movements of lesser ranking members of the pack

In a multidog household, we often see the leader of the dog pack exercise these rights on a daily basis. Does Buddy exercise any of these rights with you?

You and your family are now Buddy's pack, and someone has to be in charge — so become the leader. The principles of democracy don't apply to pack animals. Your dog needs someone he can respect and look up to for direction and guidance. You may just want to be friends, partners, or peers with your dog. You can be all of those, but for your dog's well being, you must be in charge. In today's complicated world, you can't rely on him to make the decisions.

Few dogs actively seek leadership and most are perfectly content for you to assume the role, so long as you do. But you must do so, or even the meekest of dogs will take over. Remember, it's not a matter of choice. For his safety and your peace of mind, you have to be the one in charge.

How do you know which of you is in charge? Here are a few signs to watch for:

- ✔ Does Buddy get on the furniture and then growl at you when you tell him to get off?
- ✔ Does Buddy demand attention from you, which you then give?
- ✔ Does Buddy ignore you when you want him to move out of the way, when he is in front of a door or cupboard?
- ✔ Does Buddy dash through doorways ahead of you?

If the answer to two or more of these questions is "yes," you need to become pack leader, and we show how to do that in a positive and nonconfrontational way. The next section explains how.

Being in charge with Buddy

Debbie didn't think much about the "being in charge" theory. She wanted to be pals with Thor, her Labrador Retriever. After all, he had always listened to her before and had never given her any trouble. She changed her mind when one day Thor made the decision, "Now I will chase the cat across the road," just as a car was coming. She realized that if she wanted Thor to be around for a while, he had to learn that she was in charge and that she made the decisions.

Assuming Your Role as Pack Leader

Remaining in place, in either the Sit or Down position, is one of the most important exercises you can teach your dog. Aside from its practical value, this exercise has important psychological implications.

One way a dog exerts his leadership over a subordinate dog is by restricting the movement of the subordinate, or keeping him in his place. We remember an amusing incident involving our Yorkshire Terrier, Angus. Friends had come to visit and brought their 6-month-old Doberman, Blue. Things went fine with the two dogs until we noticed that Blue was sitting in a corner with Angus lying in front of him a few feet away. Every time Blue tried to move, Angus would lift his lip, and Blue shrank back into the corner. It seems Angus had exploited the "home-field advantage" and convinced Blue that he was in charge.

Teaching your dog to stay still at your command is at the top of the list of critical exercises. Not only can you keep Buddy out from underfoot, but you also reinforce in his mind that you are the one in charge — you are the pack leader.

Using the same principle, we have successfully taught countless dog owners to become pack leader in a nonviolent and nonconfrontational way. Start the leadership exercises as soon as you get your dog. If your dog is a puppy, your job will be that much easier than if you acquired an older dog — a puppy is more readily physically handled than a grown dog. To accomplish this task, you need to learn to place your dog into a Sit and a Down. The technical term for placing your dog in the Sit or Down position is called *modeling* — you show the dog what you want him to do.

Placing your dog in a Sit and Down

For the Sit, with Buddy on your left, kneel next to him, both of you facing in the same direction. If Buddy is a small dog, you can put him on a table for these exercises. Take these steps:

1. **Place your right hand against his chest and your left hand on top of his shoulders.**

2. **Run your left hand over his back, all the way down to his knees, and with equal pressure of both hands and without saying anything, collapse him into a Sit.**

3. **Keep your hands in place to the count of five and verbally praise Buddy, saying "good dog."**

4. **Then release him with "Okay."**

This is a leadership exercise and its purpose isn't to teach Buddy the "Sit" command. To teach him to respond to the "Sit" command, see Chapter 7.

For the Down, take the following steps:

1. **With Buddy sitting on your left, kneel next to him, both of you facing in the same direction.**

2. **Reaching over his back, place your left hand behind his left foreleg; place the right hand behind the right foreleg.**

3. **Keep your thumbs up so as not to squeeze Buddy's legs, something he may not like and may cause him to resist.**

4. **Lift Buddy into the begging position and without saying anything, lower him to the ground. (See Figure 2-1.)**

5. **Keep your hands in place to the count of five and verbally praise him.**

6. **Then release him with "Okay."**

This is a leadership exercise and its purpose isn't to teach Buddy the "Down" command. To teach him to respond to the "Down" command, see Chapter 7.

Figure 2-1:
Lifting your dog to the begging position.

The Long Sit and Down exercise: A recipe for leadership

The purpose of the Long Sit and Down exercise is to teach Buddy in a nonviolent way that you are his pack leader. For this reason, it's the foundation of all further training. Training your dog is next to impossible unless he accepts you as the one in charge. It takes four weeks of practice to get the Long Sit and Down established as a routine, but as soon as you have it, it can go a long way toward helping you establish your role as pack leader. Here's what to do:

✔ **Week 1:** Five times during the course of a week, practice the Long Down exercise for 30 minutes at a time as follows:

  1. **Sit on the floor beside your dog.**

  2. **Without saying anything, place him in the Down position. (See Figure 2-2.)**

  3. **If he gets up, put him back without saying anything.**

  4. **Keep your hands off when he is down.**

  5. **Stay still.**

  6. **After 30 minutes, release him.**

Figure 2-2: Gently lowering your dog to the Down position.

As a general rule, the greater a dog's leadership aspirations, the more frequently he will try to get up and the more important this exercise becomes. Just remain calm and each time he tries to get up, replace him in the Down position.

If your dog is particularly bouncy, put him on leash and sit on a chair and the leash so your hands are free to put him back.

Some dogs immediately concede that you're the pack leader, while others need some convincing. If your dog is in the latter group, your, as well as his, first experience with the Long Down will be the hardest. As he catches on to the idea and gradually (if not grudgingly) accepts you as pack leader, each successive repetition will be that much easier.

Practice the Long Down under the following conditions:

- When your dog is tired

- After he has been exercised

- When interruptions are unlikely

- When you aren't tired

If the situation allows it, you can watch television or read, so long as you don't move.

✔ **Week 2:** On alternate days, practice three 30-minute Downs and 10-minute Sits while you sit in a chair next to your dog.

✔ **Week 3:** On alternate days, practice three 30-minute Downs and 10-minute Sits while you sit across the room from your dog.

✔ **Week 4:** On alternate days, practice three 30-minute Downs and 10-minute Sits while you move about the room but in sight of your dog.

After week 4, practice a Long Down and a Long Sit at least once a month.

We guarantee you that if you follow this regimen that your dog will unconditionally accept you as pack leader.

Chapter 3

Surviving the Puppy Period

● ●

In This Chapter

▶ Allowing your puppy to socialize

▶ Recognizing the importance of an enriched environment

▶ Understanding your puppy's growth cycles

▶ Handling the challenges your puppy throws your way

▶ Knowing whether and when to spay and neuter

▶ Wondering if your puppy will ever grow up

● ●

*E*veryone wants a super puppy, one that's well behaved and listens to every word you say — a Lassie or perhaps even a Beethoven. Of course, heredity plays a role, but so does early upbringing and environment. From birth until maturity, your dog goes through a number of developmental stages. What happens during these stages has a lasting effect on how your dog turns out, his ability to learn, his outlook on life, and his behavior.

The many scientists and behaviorists who've studied dog behavior over the last century have made important discoveries about these developmental stages and how they relate to a dog's ability to grow into a well-adjusted pet. These stages are called the *critical periods,* and what happens or doesn't happen during that time determines how the pup turns out as an adult and how he responds to your efforts to train him.

The first critical period is from birth to 49 days. During this time, the puppy needs his mother and the interaction with his littermates. He also needs to have interaction with humans. Although these particular periods aren't within your control, we briefly describe in this chapter what happens during the weaning period when the puppy learns to learn. And we also deal with the periods that follow and how they relate to training.

Understanding Your Puppy's Socialization Needs

At about the 49th day of life, when the puppy's brain is neurologically complete, that special attachment between the dog and his owner, called bonding, begins. It's one of the reasons why 49 days is the ideal time for puppies to leave the nest for their new homes so that bonding with the new owner or family can take place.

Bonding to people becomes increasingly difficult the longer a puppy remains with his mother or littermates. The dog also becomes more difficult to train. With each passing day, the pup loses a little of his ability to adapt to a new environment.

In addition, with delay, there's the potential for built-in behavior problems.

- ✓ The pup may grow up being too dog oriented.
- ✓ The pup probably won't care much about people.
- ✓ The pup may be difficult to teach to accept responsibility.
- ✓ The pup may be more difficult to train, including housetraining (see Chapter 4 for more on housetraining).

The weaning period: Weeks 3-7

You must also be wary of obtaining a puppy from a breeder who has taken a puppy away from his mother too soon, because it not only deprives the puppy of important lessons but can also affect the puppy's future health. For example, the puppy obtains antibodies to many diseases by feeding from his mother. Every sip of milk is like a vaccine that protects the puppy for many weeks after he leaves the litter and is placed in his new home.

Between 3 to 7 weeks of age, the mother teaches her puppies basic doggy manners. She communicates to the puppies what's acceptable and what's unacceptable behavior. For instance, after the puppies' teeth have come in, nursing them becomes a painful experience, so she teaches them to take it easy. She does whatever it takes, from growling, snarling, and even snapping, and she continues this lesson throughout the weaning process when she wants the puppies to leave her alone. After just a few repetitions, the puppies get the message and respond to a mere look or a curled lip from mother. The puppy learns dog language — or lip reading, as we call it — and bite inhibition, an important lesson.

The puppies also learn from each other. While playing, tempers may flare because one puppy bites another one too hard. The puppies discover from these exchanges what it feels like to be bitten and, at the same time, to inhibit biting during play (see Figure 3-1). Puppies that haven't had these lessons may find it difficult to accept discipline while growing up.

Figure 3-1:
Puppies
discover
valuable
lessons
while
playing.

Photograph by Jane Kelso

Puppies separated from their canine family before they've had the opportunity for these experiences tend to identify more with humans than with other dogs. To simplify, they don't know they're dogs, and they tend to have their own sets of problems, such as the following:

- Aggression toward other dogs
- Difficulty with housetraining
- A dislike of being left alone
- Excessive barking
- Mouthing and biting their owner
- Nervousness
- An unhealthy attachment to humans

Getting to know everyone: Weeks 7-12

Your dog is a social animal. To become an acceptable pet, the pup needs to interact with you and your family, as well as with other humans and dogs during the 7th through 12th week of life. If denied these opportunities, your dog's behavior around other people or dogs may be unpredictable — your dog may be fearful or perhaps even aggressive. For example, unless regularly exposed to children during this period, a dog may be uncomfortable or untrustworthy around them.

Socializing your puppy is critical for it to become a friendly adult dog. When your puppy is developing, expose it to as many different people as possible, including children and older people. Let him meet new dogs, too. These early experiences will pay off big time when your dog grows up.

Your puppy needs the chance to meet and have positive experiences with those persons and activities that will play a role in his life. The following are just a few examples:

- ✔ You're a grandparent whose grandchildren occasionally visit. Have your puppy meet children as often as you can.

- ✔ You live by yourself but have friends that visit you. Make an effort to let your puppy meet other people, particularly members of the opposite sex.

- ✔ You plan to take your dog on family outings or vacations. Introduce riding in a car.

We've been fortunate in that we've been able to take our puppies to our training camps. The wealth of experience they gained from the weeklong exposure to other dogs and people has made it easy for us to take our dogs anywhere. As a result, they get along with people and dogs — and are ambassadors for all dogs.

A common way for people to greet a puppy or an adult dog is to pat it on top of the head, just as they do with children. The fact is that dogs don't like this form of greeting any better than kids do. The pup will immediately scrunch down and look miserable, especially if you lean over him as well. Instead, greet your puppy by putting the palm of your hand under his chin. Stand up straight, or kneel down and greet him with a smile and a hello. When meeting a puppy or dog for the first time, slowly put the palm of your hand toward him and let him smell you.

Socialization with other dogs is equally important and should be the norm rather than the exception. It also needs to occur on a regular basis. Ideally, the puppy has a mentor, an older dog who can teach it the ropes. We've been fortunate enough in always having had a mentor dog who supervised the upbringing of a new puppy, making our task that much easier.

Puppies learn from other dogs but can only do so if they have a chance to spend time with them. Make a point of introducing your young dog to other puppies and adults on a regular basis. Many communities now have dog parks where dogs can interact and play together. If you plan on taking your puppy to obedience class or dog shows or ultimately using the dog in a breeding program, he needs to have the chance to interact with other dogs. Time spent now is well worth the effort — it will build his confidence and make your job training him that much easier.

Remember that you see Buddy as a four-legged person. Buddy sees you as a two-legged dog. You can change your perception, but Buddy can't. During this time is also when your puppy will follow your every footstep. Encourage this behavior by rewarding the puppy with an occasional treat, some petting, or a kind word.

Suddenly he's afraid: Weeks 8-12

Weeks 8 through 12 are called the *fear imprint period*. During this period, any painful or particularly frightening experience leaves a more lasting impression on your pup than if it occurred at any other time in his life. If the experience is sufficiently traumatic, it could literally ruin your pup for life.

During this time, avoid exposing the puppy to traumatic experiences. For example, elective surgery, such as ear cropping, should be done, if at all, before 8 weeks or after 11 weeks of age. When you need to take your puppy to the veterinarian, have the doctor give the puppy a treat before, during, and after the examination to make the visit a pleasant experience. Although you need to stay away from stressful situations, do continue to train your puppy in a positive and nonpunitive way.

During the first year's growth, you may see fear reactions at other times. Don't respond by dragging your puppy to the object that caused the fear. On the other hand, don't pet or reassure the dog — you may create the impression that you approve of this behavior. Rather, distract the puppy with a toy or a treat to get his mind off whatever scared him and go on to something pleasant. Practice some of the commands you've already taught him so he can focus on a positive experience. After a short time — sometimes up to two weeks — the fearful behavior will disappear.

Now he wants to leave home: Beyond 12 weeks

Sometime between the fourth and eighth months, your puppy begins to real-ize that there's a big, wide world out there. Up to now, every time you called,

Buddy probably willingly came to you. But now he may prefer to wander off and investigate. Buddy is maturing and cutting the apron strings, which is normal. He's not being spiteful or disobedient; he's just becoming an adolescent.

While he's going through this phase, keep Buddy on a leash or in a confined area until he has learned to come when called. Otherwise, not coming when called becomes a pattern — annoying to you and dangerous to Buddy. After this activity becomes a habit, breaking it is difficult; prevention is the best cure. Teaching your dog to come when called is much easier before he has developed the habit of running away. Practice calling him in the house, out in the yard, and at random times. Have a treat in your pocket to reinforce the behavior you want.

When you need to gather in a wandering Buddy, don't, under any circumstances, play the game of chasing him. Instead, run the other way and get Buddy to chase you. If that doesn't work, kneel on the ground and pretend you've found something extremely interesting, hoping Buddy's curiosity brings him to you. If you have to, approach him slowly in an upright position, using a nonthreatening tone of voice until you can calmly take hold of his collar.

Your puppy also goes through teething during this period and needs to chew anything and everything. Dogs, like children, can't help it. If one of your favorite shoes is demolished, try to control yourself. Puppies have the irritating habit of tackling many shoes, but only one from each pair. Look at it as a lesson to keep your possessions out of reach. Scolding won't stop the need to chew, but it may cause your pet to fear you.

Your job is to provide acceptable outlets for this need, such as chew bones and toys. Our dogs' favorites are marrow bones, which you can get at the supermarket. These bones provide hours of entertainment for any dog, and they keep their teeth clean. Artificial toys are also available. Kong toys (www.kongcompany.com) are a great favorite, especially the hard rubber ones that are virtually indestructible and that can be stuffed with peanut butter or kibble. They come in different sizes appropriate to the size of your dog and can keep most dogs busy for hours. Just be sure they're large enough so he can't accidentally swallow one.

Stay away from soft and fuzzy toys. Chances are, your dog will destroy them and may ingest part of them. We personally don't like rawhide chew toys that have been treated with chemicals or items that become soft and gooey with chewing because the dog can swallow them and get them stuck in the intestines.

When Buddy is going through this stage, you may want to consider crating him when he's left alone. Doing so will keep him and your possessions safe, and both of you will be happy. Crating him during this growth spurt helps with his housetraining, too. With all the chewing he does during his teething, accidents sometimes happen. (Turn to Chapter 4 for more on housetraining.)

Managing the Terrible Twos

The adolescent stage of your dog's life, depending on the breed, takes place anywhere from 4 months to 2 years and culminates in sexual maturity. Generally, the smaller the dog, the sooner he matures. Larger dogs enter (and end) adolescence later in life.

Adolescence is a time when the cute little puppy can turn into a teenage monster. He starts to lose his baby teeth and his soft, fuzzy puppy coat. He goes through growth spurts and looks gangly, either up in the rear or down in front; he's entering an ugly-duckling stage.

Depending on the size of the dog, 40 to 70 percent of adult growth is achieved by 7 months of age. If you have one of the larger breeds, you'd better start training now, before the dog gets so big that you can't manage him. As Buddy begins to mature, he starts to display some puzzling behaviors, as well as some perfectly normal but objectionable ones.

Surviving the juvenile flakies

We use the term *juvenile flakies* because it most accurately describes what's technically known as a second fear imprint period (see "Suddenly he's afraid: Weeks 8-12" earlier in this chapter about the first fear imprint period). Juvenile flakies are apprehension or fear behaviors that are usually short lived. They're caused by temporary calcium deficiencies and hormone development related to a puppy's periodic growth spurts.

The timing of this event (or events) isn't as clearly defined as the first fear imprint period, and it coincides with growth spurts; hence it may occur more than once as the dog matures. Even though he may have been outgoing and confident before, your puppy now may be reluctant to approach someone or something new and unfamiliar, or he may suddenly be afraid of something familiar.

Fear of the new or unfamiliar has its roots in evolution. In a wild pack, after the pups become 8 to 10 months of age, they're allowed to come on a hunt. The first lesson they have to learn is to stay with the pack; if they wander off, they might get lost or into trouble. They also have to develop survival techniques, one of which is fear. The message to the puppy is "if you see or smell something unfamiliar, run the other way." Apprehension or fear of the familiar is also caused by growth spurts. At this point in a puppy's life, hormones start to surge. Hormones can affect the calcium uptake in the body, and, coupled with growth, this can be a difficult time for the growing puppy.

Being patient with the flakies

One day, when our Dachshund, Manfred, was 6 months old, he came into the kitchen after having been outside in the yard. Then he noticed on the floor, near his water bowl, a brown paper grocery bag. He flattened, looked as though he'd seen a ghost, and tried to run back out into the yard.

If Manfred was going through a growth spurt at this time, which is normal at 6 months, he could've been experiencing a temporary calcium deficiency, which in turn would produce his fear reaction.

He'd seen brown paper grocery bags many times before, but this one was going to get him.

We reminded ourselves that he was going through the flakies and ignored the behavior. A few hours later, the behavior disappeared.

If you happen to observe a similar situation with your puppy, don't try to drag him up to the object in an effort to "teach" the puppy to accept it. If you make a big deal out of it, you create the impression that he has a good reason to be afraid of whatever triggered the reaction. Leave the puppy alone, ignore the behavior, and it will pass.

Puppy discovers sex

Sometime during this four-month to two-year period, depending on the size of your dog, the puppy will discover sex, and you'll be the first to know about it.

Our Landseer Newfoundland, Evo, has always enjoyed playing with other dogs. He's generally well behaved and gets along with people and all the dogs he meets. When Evo was almost 2, he fell in love. We took him to a training facility where we were to meet up with friends who had just adopted an 11-month-old female Labrador Retriever named Indy. Evo was very sweet with her, and at first they played nicely together, chasing and batting at each other with their paws. All of a sudden, a strange look came over Evo's face, and with his face crinkled up he jumped on Indy's back and with his front paws clasped her firmly around her chest. We realized that his puppy days were over.

Sex is sex in any language! Evo was a bit of a late developer because he lives with spayed females and hadn't yet had the pleasure of being involved with an unspayed female. We handled Evo by going up to him, putting his lead on, and taking him away from Indy. He wanted to go back to her and tried several times, but we occupied his mind with training and he soon forgot all about her.

When Buddy experiences a surge of hormones during training, do some heeling or retrieving to get him back into the proper frame of mind.

When hormones kick in, it's not always about sex

During the period from 4 months to a year, the male puppy's hormones surge to four times his adult level, and this surge can have important effects on his behavior. You can usually tell when he's entering this phase. The most obvious sign is that he stops listening to you. He may also try to dominate other dogs in the household or ones he meets outside. Fortunately, after this enormous surge, his hormones ultimately return to normal.

Many pet owners discover at this stage that their dog is becoming difficult to handle, and so they seek professional help or enroll Buddy in an obedience class (see Chapter 20). This stage is also a good time to consider neutering the dog (see the following section).

Some puppies begin protecting their toys, their food, or their owners. During this period puppies also aren't looking their best. With puppy fur falling out and adult fur coming in, they can appear quite moth-eaten. They get tall and gangly and aren't looking or behaving in a very lovable way.

Hormones drive behavior, which means that the intensity of behaviors increases in direct proportion to the amount of hormones coursing through his system. So if you want your male puppy to become calmer and not to assert himself quite so much, neutering him is a good idea.

Although female puppies going through puberty may show similar traits, they more often show greater dependency upon their owners. They follow their owners around, looking at them constantly, as if to say, "Something is happening to my body, but I don't know what. Tell me what to do." Females are just as apt to show mounting behavior as males, and you may consider spaying.

If you don't want to neuter your pet, the necessity for training increases. The freedom that the male puppy had before now becomes limited. The better trained he is, the easier this transition is, but it requires a real commitment on your part. The female, in turn, needs to be protected during her heat cycle, which usually occurs every 6 months and lasts around 21 days. Her attraction is so potent that you may discover unwanted suitors around your house, some of whom may have come from miles away.

Our first experience with a female in season involved our Landseer, Heidi. When we came home from work, we found a good-sized Basset Hound on our front stoop, patiently waiting for Heidi. As we approached, he made it perfectly clear that he was taking a proprietary attitude toward Heidi, as well as to the house.

A sad fact of life

The majority of dogs in animal shelters are delivered at around 8 months of age, when they are "no longer cute" and have "stopped listening." Millions of dogs are killed annually because their owners didn't want to spend 10 to 15 minutes a day working with them while they were young.

We had to enter the house via the back door. We then managed to subdue the little fellow with a few dog biscuits just long enough to check his collar. We were surprised to learn that the horny hound had traveled close to three miles to visit.

Spaying or Neutering

Unless you intend to exhibit your dog in dog shows to get a championship or to breed the dog, you need to seriously consider neutering your dog.

The advantages of neutering your pet generally outweigh the disadvantages. For the male, the advantages include the following:

- Keeps him calm and less stressed around a female who is in season
- Reduces the tendency to roam
- Diminishes mounting behavior
- Makes training easier
- Improves overall disposition, especially toward other dogs
- Reduces risk of prostate problems developing in the older male

In short, he'll be easier to live with and easier to train. Neutering also curbs the urge to roam or run away. So if the front door is left open by accident, he won't go miles to find a female in season, like our friend the Basset whom we introduced in the preceding section.

It isn't true that dogs that have been neutered lose their protective instincts — it depends on the age when the dog was neutered. Generally, dogs neutered after a year of age retain their protective instincts.

If you spay your female, she, too, will stay closer to home. Perhaps even more important are these benefits:

✔ You won't have to deal with the mess that goes with having her in season.

✔ You won't have to worry about unwanted visitors camping on your property and lifting a leg against any vertical surface.

✔ You won't have to worry about accidental puppies, which are next to impossible to place in good homes.

✔ You may have a healthier dog with less chance of getting tumors of the mammary glands and infections of the uterus.

Knowing when to spay or neuter

When you have your pet altered, make sure the operation occurs at least one month apart from his rabies shot, which shouldn't be given before 6 months of age. Until 6 months of age, the puppy is protected against rabies through the antibodies passed along in the mother's milk. Don't give your dog vaccines if he's undergoing surgery because doing so can have long-term adverse effects. So if you decide to alter your dog, think about having the surgery after 7 months of age, for both sexes.

Depending on the breed and size of the female, she'll go into her first season any time after 7 months of age. For a Yorkshire Terrier, it's apt to be sooner, and for a giant breed, it's likely to be later, sometimes as late as 18 months of age. If you want a dog to show more adult behaviors and take more responsibility — like being a protector or guard dog, training for competitive events, or working for a living — think about altering later.

A dog that hasn't been neutered until after a year of age, or a female that has gone through two seasons, is generally easier to train for competitive events such as obedience or agility trials. Dogs have become fully grown by that time, are emotionally mature, have learned more adult behaviors, and can accept more responsibility.

Disadvantages to spaying and neutering

Altering changes the hormones in the body. Some dogs that are altered develop hypothyroidism as they mature. Hypothyroidism can cause these problems:

✔ Dull, oily, smelly coats

✔ Increased shedding

✔ Separation anxiety

✔ Skin problems

✔ A tendency to gain weight

Regardless of these disadvantages, we recommend neutering a dog that isn't going to be bred simply because neutered dogs are so much easier to live with. For the males, neutering eliminates the stress they experience when they become aware of a female in season, makes training that much easier, and minimizes the unwanted roaming. For the females, spaying eliminates the violent mood swings they can experience during their cycles.

Finally He Grows Up

No matter how much you wish that cute little puppy could remain as is, your pup is going to grow up. It happens anywhere from 1 to 4 years. Over the course of those years, your dog will undergo physical and emotional changes. For you, the owner, the most important one is your dog's sense of identity — the process of becoming an individual in his own right. If you provide leadership through training, he'll reward you with many years of loyal devotion.

To breed or not to breed your dog? That's the question

Generally, don't even contemplate breeding your dog unless

✔ Your dog is purebred and registered.

✔ You didn't get your dog from an animal shelter or pet store.

✔ You have at least a three-generation pedigree for your dog.

✔ Your dog has at least four titled dogs, such as conformation or working titles, in the last three generations.

✔ Your dog is certified free of genetic disorders applicable to the breed.

✔ Your dog conforms to the standard for its breed.

✔ Your dog has a stable temperament.

Breeding dogs for the purpose of exposing your children to the miracle of birth is *not* a good idea. The world already has enough dogs that don't have homes, and finding homes for your puppies will be much more difficult than you think, if not impossible. Rent a video!

Chapter 4

Housetraining

. . . .

In This Chapter

▶ Crate-training your dog

▶ Setting up an elimination schedule and other fundamentals of housetraining

▶ Exploring an alternative to crate-training

▶ Understanding why your dog marks his territory

▶ Taking your dog for a ride

. . . .

*T*he well-trained dog's education begins with housetraining. As with any training, some dogs catch on more readily than others. Some of the toy breeds are notoriously dense in this regard and vigorously resist all efforts requiring their cooperation.

As a general rule, however, the majority of dogs don't present a problem, provided you do your part. To speed along the process, we strongly recommend that you use a crate or similar means of confinement.

Initially, you may recoil from this concept as cruel and inhumane. Nothing could be farther from the truth. You'll discover that your puppy likes his crate and that you can enjoy your peace of mind.

Using a Crate: A Playpen for Your Puppy

When Jim and Laura went to pick up their puppy, the breeder asked them what they thought was a peculiar question. "When you were raising your children, did you use a playpen?" "Of course," said Laura, "I don't know what I would have done without it." "Fine," said the breeder, "a crate for a puppy is like a playpen for a child."

Whatever your views on playpens, dogs like crates. A crate reminds them of a den — a place of comfort, safety, security, and warmth. (See Figure 4-1.)

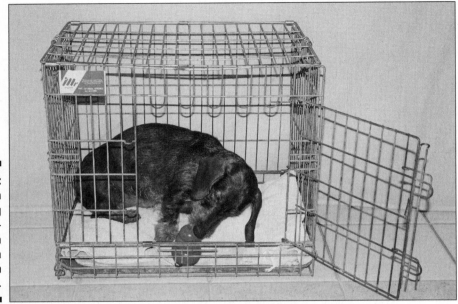

Figure 4-1:
In addition to helping with house-training, a crate is a comfy den for your dog.

Puppies, and many adult dogs, sleep most of the day, and many prefer the comfort of their den. For your mental health, as well as that of your puppy, get a crate.

Here are just a few of the many advantages to crate-training your dog:

- ✔ A crate is a babysitter — when you're busy and can't keep an eye on your dog, but want to make sure he doesn't get into trouble, put him in his crate. You can relax, and so can he.

- ✔ Using a crate is ideal for getting him on a schedule for housetraining.

- ✔ Few dogs are fortunate enough to go through life without ever having to be hospitalized. Your dog's private room at the veterinary hospital will consist of a crate. His first experience with a crate shouldn't come at a time when he's sick — the added stress from being crated for the first time can retard his recovery.

- ✔ A crate is especially helpful during the times when you have to keep your dog quiet, such as after being altered or after an injury.

- ✔ Driving any distance, even around the block, with your dog loose in the car is tempting fate. Stop suddenly and who knows what could happen. Having the dog in a crate protects you and your dog.

✔ When we go on vacation, we like to take our dog. His crate is his home away from home, and we can leave him in a hotel room knowing he won't be unhappy or stressed, and he won't tear up the room.

✔ A crate is a place where he can get away from the hustle-and-bustle of family life and hide out when the kids become too much for him.

A crate provides a dog with his own special place. It's cozy, secure, and his place to go to get away from it all. Make sure your dog's crate is available to him when he wants to nap or take some time out. He'll use it on his own, so make sure he always has access to it. Depending on where it is, your dog will spend much of his sleeping time in his crate.

Finding the right crate

Select a crate that's large enough for your dog to turn around, stand up, or lie down comfortably. If he's a puppy, get a crate for the adult size dog so that he can grow into it.

Some crates are better than others in strength and ease of assembly. You can get crates in wire mesh-type material, cloth mesh, or plastic (called *airline crates*). Most are designed for portability and are easy to assemble. Our own preference for durability and versatility is a wire mesh crate. Wire mesh crates are easy to collapse, although they're heavier than crates made out of cloth mesh or plastic.

We recommend a good-quality crate that collapses easily and is portable so that you can take it with you when traveling with your dog. If you frequently take your dog with you in the car, consider getting two crates, one for the house and one for the car. Doing so saves you from having to lug one back and forth.

Coaxing Buddy into the crate

In order to coax Buddy into the crate, use these helpful hints:

1. **Set up the crate and let your dog investigate it.**

   Put a crate pad or blanket in the crate.

2. **Choose a command, such as "Crate" or "Go to bed."**

   If your puppy isn't lured in, physically place Buddy in the crate, using the command you've chosen.

3. **Close the door, tell him what a great puppy he is, give him a bite-sized treat, and then let him out.**

   There's no rule against gentle persuasion to get your pup enthused about his crate.

4. **Use a treat to coax him into the crate.**

   If he doesn't follow the treat, physically place him in the crate and then give him the treat.

5. **Again, close the door, tell him what a great little puppy he is, and give him a bite-sized treat.**

6. **Let him out.**

   The treat doesn't have to be a dog biscuit so long as it's an object the dog will actively work for.

7. **Continue using the command and giving Buddy a treat after he's in the crate until he goes into the crate with almost no help from you.**

For the puppy that's afraid of the crate, use his meals to overcome his fear. First, let him eat his meal in front of the crate, and then place his next meal just inside the crate. Put each successive meal a little farther into the crate until he's completely inside and no longer reluctant to enter.

Helping Buddy get used to the crate

Tell your dog to go into the crate, give him a treat, close the door, tell him what a good puppy he is, and then let him out again. Each time you do this, leave him in the crate a little longer with the door closed, still giving him a treat and telling him how great he is.

Finally, put him in his crate, give him a treat, and then leave the room — first for 5 minutes, and then 10 minutes, and then 15 minutes, and so on. Each time you return to let him out, tell him how good he was before you open the door.

How long can you ultimately leave your dog in his crate unattended? That depends on your dog and your schedule, but for an adult dog, don't let it be more than eight hours.

Never use your dog's crate as a form of punishment. If you do, he'll begin to dislike the crate, and it will lose its usefulness to you. You don't want Buddy to develop negative feelings about his crate. You want him to like his private den.

Identifying the Fundamentals of Housetraining Your Puppy

The keys to successful housetraining are

- ✔ Crate-training your puppy first.
- ✔ Setting a schedule for feeding and exercising your dog.
- ✔ Sticking to that schedule, even on weekends — at least until your dog is housetrained and mature.
- ✔ Vigilance, vigilance, and vigilance until your dog is trained.

Using a crate to housetrain your puppy is the most humane and effective way to get the job done. It's also the easiest way because of the dog's natural desire to keep his den clean. The crate, combined with a strict schedule and vigilance on your part, ensures speedy success (see "Using a Crate: A Playpen for Your Puppy" earlier in this chapter for tips on crate-training your puppy).

Over the course of a 24-hour period, puppies have to eliminate more frequently than adult dogs. A puppy's ability to control elimination increases with age, at approximately the rate of one hour per month. During the day, when active, the puppy can last for only short periods. Until he is 6 months of age, expecting him to last for more than four hours during the day without having to eliminate is unrealistic. When sleeping, most puppies can last through the night. If you have a female puppy and you notice frequent accidents (urine), it could be a sign of a bladder infection called *cystitis,* which requires a trip to the vet.

Set up an elimination schedule

Dogs thrive on a regular routine. By feeding and exercising Buddy at about the same time every day, he'll also relieve himself at about the same time every day.

Set a time to feed the puppy that's convenient for you. Always feed at the same time. Until he's 4 months of age, he needs four meals a day; from 4 to 7 months, three daily meals are appropriate. From then on, feed twice a day, which is healthier than feeding only once and helps with housetraining.

A sample feeding schedule follows:

- ✔ 7 weeks through 4 months — four times a day
- ✔ 4 months to 7 months — three times a day
- ✔ 7 months on — two times a day

Feed the right amount — loose stools are a sign of overfeeding; straining or dry stools a sign of underfeeding. After ten minutes, pick up the dish and put it away. Don't have food available at other times. Keep the diet constant. Abrupt changes of food may cause digestive upsets that won't help your housetraining efforts. (For tips on how often and how much to feed, look in Chapter 18.)

For the sake of convenience, you may be tempted to put your puppy's meal in a large bowl and leave it for him to nibble as he sees fit, called *self-feeding*. Although convenient, for purposes of housetraining, don't do it because you won't be able to keep track of when and how much he eats. You won't be able to time the in with the out.

Fresh water must be available to your dog at all times during the day. When left in his crate for more than two hours, leave him a dish of fresh water in the crate. You can also attach a little water bucket to the inside of the crate. After 8 p.m., remove his water dish so he can last through the night. If you work all day and are unable to follow this schedule, see the section, "Using an Exercise Pen for Housetraining" later in this chapter.

A strict schedule for your dog is a great asset in housetraining. If you feed your dog and take him out for exercise at the same times every day, he'll tend to eliminate at the same times every day. After you and your dog have established a schedule, you can project when he'll need to relieve himself and help him to be in the right spot at the right time.

Establish a regular toilet area

Start by selecting a toilet area and always take Buddy to that spot when you want him to eliminate. If possible, pick a place in a straight line from the house. Carry your puppy or put him on leash. Stand still and let him concentrate on what he's doing. Be patient and let him sniff around. After he's done, tell him what a clever puppy he is and play with him for a few minutes. Don't take him directly back inside so that he doesn't get the idea that he only gets to go outside to do his business and learns to delay the process just to stay outside.

Witnessing the act of your puppy relieving himself outside, followed by play-time, is perhaps one of the most important facets of housetraining. The first sign of not spending enough time outside with your puppy is when he comes back inside and has an accident. Letting the puppy out by himself isn't good enough — you have to go with him until his schedule has been developed.

Where you live will dictate your housetraining strategies. In a city, where dogs have to be curbed to relieve themselves, you need to keep Buddy on leash. You also need to pick up after him, *please!* If you walk your dog in a park or through a neighborhood, you also need to pick up after him. Don't let him do his business in a neighbor's yard — not even in the yard of that old crotchety neighbor who yelled at your children.

Even in your own yard, unless you have oodles of land, you need to pick up after him for sanitary reasons. If you have a fenced yard and don't mind where he goes, you can let him off leash. If you want him kept to a particular spot, keep him on leash and then clean up.

You may also want to teach Buddy a command, such as "Hurry up," so that you can speed up the process when necessary. Time the command to just before he starts and then lavishly praise when he has finished. After several repetitions, Buddy will associate the command with having to eliminate.

Keep your eyes open for signs

Take your puppy to his toilet area after waking up, shortly after eating or drinking, and after he has played or chewed. A sign that he has to go out is sniffing the ground in a circling motion.

Setting up a housetraining schedule

First thing in the morning, Mary takes her 12-week-old poodle puppy, Colette, out of her crate and straight outside to her toilet area. Fifteen minutes after Colette's morning meal, she's let out again. Mary then crates Colette and leaves for work.

On her lunch break, Mary goes home to let Colette out to relieve herself, and she plays with her for a few minutes. She then feeds her and, just to make sure, takes her out once more. For the afternoon, Colette is crated again until Mary returns. Colette is then walked and fed, after which she spends the rest of the evening in the house where Mary can keep an eye on her. Before bedtime, Colette goes out to her toilet area one more time and is then crated for the night.

When Colette becomes 7 months old, Mary will drop the noontime feeding and walk. From that age on, most dogs only need to go out immediately or soon after waking up in the morning, once during the late afternoon, and once again before bedtime.

When you see your puppy sniffing and circling, take note! He's letting you know that he's looking for a place to go. Take him out to his toilet area so he doesn't make a mistake.

Special care is required when it's raining or is very cold because many dogs, particularly those with short hair, don't like to go out in the wet anymore than you do. Make sure the puppy actually eliminates before you bring him back into the house.

An accident is an accident is an accident

No matter how conscientious and vigilant you are, your puppy will have an accident. Housetraining accidents may be simple mistakes, or they can be indicative of a physical problem. The key to remember is that, as a general rule, dogs want to be clean.

When Buddy has had an accident in the house, don't call him to you to punish him. It's too late. If you do punish your dog under these circumstances, it won't help your housetraining efforts, and you'll make him wary of wanting to come to you.

A popular misconception is that the dog knows "what he did" because he looks "guilty." *Absolutely not so!* He has that look because from prior experience he knows that when you happen to come across a mess, you get mad at him. He has learned to associate a mess with your response. He hasn't and can't make the connection between having made the mess in the first place and your anger. Discipline after the fact is the quickest way to undermine the relationship you're trying to build with your dog.

Dogs are smart, but they don't think in terms of cause and effect. When you come home from work and yell at your dog for having an accident in the living room, you aren't encouraging your dog to use his toilet area. All you're doing is letting him know that sometimes you're really nice and sometimes you're really mean. Swatting your dog with a rolled-up newspaper is cruel and only makes him afraid of you and rolled-up newspapers. Rubbing his nose in it is unsanitary and disgusting. Dogs may become housetrained in spite of such antics, but certainly not because of them.

When you come upon an accident, always keep calm. Put your dog out of sight so he can't watch you clean up. Use white vinegar or a stain remover. Don't use any ammonia-based cleaners, because the ammonia doesn't neutralize the odor and the puppy will be attracted to the same spot.

Accidents are just that — accidents. The worst thing you can do is call your dog to you to punish him. Your dog didn't do it on purpose, and most dogs are just as horrified by what happened as you are.

Be ready for regressions

Regressions in housetraining do occur, especially during teething. Regressions after 6 months of age may be a sign that your dog is ill. If accidents persist, take him to your vet for a checkup.

What to do if you catch Buddy in the act

If you catch your dog in the act, sharply call his name and clap your hands. If he stops, take him to his toilet area. If he doesn't, let him finish and don't get mad. Don't try to drag him out because that will make your clean-up job that much more difficult. Until your puppy is reliable, don't let him have the run of the house unsupervised.

How to train an adult dog

If you've obtained an adult dog from a shelter or other source, he may not be housetrained. For example, if he was tied on a chain outside, he most certainly won't be.

The rules for housetraining an adult dog are the same as for a puppy, but the process should go much more quickly. The adult dog's ability to control elimination is obviously much better than a puppy's.

What to do about an apartment dog

Many dogs live in apartments, and their owners have to jump through a variety of hoops to get their dogs outside, such as elevators, stairs, and so on. Moreover, if the owner is mobility impaired, taking the dog outside may be a real challenge.

Presumably, an apartment dog is a small dog. In any event, the easiest way to housetrain an apartment dog is to first follow the regimen by using a crate, and after that by using an X-pen (see the following section).

Using an Exercise Pen for Housetraining

Although a puppy can last in his crate for the night when he's asleep, you can't leave a puppy in his crate for purposes of housetraining for longer than four hours at a time during the day. Your puppy will soil his crate, which definitely isn't a habit you want to establish.

If your schedule is such that you can't keep an eye on Buddy during the day or come home to let the puppy out in time, the alternative is an exercise pen. An X-pen (see Figure 4-2) is intelligent confinement and uses the same principle as a crate, except it's bigger and has no top. An X-pen can also be used outdoors. For the super athlete who either climbs over or jumps out of the X-pen, you do have to cover the X-pen.

First, you need to acquire an X-pen commensurate to the size of your dog. For example, for a dog the size of a Labrador, the X-pen needs to be 10 square feet. Set up the X-pen where the puppy will be confined during your absence.

Figure 4-2:
An X-pen is another form of containment.

To get your dog comfortable in his X-pen, follow the same procedure as you did in introducing him to his crate (see "Coaxing Buddy into the crate" earlier in this chapter). When Buddy is "at home" in the X-pen and you're ready to leave him for the day, cover one-third of the area with newspapers for Buddy to use to eliminate on (no, he's not going to read the sports section). Cover one-third of the remaining area with a blanket, and leave one-third uncovered. The natural desire of your dog is to keep his sleeping area clean.

Buddy needs to have access to water during the day, so put his water dish on the uncovered area in the corner of the X-pen (some water is bound to splash out, and the uncovered floor is easy to clean). Before you leave, place a couple toys on Buddy's blanket, put him into X-pen with a dog biscuit, and leave while he's occupied with the biscuit. Don't make a big deal out of leaving — simply leave.

Some people try to rig up confinement areas by blocking off parts of a room or basement or whatever. Theoretically, this works, but it does permit Buddy to chew the baseboard, corners of cabinets, or anything else he can get his teeth on. Furthermore, leaving a dog on a concrete surface isn't a good idea. There's something about concrete that impedes housetraining; many dogs don't understand why it can't be used as a toilet area. Concrete also wreaks havoc on the elbows of large breeds.

You may want to confine your dog to part of a room with baby gates. This option works well for some people and some dogs, but remember it's no holds barred for whatever items Buddy can access. Lots of chew toys are a must!

Whatever barrier you decide to try, don't use an accordion-type gate — he could stick his head through it and possibly strangle himself.

You'll find that in the long run, your least expensive option — as is so often the case — is the right way from the start. Don't be penny-wise and pound-foolish by scrimping on the essentials at the risk of jeopardizing more expensive items. Splurging for an X-pen now will probably save you money on your home improvement budget later down the road.

Managing Marking Behavior

Marking is a way for your dog to leave his calling card by depositing a small amount of urine in a particular spot, marking it as his territory. The frequency with which dogs can accomplish marking never ceases to amaze us. Male dogs invariably prefer vertical surfaces, hence the fire hydrant. Males tend to engage in this behavior with more determination than females.

Doing your doody

Being a good dog neighbor means not letting Buddy deface the property of others and using only those areas specifically designed for that purpose. Even diehard dog lovers object to other dogs leaving their droppings on their lawn, the streets, and similar unsuitable areas. They also object to having their shrubbery or other vertical objects on their property doused by Buddy.

Part of responsible dog ownership is curbing and cleaning up after your dog. Don't let Buddy become the curse of your neighborhood. Do unto others as you would have them. . . .

Behaviorists explain that marking is a dog's way of establishing his territory, and it provides a means to find his way back home. They also claim that dogs are able to tell the rank order, gender, and age — puppy or adult dog — by smelling the urine of another dog.

Those people who take their dogs for regular walks through the neighborhood quickly discover that marking is a ritual, with favorite spots that have to be watered. It's a way for the dog to maintain his rank in the order of the pack, which consists of all the other dogs in the neighborhood or territory that come across his route.

Adult male dogs lift a leg, as do some females. For the male dog, the object is to leave his calling card higher than the previous calling card. This can lead to some comical results, as when a Dachshund or a Yorkshire Terrier tries to cover the calling card of an Irish Wolfhound or Great Dane. It's a contest.

Annoying as this behavior can be, it's perfectly natural and normal. At times, it can also be embarrassing, such as when Buddy lifts his leg on a person's leg, a not-uncommon occurrence. What he's trying to communicate here we'll leave to others to explain.

When this behavior is expressed inside the house, it becomes a problem. Fortunately, this behavior is rare, but it does happen.

Here are the circumstances requiring special vigilance:

- Taking Buddy to a friend's or relative's house for a visit, especially if that individual also has a dog or a cat
- When there's more than one animal in the house — another dog or dogs, or a cat

- ✔ When you've redecorated the house with new furniture and/or curtains
- ✔ When you've moved to a new house

Distract your dog if you see that he's about to mark in an inappropriate spot. Call his name, and take him to a place where he can eliminate. When you take Buddy to someone else's home, keep an eye on him. At the slightest sign that he's even thinking about it, interrupt his thought by clapping your hands and calling him to you. Take him outside and wait until he's had a chance to relieve himself.

If you catch Buddy in the act in your own house, you already know what to do (see "Identifying the Fundamentals of Housetraining Your Puppy" earlier in the chapter). If this behavior persists, you need to go back to basic house-training principles, such as the crate or X-pen, until you can trust him again.

Traveling by Car with Buddy

The same rules of housetraining apply when you're traveling with your dog. In the car, crate Buddy for his and your safety. If he's still a puppy, be prepared to stop about every two hours. An older dog can last much longer.

When we travel with one or more of our dogs, we make a point to keep to their feeding schedule and exercising routine as closely as possible. Sticking to customary daily rhythm prevents digestive upsets that can lead to accidents. For a great deal more information on this subject, see Susan McCullough's *Housetraining For Dummies* (Wiley).

Chapter 5

Understanding Your Dog's Mind

*T*o train Buddy, you need some insight into what is happening at any given moment in his little brain. Here, your powers of observation can help you. In many instances, Buddy's behavior is quite predictable based on what he has done in similar situations before. You may be surprised at what you already know. You can almost see the wheels turning when he's about to chase a car, bicycle, or jogger. If you're observant, Buddy will give you just enough time to stop him.

You don't, however, have to rely on observation alone. To help you understand how Buddy's mind works, we've devised a simple Personality Profile that's an amazingly accurate predictor of his behavior, such as his propensity to chase moving objects.

Such is the stuff of this chapter. Read on.

Recognizing Your Dog's Instinctive Behaviors

Your dog and every other dog is an individual animal that comes into the world with a specific grouping of genetically inherited, predetermined behaviors. How those behaviors are arranged, their intensity, and how many components of each determine the dog's temperament, personality, and suitability for the task required. Those behaviors also determine how the dog perceives the world.

Can dogs "reason"?

As much as you would want your dog to be able to reason, the answer is no, not in the sense that humans can. Dogs can, however, solve simple problems. By observing your dog, you learn his problem-solving techniques. Just watch him try to open the cupboard where the dog biscuits are kept. Or see how he works at trying to retrieve his favorite toy from under the couch. During your training, you'll also have the opportunity to see Buddy trying to work out what you're teaching him.

Our favorite story involves a very smart English Springer Spaniel who had been left on our doorstep. The poor fellow had been so neglected that we didn't know he was a pure-bred Spaniel until after he paid a visit to the groomer. He became a delightful member of the family for many years. One day, his ball had rolled under the couch. He tried everything — looking under the couch, jumping on the back-rest to look behind it, and going around to both sides. Nothing seemed to work. In disgust, he lifted his leg on the couch and walked away. So much for problem solving.

To give you a better understanding of your dog, we group instinctive behaviors into three drives:

- ✔ Prey
- ✔ Pack
- ✔ Defense

These *drives* reflect instinctive behaviors that your dog has inherited and that are useful to you in teaching him what you want him to learn. Each one of these drives is governed by a basic trait.

Prey drive

Prey drive includes those inherited behaviors associated with hunting, killing prey, and eating. The prey drive is activated by motion, sound, and smell. Behaviors associated with prey drive (see Figure 5-1) include the following:

- ✔ Air scenting and tracking
- ✔ Biting and killing
- ✔ Carrying
- ✔ Digging and burying
- ✔ Eating

- High-pitched barking
- Jumping up and pulling down
- Pouncing
- Seeing, hearing, and smelling
- Shaking an object
- Stalking and chasing
- Tearing and ripping apart

You see some of these behaviors when Buddy is chasing the cat or gets excited and barks in a high-pitched tone as the cat runs up a tree. Buddy may also shake and rip up soft toys or bury bones in the couch.

Figure 5-1: A dog exhibits typical prey drive behaviors.

Pack drive

Pack drive consists of behaviors associated with reproduction, being part of a group or pack, and being able to live by the rules. Dogs, like their distant ancestors the wolves, are social animals. To hunt prey that's mostly larger than themselves, wolves have to live in a pack. To assure order, they adhere to a social hierarchy governed by strict rules of behavior. In dogs, this translates into an ability to be part of a human group and means a willingness to work with people as part of a team.

Pack drive is stimulated by rank order in the social hierarchy. Behaviors associated with this drive include the following:

- Being able to breed and to be a good parent
- Demonstrating behaviors associated with social interaction with people and other dogs, such as reading body language
- Demonstrating reproductive behaviors, such as licking, mounting, washing ears, and all courting gestures
- Exhibiting physical contact with people and/or other dogs
- Playing with people and/or other dogs

A dog with many of these behaviors is the one that follows you around the house, is happiest when with you, loves to be petted and groomed, and likes to work with you. (Check out Figure 5-2.) A dog with these behaviors may be unhappy when left alone too long, which is a feeling that can express itself in separation anxiety.

Figure 5.2:
A dog exhibits typical pack drive behaviors.

Defense drive

Defense drive is governed by survival and self-preservation and consists of both fight and flight behaviors. Defense drive is complex because the same stimulus that can make a dog aggressive (fight) can elicit avoidance (flight) behaviors, especially in a young dog.

Fight behaviors aren't fully developed until the dog is sexually mature or about 2 years old. You may notice tendencies toward these behaviors at an earlier age, and life experiences determine their intensity. Behaviors associated with fight drive include the following:

- ✔ Disapproving of being petted or groomed
- ✔ Hackling up from the shoulder forward
- ✔ Growling at people or dogs when he feels his space is being violated
- ✔ Guarding food, toys, or territory against people and dogs
- ✔ Lying in front of doorways or cupboards and refusing to move
- ✔ Putting his head over another dog's shoulder
- ✔ Standing tall, weight forward on front legs, tail high, and staring at other dogs
- ✔ Standing his ground and not moving

Flight behaviors demonstrate that the dog is unsure, and young dogs tend to exhibit more flight behaviors than older dogs. The following behaviors are associated with flight drive:

- ✔ Demonstrating a general lack of confidence
- ✔ Disliking being touched by strangers
- ✔ Flattening of the body with the tail tucked when greeted by people or other dogs
- ✔ Hackling that goes up the full length of the body, not just at the neck
- ✔ Hiding or running away from a new situation
- ✔ Urinating when being greeted by a stranger or the owner

Freezing — not going forward or backward — is interpreted as inhibited flight behavior.

Whoa! Buddy's got his hackles up

Hackles refer to the fur along the dog's spine from the neck to the tip of his tail. When a dog is frightened or unsure, the fur literally stands up and away from his spine. In a young dog, it may happen frequently because the dog's life experiences are minimal. When he meets a new dog, for example, he may be unsure whether or not that dog is friendly, and so his hackles go up. His whiskers are also a good indication of his insecurity; they're pulled back, flat along his face. His ears are pulled back, and his tail is tucked.

And he cringes, lowering his body posture and averting his eyes. All in all, he'd rather be somewhere else.

On the flip side, when the hackles go up only from the neck to the shoulders, the dog is sure of himself. He's the boss, and he's ready to take on all comers. His ears are erect, his whiskers are forward, all his weight is on his front legs, his tail is held high, and he stands tall and makes direct eye contact. He's ready to rumble.

How the drives affect training

Because dogs were originally bred for a particular function and not solely for appearance, you can, as a general rule, predict the strength or weakness of the individual drives. For example, the northern breeds, such as Alaskan Malamutes and Siberian Huskies, were bred to pull sleds. They tend to be low in pack drive, and training them not to pull on the leash can be a bit of a chore. Herding dogs were bred to herd livestock under the direction of their master. Although high in prey drive, they also tend to be high in pack drive and should be relatively easy to train not to pull on the leash. The guarding breeds, such as the German Shepherd, Doberman, and Rottweiler, were bred to work closely with man, so they tend to be high in fight drive with a desire to protect family and property. They can be easily taught to walk on a leash. The Retrievers tend to be high in prey as well as pack drive and generally love to retrieve. They too can be easily taught to walk on a leash.

Many of the behaviors for which dogs were bred, such as herding and hunting, are the very ones that get them into trouble today. These behaviors involve prey drive and result in chasing anything that moves. A guard dog may guard your home against intruders and protect your children, but those "intruders" may include the children's friends.

Clearly, these generalizations don't apply to every dog of a particular breed. Today, many dogs of different breeds were bred solely for appearance and without regard to function, so their original traits have become diluted.

Determining Your Dog's Personality Profile

To help you understand how to approach your dog's training, we created *Volhards' Canine Personality Profile.* The profile catalogs ten behaviors in each drive that influence a dog's responses and that are useful in training. The ten behaviors chosen are those that most closely represent the dog's strengths in each of the drives. The profile doesn't pretend to include all behaviors seen in a dog, nor the complexity of their interaction. For example, what drive is Buddy in when he's sleeping? For purposes of training, we don't care. Although our Personality Profile is an admittedly crude tool for predicting Buddy's behavior, you'll find it surprisingly accurate.

The results of the profile can give you a better understanding of why Buddy is the way he is and the most successful way to train him. You can then make use of his strengths, avoid needless confusion, and greatly reduce training time.

When completing the profile, keep in mind that we devised it for a house dog or pet with an enriched environment, perhaps even a little training, and not a dog tied out in the yard or kept solely in a kennel — such dogs have fewer opportunities to express as many behaviors as a house dog. Answers should indicate those behaviors Buddy would exhibit if he'd not already been trained to do otherwise. For example, did he jump on people to greet them or jump on the counter to steal food before he was trained not to do so?

The possible answers and their corresponding point values are as follows:

- ✔ Almost always — 10
- ✔ Sometimes — 5 to 9
- ✔ Hardly ever — 0 to 4

For example, if Buddy is a Beagle, the answer to the question "When presented with the opportunity, does your dog sniff the ground or air?" is probably "almost always," giving him a score of 10.

You're now ready to find out who Buddy really is. You may not have had the chance to observe all these behaviors, in which case you leave the answer blank.

When presented with the opportunity, does your dog

1. Sniff the ground or air? _____
2. Get along with other dogs? _____
3. Stand his ground or show curiosity in strange objects or sounds? _____
4. Run away from new situations? _____
5. Get excited by moving objects, such as bikes or squirrels? _____
6. Get along with people? _____
7. Like to play tug-of-war games to win? _____
8. Hide behind you when he feels he can't cope? _____
9. Stalk cats, other dogs, or things in the grass? _____
10. Bark when left alone? _____
11. Bark or growl in a deep tone of voice? _____
12. Act fearfully in unfamiliar situations? _____
13. Bark in a high-pitched voice when excited? _____
14. Solicit petting, or like to snuggle with you? _____
15. Guard his territory? _____
16. Tremble or whine when unsure? _____
17. Pounce on his toys? _____
18. Like to be groomed? _____
19. Guard his food or toys? _____
20. Cower or turn upside down when reprimanded? _____
21. Shake and "kill" his toys? _____
22. Seek eye contact with you? _____
23. Dislike being petted? _____
24. Act reluctant to come close to you when called? _____
25. Steal food or garbage? _____
26. Follow you around like a shadow? _____
27. Guard his owner(s)? _____
28. Have difficulty standing still when groomed? _____
29. Like to carry things in his mouth? _____
30. Play a lot with other dogs? _____
31. Dislike being groomed or petted? _____
32. Cower or cringe when a stranger bends over him? _____

33. Wolf down his food? _____
34. Jump up to greet people? _____
35. Like to fight other dogs? _____
36. Urinate during greeting behavior? _____
37. Like to dig and/or bury things? _____
38. Show reproductive behaviors, such as mounting other dogs? _____
39. Get picked on by older dogs when he was a young dog? _____
40. Tend to bite when cornered? _____

Score your answers by using Table 5-1.

Table 5-1	Scoring the Profile		
Prey	*Pack*	*Fight*	*Flight*
1.	2.	3.	4.
5.	6.	7.	8.
9.	10.	11.	12.
13.	14.	15.	16.
17.	18.	19.	20.
21.	22.	23.	24.
25.	26.	27.	28.
29.	30.	31.	32.
33.	34.	35.	36.
37.	38.	39.	40.
Total Prey	Total Pack	Total Fight	Total Flight

After you've obtained the totals, enter them into the appropriate column of the profile at a glance that's shown in Table 5-1. (Check out Figure 5-3 to see your dog's profile at a glance.)

To make best use of the concept of drives in your training, you need to know what you want Buddy to do or stop doing. Usually, you want him to be in pack drive, and he wants to be in prey. After you've mastered how to get him out of prey and into pack, you have a well-trained dog.

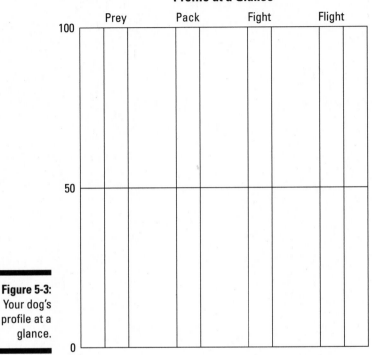

Profile at a Glance

Figure 5-3:
Your dog's
profile at a
glance.

Deciding How You Want Buddy to Act

Before you can use the results of the profile, you need to look at what you want Buddy to do or — and this is often more important — stop doing. For example, when you walk Buddy on leash and want him to pay attention to you, he has to be in pack drive. Buddy, on the other hand, wants to sniff, maybe follow a trail, or chase the neighbor's cat; he is in prey drive.

For most of what you want Buddy to do, such as the following, he needs to be in pack drive:

- ✔ Come
- ✔ Down
- ✔ Sit
- ✔ Stay
- ✔ Walk on a loose leash

For most of what Buddy wants to do, such as the following, he's going to be in prey drive:

- ✔ Chase a cat
- ✔ Dig
- ✔ Follow the trail of a rabbit
- ✔ Retrieve a ball or stick
- ✔ Sniff the grass

You can readily see that those times when you want him to behave, you have to convince Buddy to forget about being in prey drive. Dogs high in prey drive usually require quite a bit of training. The dog with high pack and low prey drive rarely needs extensive training, if any at all.

Such a dog doesn't do the following:

- ✔ Chase bicycles, cars, children, or joggers
- ✔ Chase cats or other animals
- ✔ Chew your possessions
- ✔ Pull on the leash
- ✔ Roam from home
- ✔ Steal food

In other words, he's a perfect pet.

Theoretically, Buddy doesn't need defense drive (fight) behaviors for what you want him to learn, but the *absence* of these behaviors has important ramifications. A very low defense drive determines how Buddy has to be trained. For example, our first Labrador, Bean, was low in defense drive. If we, or anyone else, would lean over him, he would collapse on the floor and act as though he had been beaten. Katharina, our German Shepherd, on the other hand, who was high in fight drive, would just look at you if you leaned over her, as though to say, "Okay, what do you want?"

Training each dog required a different approach. With Bean, a check on his leash caused him to literally collapse — he didn't have enough fight behaviors to cope with the check. A slight tug on the leash or a quietly spoken command was sufficient to get him to ignore chasing our proverbial rabbit. Katharina required a firm check to convince her to forget about the rabbit. The only difference between the two dogs was their score in fight drive on their Personality Profile. (Refer to the following sections for the different profiles and how to deal with them.)

The beauty of the drives theory is that, if used correctly, it gives you the necessary insight to overcome areas where you and your dog are at odds with each other as to appropriate behavior. A soft command may be enough for one dog to change the undesired behavior, whereas a check is required for another.

Bringing out drives

When you grill hamburgers on the barbecue, the aroma stimulates your appetite, as well as everyone else's in the neighborhood. In effect, it brings out your prey drive. The smell becomes a cue. Incidentally, the smell also brings out Buddy's prey drive.

Following is a short list of cues that bring out each of the dog's major drives:

- **Prey drive** is elicited by the use of motion — hand signals (except "Stay") — a high-pitched tone of voice, the movement of an object of attraction (stick, ball, or food), chasing or being chased, and leaning or running backwards as your dog comes to you.

- **Pack drive** is elicited by calmly and quietly touching, praising and smiling, grooming, and playing and training with your body erect.

- **Defense drive** is elicited by a threatening body posture, such as leaning or hovering over the dog either from the front or the side, staring at the dog with direct eye contact (this is how people get bitten), leaning over and wagging a finger in the dog's face while chastising him, checking the dog, using a harsh tone of voice, and exaggerating the use of the "Stay" hand signal (see Chapter 7).

Switching drives

Buddy can instantaneously switch himself from one drive to another. Picture this scene — Buddy is lying in front of the fireplace:

He's playing with his favorite toy.

The doorbell rings; he drops the toy, starts to bark, and goes to the door.

You open the door; it's a neighbor, and Buddy goes to greet him.

He returns to play with his toy.

Buddy has switched himself from prey into defense into pack and back into prey.

During training, your task is to keep Buddy in the right drive, and if necessary, switch him from one drive into another. For example, you're teaching Buddy to walk on a loose leash in the yard when a rabbit pops out of the hedge. He immediately spots it, runs to the end of the leash, straining and barking excitedly in a high-pitched voice. He's clearly in full-blown prey drive.

Now you have to get him back into pack, where he needs to be to walk at your side. The only way you can do that is by going through defense. You can't, for example, show him a cookie in an effort to divert his attention from the rabbit. The rabbit is going to win out.

The precise manner in which you get Buddy back into pack drive — you must go through defense — depends on the strength of his defense drive. If he has a large number of defense (fight) behaviors, you can give him a firm tug on the leash, which switches him out of prey into defense. To then get him into pack, touch him *gently* on the top of his head (don't pat), smile at him, and tell him how clever he is. Then continue to work on your walking on a loose leash.

If he's low in defense (fight) behaviors, a check may overpower him, and a voice communication, such as "Ah, ah" will be sufficient to get him out of prey into defense, after which you put him back into pack drive.

For the dog that has few fight behaviors and a large number of flight behaviors, a check on the leash is often counterproductive. Body postures, such as bending over the dog or even using a deep tone of voice, are usually enough to elicit defense drive. By his response to your training — cowering, rolling upside down, not wanting to come to you for the training session — your dog will show you when you overpower him, thereby making learning difficult, if not impossible.

Here are the basic rules for switching from one drive to another:

- **From prey into pack:** You must go through defense.

  How you put your dog into defense depends on the number of defense (fight) behaviors he has. As a general rule, the more defense (fight) behaviors the dog has, the firmer the check needs to be. As the dog learns, a barely audible voice communication or a slight change in body posture will suffice to encourage your dog to go from prey through defense into pack drive.

- **From defense into pack:** Gently touch or smile at your dog.

- **From pack into prey:** Use an object (such as food) or motion.

Applying the concept of drives, learning which drive Buddy has to be in and how to get him there speeds up your training process enormously. As you become aware of the impact your body stance and motions have on the drive he's in, your messages will be perfectly clear to your dog. Your body language is congruent with what you're trying to teach. Because Buddy is an astute observer of body motions, which is how dogs communicate with each other, he'll understand exactly what you want.

Applying drives to your training

By looking at your dog's profile (see the questionnaire earlier in this chapter), you know the training techniques that work best and are in harmony with your dog's drives. You now have the tools to tailor your training program to your dog.

- **Defense (fight) — more than 60:** A firm hand doesn't bother your dog much. Correct body posture isn't critical, although incongruent postures on your part can slow down the training. Tone of voice should be firm, but pleasant and nonthreatening.

- **Defense (flight) — more than 60:** Your dog won't respond to strong corrections. Correct body posture and a quiet, pleasant tone of voice are critical. Avoid using a harsh tone of voice and any hovering — either leaning over or toward your dog. There's a premium on congruent body postures and gentle handling.

- **Prey — more than 60.** Your dog will respond well to a treat or toy during the teaching phase. A firm hand may be necessary, depending on strength of defense drive (fight), to suppress prey drive when in high gear, such as when chasing a cat or spotting a squirrel. This dog is easily motivated, but also easily distracted by motion or moving objects. Signals will mean more to this dog than commands. There's a premium on using body, hands, and leash correctly so as not to confuse the dog.

- **Prey — less than 60.** Your dog probably isn't easily motivated by food or other objects, but also isn't easily distracted by or interested in chasing moving objects. Use praise to your advantage in training.

- **Pack — more than 60.** This dog responds readily to praise and physical affection. The dog likes to be with you and will respond with little guidance.

- **Pack — less than 60.** Start praying. Buddy probably doesn't care whether he's with you or not. He likes to do his own thing and isn't easily motivated. Your only hope is to rely on prey drive in training. Limited pack drive is usually breed-specific for dogs bred to work independently of man.

Dogs with defense drive of less than 60 rarely get into trouble — in fact, they avoid it. Many young dogs without life experience fall into this category, and although their numbers may be quite low as pups, they may vary slightly with age. With such a dog, a straight body posture is more important, and to greet him, you need to squat down — as opposed to bending at the waist — to the dog's level.

If your dog is high in both prey and defense (fight), you may need professional help. He's by no means a bad dog, but you may become exasperated with your lack of success. The dog may simply be too much for you to train on your own. (See Chapter 20 for advice on finding help.)

Dogs that exhibit an overabundance in prey or pack are also easily trained, but you'll have to pay more attention to the strengths of their drives and exploit those behaviors most useful to you in training. You now have the tools to do it!

Here are some other important hints to keep in mind when planning your training strategy:

- ✔ If your dog is high in defense (fight), you need to work especially diligently on your leadership exercises and review them frequently (see Chapter 2).

- ✔ If your dog is high in prey, you also need to work on these leadership exercises to control him around doorways, moving objects, and similar distractions.

- ✔ If your dog is high in both prey and defense (fight), you may need professional help with your training.

Following are the nicknames for a few of the profiles. See if you can recognize your dog.

- ✔ **The Couch Potato — low prey, low pack, low defense (fight):** This dog is difficult to motivate and probably doesn't need extensive training. He needs extra patience if training is attempted because he has few behaviors with which to work. On the plus side, this dog is unlikely to get into trouble, doesn't disturb anyone, makes a good family pet, and doesn't mind being left alone for considerable periods of time.

- ✔ **The Hunter — high prey, low pack, low defense (flight):** This dog gives the appearance of having an extremely short attention span but is perfectly able to concentrate on what he finds interesting. Training requires the channeling of his energy to get him to do what you want. You need patience, because you have to teach the dog through prey drive.

✔ **The Gas Station Dog — high prey, low pack, high defense (fight):** This dog is independent and not easy to live with as a pet. Highly excitable by movement, he may attack anything that comes within range. He doesn't care much about people or dogs and works well as a guard dog. Pack exercises, such as walking on a leash without pulling, need to be built up through his prey drive. This dog is a real challenge.

✔ **The Runner — high prey, low pack, high defense (flight):** Easily startled and/or frightened, this dog needs quiet and reassuring handling. A dog with this profile isn't a good choice for children.

✔ **The Shadow — low prey, high pack, and low defense (fight):** This dog follows you around all day and is unlikely to get into trouble. He likes to be with you and isn't interested in chasing much of anything.

✔ **Teacher's Pet — medium (50 to 75) prey, pack, and defense (fight):** This dog is easy to train and motivate, and mistakes on your part aren't critical. Teacher's Pet has a nice balance of drives. He's easily motivated and therefore quite easy to train — even when your training skills aren't particularly keen. At our training camps and seminars, we have the owners put the profile of their dogs in graph form for easy reading. Figure 5-4 shows the graph for Teacher's Pet.

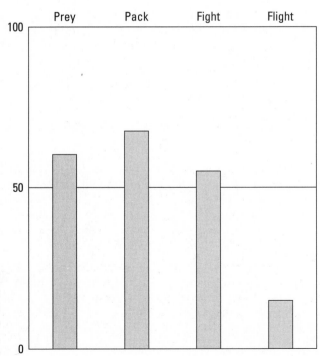

Figure 5-4:
A typical Teacher's Pet profile.

By now, you've gathered that the easiest dogs are those that are balanced among all drives. No matter what you do, the dog seems to be able to figure out what you want. If you're lucky enough to have such a dog, take good care of him. By applying the principles of drives, he'll be easy to turn into a well-trained pet.

People frequently ask us, "Can you change a dog's drives — either reduce or enhance a particular drive?" There are a few instances where you can enhance a drive through training. For example, after you've taught a dog with few prey behaviors to retrieve, he *may* be more inclined to participate in fetch games. As a general rule, however, the answer is "No." You see what you get and you get what you see.

Chapter 6

Equipping for Training Success

. . . .

In This Chapter

▶ Getting yourself (and your dog) ready for training

▶ Distinguishing between leashes and collars

▶ Balancing fit and safety concerns

▶ Taking advantage of training treats

. . . .

Dog training is no different from any other activity — you need the right equipment for the job. Many choices are available to you, and in this chapter, we address the factors that determine what training equipment to use under what circumstances.

Just because it's a collar or a leash doesn't mean you can use it to *train* your dog. In Chapter 2, we discuss how the mother dog teaches her puppies to stop doing something she doesn't want them to do. She uses a correction, something the puppies perceive as unpleasant, to get them to stop. This unpleasant experience, in turn, teaches the puppies the responsibility for their own behavior. A puppy says to himself, "If I use my teeth on Mommy, I'll get nailed. If I don't, mommy will lick my face." So puppy chooses not to use his teeth on Mommy. That, at any rate, is the gist of what we think is the puppy's thought process.

Teaching your dog the responsibility for his own behavior is the key to training. Therefore, the dog has to perceive the correction as unpleasant so he can avoid it. (See Chapter 2 for training descriptions and definitions.) If he doesn't perceive it as unpleasant, there's nothing to avoid, and the objectionable behavior continues. Hence, the importance of the right training equipment.

Choosing the Right Training Equipment

The type of training collar and leash you need depends on a number of factors, including the ones in the following list:

- Your dog's Personality Profile (see Chapter 5)
- Your dog's touch sensitivity or threshold of discomfort
- Your dog's size and weight in relation to your size and weight
- The equipment's effectiveness
- Your dog's safety
- Your aptitude for training your dog

Keep in mind that training isn't a matter of strength but finesse. For you, Buddy's trainer, it doesn't have to be a heavy aerobic workout.

Pulling on leashes

Leashes come in an assortment of styles, materials, widths, and lengths. The following are the most common materials:

- **Canvas:** Canvas leashes are readily available in pet stores and through catalogs and Web sites. They come in a variety of colors, although olive green seems to be the most common. We get ours from Handcraft Collars (www.handcraftcollars.com).

  The best training leash is a six-foot canvas leash — it's easy on the hands, easily manipulated, and just the right length. It's also the most economical. For the average-size or larger dog, such as a Labrador, we use a canvas leash that's ½-inch wide. For toy dogs, such as a Yorkshire Terrier, we use a leash that's ¼-inch wide.

- **Nylon:** For a training leash, our materials of choice are canvas or nylon. Both can be readily manipulated, an important factor for the method we use, and they're economical. Canvas, especially with larger dogs, is easier on your hands than nylon.

- **Leather:** Leather leashes are also quite popular, although they're more expensive than canvas leashes. They're usually bulkier than canvas or nylon but do not readily lend themselves to our approach to training.

> ✔ **Chain:** We've never quite understood the purpose of chain leashes or why anyone would want to use them, but they exist. Chain leashes are often used with large dogs, but they're heavy, unwieldy, and hard on the hands. For example, if you wanted to fold the leash neatly into one hand or the other, as required by the training techniques we teach in this book, you wouldn't be able to do so without considerable discomfort. It's definitely not a leash you can use for training Buddy.

Choosing among collars

Collars also come in a dazzling assortment of styles, colors, and materials. We distinguish between two types of collars:

✔ Training collars

✔ Collars for the trained dog, which can be ornamental

The purpose of a *training* collar is for you to be able to guide your dog and, if necessary, to check your dog. (A *check* is a crisp snap on the leash, followed by an immediate release of tension.) A check is used mainly for abstention training, when you want your dog to stop doing something that he wants to do but that you don't want him to do (see Chapter 2). The check creates an unpleasant experience for the dog, which he can avoid by stopping the unwanted behavior, similar to a mother dog snapping at a puppy.

Collars for the trained dog are *buckle collars,* and they can be leather, nylon, or canvas. For the untrained dog, buckle collars are virtually useless. Picture yourself trying to hang on as a fully-grown Rottweiler decides to take off after a cat. Trying to control that dog with a buckle collar would definitely be a heavy aerobic workout.

Some owners prefer a harness, which is perfectly fine for dogs that don't pull or for small dogs, where pulling isn't terribly objectionable. But for a medium-sized or large dog that pulls, harnesses aren't a good idea because you give up the control you're trying to achieve. The dog literally leans into the harness and happily drags you wherever he wants to go. The only exception we can think of for using a harness on an untrained dog is if the dog has a neck injury.

Use the two types of collars — training collars and buckle collars — correctly. Remove the training collar when you aren't training your dog or when you can't supervise him. When not training, your dog should wear his buckle collar with ID tags attached.

You can find any number of training collars. We describe the advantages and disadvantages of each in the following sections.

Chain or nylon slip-on collars

A *slip-on collar,* usually made of chain or nylon, is one that slips over the dog's head. Because such a collar has to fit over the dog's neck, it has the tendency to slide down the dog's neck. The strongest part of a dog's body is where the neck joins the shoulder blades. The farther the collar slides down the neck, the more difficult controlling the dog becomes and the less effective the collar is as a training tool. Table 6-1 lists the pros and cons of this type of collar.

Table 6-1	Pros and Cons of Slip-On Collars
Advantages	*Disadvantages*
Readily available in pet stores and through catalogs	Not very effective
Inexpensive	Great potential for damaging the dog's trachea and neck
Easy to put on	Therefore, easy to come off — not very helpful when trying to make Buddy walk without pulling

Not only are slip-on collars ineffective for purposes of training, but when improperly used, they also pose a danger to your dog's trachea and spine. Avoid them! Animal chiropractors have made similar observations of spinal misalignment caused by this collar. Because slip-on collars aren't very effective to begin with and have a poor safety record, we recommend you save your money and get something that works, such as the nylon snap-around collar.

If you do decide to use a slip-on collar, put it on by taking the live ring, the one that pulls the collar tighter, and pass it over the dog's neck from left to right. In this position, the weight of the dead ring will automatically release the collar when pressure is released from the live ring. When worn the other way, the pressure from the live ring won't release promptly.

Nylon snap-around collars

The principal difference between a slip-on and a nylon, snap-around collar is that the latter has a clasp that enables you to fasten the collar around the dog's neck instead of having to slip it over his head. That way, you can fit the collar high on your dog's neck where you have the most control. It should fit high on his neck, just below his ears, as snug as a turtleneck sweater, for maximum control. Table 6-2 presents some other advantages (and disadvantages) to a snap-around collar.

The snap-around collar is our first choice collar because of its effectiveness and versatility. For more than 30 years we've used the same source — Handcraft Collars — because of the quality and durability (see www. handcraftcollars.com for more information).

Table 6-2	Pros and Cons of Nylon Snap-Around Collars
Advantages	*Disadvantages*
Fairly inexpensive	A puppy will grow out of it quickly, and you may have to purchase others
Can be fitted exactly to your dog's neck	Not as easy to put on as a slip-on collar
Very effective	
Quite safe	

The snap-around collar is guaranteed to fit your dog properly. The collar should sit just below your dog's ears. Measure the circumference of your dog's neck directly behind his ears with sewing tape, or a piece of string that you can then measure with a ruler. The collars from Handcraft come in half-inch increments.

The snap-around collar comprises

✔ A clasp on one side

✔ A ring on the other side

✔ A loose or floating ring

Start with you and your dog facing each other. Then follow these steps to place a snap-around collar on your dog:

1. **Take the clasp in your left hand and the two rings in your right hand.**

2. **Place the collar under your dog's neck and bring the ends up to the top of his neck, directly behind the ears.**

   When you begin to put on the collar, the dog flexes his neck muscles, expanding the circumference of the neck by as much as a half inch, creating the impression that the collar is much tighter than it actually is (similar to the effect produced by a horse taking in air as it's being saddled).

3. Attach the clasp to the floating ring.

The smooth side of the clasp needs to be next to the dog's skin.

TIP

You may get the impression that the collar is much too tight and that you can barely get it around Buddy's neck. We suggest that after the first time you put the collar on, you wait for five minutes. After the dog has relaxed, you then can test for correct snugness. You need to be able to slip two fingers between the collar and your dog's neck (one finger if you have a toy dog). If you can't, the collar is too tight; if you can get three or more fingers through, the collar is too loose. One way to make the collar smaller is to tie a knot in it.

After you have the collar on, you can use it as a training collar by attaching the leash to the *live ring* of the collar or as a buckle collar by attaching it to the *dead ring* of the collar.

The *live ring* of the training collar is the floating ring; the *dead ring* of the collar is the stationary ring (see Figure 6-1).

Some dogs don't respond to a check on a snap-around collar — that is, the check doesn't create an unpleasant experience for the dog and change his behavior. The dog may be touch-insensitive and have a high discomfort threshold. Or, the dog's size and weight in relation to your size and weight may be such that he doesn't feel your check. When that happens, you may need to consider a pinch collar.

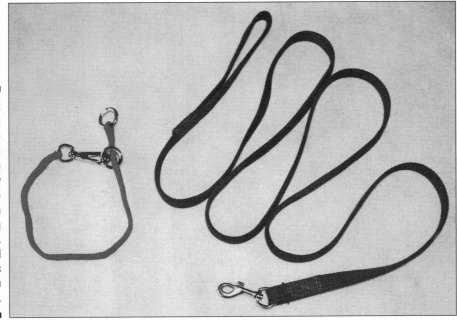

Figure 6-1:
The floating ring is the live ring and the stationary ring is the dead ring on a training collar (left). An ideal leash is shown on the right.

Take the training collar off your dog when he isn't being trained and whenever he isn't under your direct supervision. Don't attach any tags to the training collar. When you're not training your dog, use a buckle collar you've attached his tags to.

Pinch collars

For old-time trainers, the pinch collar was the only collar to use. Also called a prong collar, a pinch collar certainly is an effective and efficient training tool. Those who use one for the first time often refer to it as power steering. We jokingly call it the *religious collar* because it makes an instant convert out of the dog.

According to our vet, who is also a certified animal chiropractor, the pinch collar is generally the safest training collar. From our perspective, it's also the most effective training collar. Table 6-3 offers some of the highlights and lowlights of using the pinch collar.

Table 6-3	Pros and Cons of Pinch Collar
Advantages	*Disadvantages*
Readily available in pet stores and through catalogs	Looks like a medieval instrument of torture
Very effective	Twice as expensive as a snap-on collar
Can be fit to the exact size of the dog's neck	
Very safe — it's self-limiting in that it constricts very little and not to the point where the dog's air can be cut off	

Pinch collars come in four sizes: large, medium, small, and micro. We've never used or recommended the large size because it appears to have been made for elephants. For a large, strong, and rambunctious dog, the medium size is more than adequate. For Golden Retriever–sized or smaller dogs, the small size is sufficient. For toy dogs, use the micro version, which must be ordered.

Any collar or piece of training equipment can be misused or abused. The intent of the user is the key to achieving a harmonious relationship through training.

Clara's story

When we met Clara, she was in her mid-60s. She lived in a large house outside of town, fairly isolated, although she could see some of her neighbors. We discovered that Clara had had a number of dogs during her life and after her last dog died, had acquired a German Shepherd puppy. Clara felt that she needed a dog that would protect her. She named the puppy Ursa. Whenever we talked, Clara would extol Ursa's virtues — how sweet she was, how easy she was to train, how well she played with the grandchildren, and how many tricks she'd learned.

As time went by, we found out more about Clara. She'd had back surgery with steel rods implanted, and she frequently had to wear a neck brace. She then told us that she had to put Ursa on a pinch collar to walk her. Clara said,

"She just got too strong for me. Every time we went for a walk, she would sniff the ground where the deer had been and she would pull so hard that I didn't think I could hold her. So, I put her on a pinch collar to control her and now, after two weeks, I can walk her on her regular collar and she no longer pulls me off my feet. Without the pinch collar to help me, who knows what I would have done. I even thought that I might have to give her up, a thought I couldn't bear. Who knows what would have happened to her?"

Now when we meet Clara, she often has Ursa with her, and according to Clara, the dog is a saint. She said, "Instead of being frustrated and angry with her, I tell her what a good girl she is. I'm happy, and she is happy."

The pinch collar does rub some people the wrong way, because it looks like a medieval instrument of torture. Others consider it inhumane. People's perception of a given piece of equipment, however, is immaterial. What counts is the dog's perception, and your dog will tell you. Does your check have the desired effect on the dog's behavior? Are you putting your dog in a position where you can sincerely praise him for the correct response, or are you angry with him and calling him names? Yes, dogs have feelings, too!

In selecting training equipment, keep in mind the circumstances. A dog's *touch sensitivity,* or threshold of discomfort, increases proportionally with the interest the dog has in what interests him (see Chapter 5 for more info about understanding your dog's mind). For example, when you train Buddy in your backyard, where there are few distractions, a buckle collar may be sufficient to get him to respond. When he's out in the real world and wants to chase another dog, you may have to use a training collar to get him to mind.

Does all this mean that the pinch collar is the right solution for every training problem or every dog? Not at all, but it's the right solution under certain circumstances.

For many dogs, the pinch collar is the most humane training collar, especially if it saves them from a one-way trip to the shelter. If you have to use a pinch collar, put it on the same way you put on the snap-around collar. Simply expand or contract it by adding or removing links, respectively.

Electronic collars

We don't recommend that you use an electronic collar to train your dog. To use such a collar requires a great deal of skill and experience. Moreover, they're quite expensive.

We do, however, recommend an electronic bark collar for uncontrollable barking — it's a lot cheaper than being evicted. They typically cost about $50.

Citronella collars

Another training tool is a citronella collar, which costs about $100 and comes in basically two versions: a bark collar and a "deterrent to chasing" collar.

The vibrations of the dog's throat activate the bark collar, and it emits a puff of citronella in the direction of the dog's nose. The expectation is that the dog considers the puff of citronella sufficiently unpleasant and therefore stops barking.

The "deterrent to chasing" collar operates on the same principal except by remote control. Dog chases car, and just before he gets there, the owner presses the button and the dog gets a whiff of citronella. Again, the expectation is that the dog considers the puff of citronella unpleasant enough to stop chasing.

Do citronella collars work? No one piece of training equipment results in success every time with every dog, and citronella collars are no exception. They do, however, work with about 75 percent of dogs, thus making them another effective training tool.

Hedging toward head halters

The head halter is a hybrid piece of equipment, an adaptation from head halters used for horses. It works on the premise that where the dog's head goes, eventually the rest of the body has to follow.

Whereas the pinch collar looks downright menacing, the head halter looks quite inviting and user-friendly. Interestingly, your dog's reaction (and he's the one that counts) is likely to be quite the opposite. He'll readily accept a pinch collar but vigorously and vociferously object to the halter, at least initially.

The following list describes the principal advantages of the halter, after your dog has learned to accept the effect it has on him:

- **Calming and tranquilizing:** Helpful with nervous, timid, shy, or hyperactive dogs

- **Equalizing:** Helps smaller handlers with larger dogs, senior citizens, and handicapped handlers control their dogs

- **Muzzling:** Helps with inappropriate sniffing behavior, whining or barking, some forms of aggression, and play biting or nibbling

Table 6-4 provides some additional advantages of the head halter, as well as some disadvantages.

Table 6-4	Pros and Cons of the Head Halter
Advantages	**Disadvantages**
Readily available in pet stores and through catalogs	Greatest potential for serious damage to your dog's neck
Not very expensive	Transition tool only
Minimum strength required to use it	The dog doesn't learn to accept responsibility for his behavior. When the halter is removed, the dog reverts to previous behavior.

The great potential for damage is due to the nature of the halter. Because it controls the head, a strong pull by the dog or the handler can do serious damage to the dog's neck. In this regard, it isn't quite the same principle as the head halter for horses. Because most people are smaller than horses, the halter is used to control the horse's head from below.

In contrast, most people are taller than dogs, and any pull or tug is going to be upward and, at times, simultaneously to the side. Tugging the dog's neck in this way creates great potential for injury. In relation to a person, a horse's neck is also correspondingly stronger than a dog's. We feel that the halter can and often does have a depressing effect on the dog. The irony here is that this highly marketable tool has great potential for damage, while the torturous-looking pinch collar is the safest.

Finally, the halter is a transition tool, at best, because it doesn't teach the dog to assume the responsibility for his behavior. Take the halter off, and the dog will revert to his previous and presumably undesired behavior.

Treats Are Your Training Buddies

Other than your ingenuity and intellect, treats are the most powerful training tool you can use. If your dog isn't interested in food, see Chapter 2 for the definition of *object of attraction*.

You can use treats in one of two ways:

- ✔ **As a reward for a desired response:** When you use it as a reward, you keep the treat hidden from the dog, who doesn't know whether or not he's going to get it. For example, you say "Down," and Buddy lies down. He may get a treat, or he may not.

  When conditioning your dog to a particular command, to be effective, the treat has to *immediately* follow the desired response so the dog understands that he's being rewarded for that particular response. Don't diddle around fumbling for a treat and give it to him just as he's getting up again. You'd be rewarding Buddy for getting up, not what you wanted at all.

- ✔ **As a lure or inducement to obtain a desired response:** Now the treat is in the open and you use it to entice the dog to lie down, and when he does, he gets the treat. When used as an inducement, it's within the dog's control whether he gets the treat or not.

Because you're going to use treats both as a reward and as an inducement, you need to decide where to carry them. Some people use fanny packs, some a trouser pocket, and still others a shirt pocket. All these options are fine so long as you realize that as soon as your hand moves, your dog will focus on where you keep the treats. Wherever you keep them, you must be able to reach them quickly to reward the desired response. Having a few in the palm of your hand when working on a particular exercise isn't a bad idea. The key is to use the treat *before* the dog does something you don't intend to reward. If you can't get to the treat quickly, there's a good chance that Buddy will do something you don't want to reward — and you'll have lost the moment to reinforce the right behavior. We make a habit of having some treats with us at all times.

Selecting the ideal treat

We like to use dry treats rather than something moist or soggy, and many dry and semidry treats are available. You do, however, need to be careful of both salt and sugar content so that treats don't ruin your dog's diet. Experiment to find out what your dog likes and what he responds to. Trying to train a dog with treats he doesn't like is pointless. Treats also aren't going to be very effective after Buddy has just been fed.

Our dogs' favorites are homemade liver treats, which we use sparingly so as not to upset their stomachs. They're simple to make using the following steps and contain no salt or sugar:

1. **Parboil some beef liver and let cool.**

2. **Cut liver into ¼-inch cubes.**

3. **Place on a baking sheet and liberally sprinkle with garlic powder.**

4. **Bake in a 250-degree oven until dry, about one hour.**

5. **Store in the refrigerator.**

Our dogs also like carrots (actually, anything that's edible), but obviously not as much as they like liver.

Kong treats

Next to pure liver, our dogs like the TOTs (Training Opportunity Treats) made by the Kong Company (kongcompany.com). TOTs are made of liver and *milo* — a gluten-free grain that's highly digestible — and contain no salt or sugar. (Milo is a variety of sorghum that resembles millet.) TOTs are just the right size for a training treat and are dry and don't need to be refrigerated. Unless exposed to moisture, they have a good chance of lasting a long time. Few dogs can resist this treat.

thedog8it!

Another excellent training treat is made by thedog8it! Inc. (thedog8it.com). The treats are called Bribery Bits, and they're also dry and don't require refrigeration. They're made with human-grade ingredients and are organic whenever possible. Bribery Bits come in different flavors, such as Chicken Liver & Garlic and Cheese & Herb, and the original recipe is made with whole smoked kipper fillets. They sound so good, it's hard to believe they're intended just for dogs. The base grain is organic barley flour. Dogs love them.

When treats don't work

Some dogs don't respond as well to treats as they do to other objects, such as a ball, Frisbee, stone, or stick. In that case, use whatever turns your dog on, so long as it doesn't become a hindrance in your training.

Our German Shepherd, Katharina, wouldn't take treats in training. She would, however, respond to a stick or a toy, so that's what we used (see Chapter 2 for the definition of an *object of attraction*).

Chapter 7

Mastering Basic Training

∙∙

In This Chapter
▶ Using a leash
▶ Teaching the basic skills: sitting and staying
▶ Keeping your dog from bolting
▶ Behaving at the dinner table

∙∙

*O*ne question almost every dog owner asks is, "How do I keep my dog from jumping up on people?" Dogs jump on people as a form of greeting, like saying, "Hello, nice to meet you!"

Dogs have perfected different styles of greeting behaviors. Bean, our Labrador, would literally launch himself from a distance of about six feet to greet us. Cece, our Dachshund, would jump up and scratch our legs. Neither style is acceptable.

Dogs perceive jumping on people as a friendly gesture, a dog's way of letting the object of his affection know how happy he is to see him or her. He's literally jumping for joy. You can train your dog to greet people in a less rambunctious fashion, but you don't want to punish your happy pet simply because he's glad to see you.

Even more annoying is the dog's habit of sniffing parts of our anatomy we prefer he didn't. Although this behavior may be normal for the dog — he uses his nose to identify the rank, gender, and age of other dogs he meets — you need to insist that he gets this information from people in a less intrusive way.

So how do you get him to stop these behaviors without dampening his enthusiasm? By teaching him to Sit and Stay on command. Your dog can't jump on you when he's sitting — the two behaviors are mutually exclusive.

You also need to teach Buddy a release word to let him know he can move again after you've told him to stay. If you don't release him from the command after a reasonable period of time, he'll release himself, and the length of time he stays will become shorter and shorter. Our release word is "Okay," meaning "You can move now." Another frequently used release word is "Free," or "Free dog."

The First Step: Leash Training Your Dog

The majority of dogs readily accept the leash. Some, especially puppies, need a little time to get used to it. If your dog hasn't already been leash trained, you need to do it now.

Attach his six-foot leash to the *dead ring* of his training collar (see Chapter 6), and let him drag it around. You need to supervise him so that he doesn't get tangled up. Do this over a period of a few days. After he ignores the leash, pick up the other end and follow him around. He'll happily wander off wherever his fancy takes him.

You're now ready to show him where you want him to go. First, use a treat to entice him to follow you, and then gently guide him with the leash, telling him what a good puppy he is. If you're teaching him outside, use the treat to coax him away from the house, and use the leash to guide him back toward the house. Before you know it, he'll not only walk on the leash in your direction, but he'll actually pull you along. See Chapter 8 for teaching your dog not to pull.

Puppies are sometimes reluctant to go away from the house, even for a treat. In that case, pick up your puppy, carry him away from the house, put him down, and he'll lead you back to the house. (Chapter 8 gives you even more information on leash training and more advanced techniques you can try.)

Teaching the Basics

Of all the commands your dog could learn, he must know the following to be a good house pet and socially acceptable:

- ✔ Sit
- ✔ Stay
- ✔ Okay (the release word)
- ✔ Down
- ✔ Go lie down

Sitting

The Sit and Stay is one of the simplest and yet most useful commands you can teach your dog. It gives you a wonderfully easy way to control him when you need to most. It's also one of the most basic commands that you and your dog can quickly accomplish.

The importance of teaching a dog to sit and stay can't be overemphasized. Not only does Buddy stop jumping up on Grandma when she walks into the house, but when the door opens, he won't run into the street.

Use the "Sit and Stay" command when you want your dog to remain quietly in one spot. For example, Kaiser, a German Shepherd, would become so excited when Jane was about to feed him that he sent the dish flying out of her hands. After teaching him the Sit and Stay, he sat like a perfect gentleman when she put his dish down.

Getting your dog to sit — the easy part

Teaching your dog to sit on command is quite simple.

1. **Show your dog a small, bite-sized treat, holding it just a little in front of his eyes, slightly over his head.**

2. **Say "Sit" as you bring your hand above his eyes.**

   When your dog looks up at the treat, he should sit.

3. **When he sits, give him the treat and tell him what a good puppy he is.**

   Tell him without petting him. If you pet him at the same time as you praise him, he'll probably get up, but what you really want him to do is sit. *Praising* is verbal, such as saying "good" or "good dog" in a pleasant tone of voice. *Rewarding* is giving the dog a treat for a correct response while he's still in position. For example, if your dog gets up after you told him to sit, and you then give him a treat, you're rewarding his getting up and not the Sit.

   When using this method of teaching your dog to sit, position your hand properly in relation to the dog's head. If your hand is held too high, your dog will jump up; if it's too low, he won't sit. Hold your hand about two inches above his head.

4. **If your dog doesn't respond on his own, say "Sit" again and physically place your dog into a Sit position by placing your left hand under his tail and behind his knees and your right hand on his chest, and then tuck him into a Sit (see Chapter 2).**

5. **Keep your hands still and count to five, before giving him the treat.**

6. **Practice making your dog sit five times in a row for five days.**

   Some dogs catch on to this idea so quickly that they sit in front of their owner whenever they want a treat.

Getting your dog to sit on command — the next part

When your dog understands what the word "Sit" means, you can start to teach him to obey your command.

1. **Put the treat in your right hand and keep it at your side.**

2. **Put one or two fingers, depending on the size of your dog, of your left hand through his training collar at the top of his neck, palm facing up, and tell him to sit.**

   If he sits, give him a treat and tell him how good he is while taking your hand out of the collar. If he doesn't sit, pull up on his collar and wait until he sits, and then praise and reward him with a treat.

3. **Practice until he sits on command — that is, without having to pull up on or touch the collar.**

4. **Give him a treat and praise him for every correct response, keeping him in position to the count of five.**

As your dog demonstrates that he has mastered sitting on command, start to reward the desired response every other time. Finally, reward him on a *random* basis — every now and then give him a treat after he sits on command. A random reward is the most powerful reinforcement of what your dog has learned. It's based on the premise that hope springs eternal. To make the random reward work, all you have to do is use it and keep using it!

Now when Buddy wants to greet you by jumping up, tell him to sit. When he does, praise him, scratch him *under* the chin, and then release him. Following this simple method consistently, you can change your dog's greeting behavior from trying to jump on you to sitting to being petted.

Staying

As a part of Buddy's education, he has to learn the Sit-Stay in a more formal manner — not just at home, but anywhere. Because he already knows the "Sit" command, teaching the Sit-Stay should go relatively quickly.

How much time you have to spend and how many repetitions it takes for each progression depend on your dog's Personality Profile (see Chapter 5). How much time do you need to spend at any given session? The rule we follow is as long as we and the dog enjoy it. You can also practice several different exercises at the same session — the Sit-Stay, the Down, Walking On Leash without pulling, and the Come. Whatever you do, there's no point advancing to the next progression until Buddy has mastered the previous one.

Here are the steps for mastering the Sit-Stay:

1. **With your dog sitting at your left side, both of you facing in the same direction (called Heel position), put the rings of his training collar on top of his neck and attach the leash to the dead ring of the collar.**

The Heel position is when the area from the dog's head to his shoulder is in line with your left hip, with both of you facing in the same direction.

2. **Put the loop of the leash over the thumb of your left hand and fold the leash accordion-style into your hand with the part of the leash going toward the dog coming out at the bottom of your hand.**

Hold your hand as close to the dog's collar as you comfortably can. The farther away from the dog's collar you hold your hand, the less control you have.

3. **Apply a little upward tension on the collar — just enough to let him know the tension is there, but not enough to make him uncomfortable.**

4. **Say "Stay" and give the "Stay" signal — a pendulum motion with the right hand, palm facing the dog, stopping in front of the dog's nose, and then returning to your right side (check out Figure 7-1).**

Figure 7-1: Giving the "Stay" signal.

Keep your body as straight as you can, and don't bend over your dog. Before you step away from your dog, make sure your right hand is at your side again.

5. **Take a step to the right, keeping the tension on the collar, count to ten, return to your dog's side, release tension, praise him, and release your dog, taking several steps forward.**

6. **Repeat, only this time step directly in front of your dog, count to ten, step back to Heel position, release tension, praise, and release.**

7. **With your dog in Heel position, put the rings of the training collar under your dog's chin and attach the leash to the *live* ring of the collar.**

8. **Neatly fold your leash accordion-style into your left hand, and place it against your belt buckle, allowing one foot of slack.**

9. **Say and signal "Stay," and then place yourself one foot in front of your dog, keeping your left hand at your belt buckle and your right hand at your side, palm open, facing your dog.**

When you see that your dog's attention is drifting, there's a good chance he's about to move. You can tell your dog is thinking about moving when he starts to look around and begins to focus on something other than you. Any time you see that lack of attention, reinforce the "Stay" command by slapping the leash straight up with your right hand. Don't say anything, but smile at your dog when he's in position. Return your right hand to your side.

If your dog is thinking about moving or actually tries to move, take a step toward your dog with your right foot and, with your right hand, slap the leash straight up to a point directly above his head. Bring back your right foot and right hand to their original positions without repeating the "Stay" command. Count to 30 and pivot back to your dog's right side. Count to five, praise, and release.

Until you discover how to recognize the signs that Buddy is going to move, chances are you'll be too late in reinforcing the Stay, and he'll have moved. When that happens, without saying anything, put him back to the spot where he was supposed to stay, stand in front of him, count to ten, return to heel position, count to five, and release him. Repeat over the course of several training sessions until your dog is steady on this exercise.

Playing the Sit-Stay game

The following steps, using the leash on the *dead* ring of the collar, involve testing your dog's understanding of "Stay," while extending the time and distance of the "Stay" command:

1. **Starting in Heel position, with your left hand holding the leash and placed against your belt buckle, say and signal "Stay," and then step three feet in front of your dog, with no tension on the leash.**

2. **Slightly rotate your left hand downwards, against your body, to apply tension on the leash.**

   This is called the Sit-Stay test. If your dog moves to come to you, reinforce the Stay with your right hand. Test three times, increasing the tension until you get physical resistance on the part of your dog.

Your tension needs to be commensurate to your dog's size and weight. In other words, small terrier-strength tension applied to your Golden Retriever isn't going to produce the desired results.

For the Sit-Stay test, use a downward rotation of the left wrist. Maintain tension for a few seconds, and then slowly release tension. You're looking for physical resistance from your dog. From now on, practice this quick test before you do a Sit-Stay. Remember to release at the end of the exercise.

3. **Starting in Heel position, with the leash now on the live ring, go three feet in front of your dog.**

    The goal is to have him stay for one minute. If he moves, reinforce the Stay.

4. **Move six feet in front, to the end of the leash.**

You need to practice the Sit-Stay on a fairly regular basis, but you don't want to bore yourself or the dog. After Buddy understands what you want, once or twice a week is perfectly adequate. Start with the Sit-Stay test to refresh Buddy's recollection of what you expect from him. When he's reliable on leash, try him off leash in a safe place. First practice three feet in front, and then gradually increase the distance and the time you expect him to stay.

Releasing: The magic word is "Okay"

"Okay" is the release word we use. When you say the release word, your dog will know that he can move now and is on his own time. Make it a strict rule to give him the Release word, which allows him to move again, every time after you told him to stay. If you get lax about releasing and forget, Buddy will get into the habit of releasing himself. That teaches him that he can decide when to move — not a good idea and the opposite of what you want him to learn.

Buddy also needs to learn the difference between being praised for responding correctly and being released. Praise isn't an invitation to move. You say "good boy" when Buddy responds to a command. Praise is when you use your voice, not to be confused with petting, when you use your hands. You release him when the exercise is finished.

As quickly as you can, get into the habit of using only one command. If you don't get the desired response on the first command, show your dog what you want without repeating the command. Repeating commands teaches your dog to ignore you. By being consistent early on, your dog learns he has to respond to the first command.

Getting the dog down (but not out)

Your dog already knows how to lie down, but he needs to be taught to lie down on command. "Down" is the command used when you want your dog to lie down in place, right now, and stay there until you release him.

The following steps can help you teach this command to Buddy. If you've taught him the "Long Down," he'll quickly learn the command (see Chapter 2).

1. **With your dog sitting at your left side and a treat in your right hand, put one or two fingers of your left hand, palm facing you, through his collar at the side of his neck.**

   Show him the treat and lower it straight down and in front of your dog as you apply gentle downward pressure on the collar, at the same time saying "Down."

2. **When he lies down, give him the treat and praise him by telling him what a good puppy he is.**

   Keep your left hand in the collar and your right hand off your dog while telling him how clever he is so that he learns he's being praised for lying down. With a small dog, you may want to do this on a table. If Buddy is reluctant to cooperate, see Chapter 2 for physically placing him in the Down position.

3. **Reverse the process by showing him a treat and bringing it up slightly above his head with upward pressure on the collar as you tell him to sit.**

   Practice having your dog lie down at your side five times in a row for five days, or until he does it on command with minimal pressure on the collar. Praise and reward with a treat every time.

4. **Sit your dog at your left side and put two fingers of your left hand, palm facing you, through his collar at the side of his neck.**

   Keep your right hand with the treat at your right side.

5. **Say "Down" and apply downward pressure on the collar.**

   When he lies down, praise and give him a treat every other time. Practice over the course of several days until he lies down on command without any pressure on the collar.

Make a game out of teaching your dog to lie down on command. Get him eager about a treat, and in an excited tone of voice say, "Down." Then give him his treat. After that, when he lies down on command, you can randomly reward him.

Although the Sit-Stay is used for relatively short periods, the Down-Stay is used for correspondingly longer periods. Traditionally, the Down-Stay is also taught as a safety exercise — to get Buddy to stop wherever he is and stay there. For example, Buddy finds himself on the other side of the road. He sees you and is just about to cross the road when a car comes. You need a way to get him to stay on the other side until the car has passed by.

The object of the Down-Stay command is to have your dog respond to your command whether he is up close or at a distance. Pointing to the ground won't work from a distance, so you need to train your dog to respond to an oral command. This is where the Down-Stay command comes in — the theory being that the dog is least likely to move in the Down position. Be that as it may, you'll find this command not that hard to teach, and you do want to be able to stop your dog in his tracks.

Go lie down, doggy!

The "Go Lie Down" is a useful command when you want Buddy to go to a specific spot and remain there for an extended period until you release him. Use the command whenever you don't want Buddy underfoot, such as at mealtimes or when you have visitors and don't want him making a pest of himself.

Select the spot where you want Buddy to hang out — his crate, bed, favorite chair, whatever.

1. **Depending on your needs, you can also use a movable object — a dog bed, crate pad, or blanket, which allows you to change locations.**

   Assume you're going to use a dog bed.

2. **Start by taking your dog to the bed and tell him "Go lie down."**

   You may have to coax him with a treat.

3. **When he lies down on the bed, praise, give him the treat, count to five, and release him.**

4. **Repeat until he readily lies down on the bed.**

5. **Next, start three feet from the bed, give the command "Go lie down," and lure him onto the bed with a treat.**

6. **Praise him when he lies down, give him the treat, count to ten, and release him.**

7. **Repeat several times, gradually increasing the time between the praise and the giving of the treat, from a count of 10 to a count of 30.**

   Stop for now — you're getting bored and so is Buddy — and come back to it at another time.

For your next session, review the last progression two or three times and then send Buddy from three feet. Stand still, but motion him to go to his bed. He may surprise you and actually go to his bed and lie down. If he does, praise him enthusiastically and give him a treat. If he just stands there with a befuddled look on his face, put one finger through his collar, guide him to his bed and when he lies down, praise and give him a treat. You may have to repeat this process several times until he responds to the command.

When Buddy responds reliably from three feet, gradually and over the course of several sessions, increase the distance from the bed, as well as the length of time — up to 30 minutes — you want him to stay there. If he gets up without being released, just put him back (finger through the collar).

The "Go Lie Down" command, although practical, isn't the most exciting exercise. Use common sense, and don't make it drudgery.

You must release him from the spot when he can move again. If you forget, he'll get into the habit of releasing himself, thereby undermining the purpose of the exercise.

Dashing Your Dog's Dashing Habits

Almost as annoying as unrestrained greeting behavior, but far more dangerous, is the dog's habit of dashing through doors just because they're open, racing up and down stairs — ahead, or behind you — and jumping in and out of the car without permission. These behaviors are dangerous to your dog because he may find himself in the middle of the road and get run over. These behaviors are dangerous to you because you may get knocked over or down the stairs.

Prevent such potential accidents by teaching Buddy to sit and stay while you open the door and to wait until you tell him it's okay to go out.

Door and stair manners

After your dog knows the Sit-Stay, you can easily teach him door manners:

1. **Put your dog on leash, using the dead ring of the training collar, and review the Sit-Stay test described in "Teaching the Basics," earlier in the chapter.**

2. **Neatly fold the leash, accordion-style, into your left hand, and approach the closed door you normally use to let him out.**

   Follow the same procedure as you did for Sequence 1 of the Sit-Stay. Place yourself in such a way that you can open the door without your dog having to get out of its way.

3. **With a little upward tension on the collar, tell Buddy to stay, and open the door.**

Release the tension, and he should stay. If he doesn't, apply a little upward tension. Close the door and try again.

4. **When Buddy stays without any tension on the leash facing the open door, slowly walk through the door.**

    If he tries to follow, apply upward tension on the leash to remind him to stay. Repeat until he stays without having to be reminded.

5. **Walk through the door and release him so he can follow you.**

6. **Repeat the entire sequence off leash, beginning with step 1.**

You'll find that after several repetitions, he begins to get the message and will sit and stay on his own as you approach the door.

Motion means more to dogs than words, so make sure you stand still when releasing your dog. For this exercise, you don't want him to associate your moving with the release. Dogs are also time conscious, so vary the length of time you make him wait before releasing him.

Some people prefer to go through the doorway first, while others want the dog to go through first. It makes no difference, so long as your dog stays until you release him. Practice through doors your dog uses regularly, including the car door, especially exiting the car. Every time you make him sit and stay, you reinforce your position as pack leader and the one in charge.

If you have stairs, start teaching Buddy to stay at the bottom while you go up. First sit him and tell him to stay. When he tries to follow, put him back and start again. Practice until you can go all the way up the stairs with him waiting at the bottom before you release him to follow. Repeat the same procedure for going down the stairs.

After Buddy has been trained to wait at one end of the stairs, you'll discover that he'll anticipate the release. He'll jump the gun and get up just as you're thinking about releasing him. Before long, he'll only stay briefly and release himself when he chooses. It may happen almost as soon as he grasps the idea, or it may take a few weeks or even months, but it will happen.

When it does, stop whatever you're doing and put him back, use the stairs, turn, count to ten, and release him. Don't let him get into the habit of releasing himself. Consistency is just as important here as it is teaching any other exercise.

The doorbell and guests

Buddy now knows to sit and stay when you open the door. It's doubtful, however, that he'll obey these commands when the doorbell rings or someone knocks on the door. If your dog is anything like ours, the doorbell causes an immediate charge amidst paroxysms of barking. Even though most people want their dog to display his protective side, they then also want him to stop, sit, and stay, so they can answer the door.

To accomplish this goal, you need to enlist the aid of a friend or neighbor to ring the doorbell.

1. **Agree on a time and then put Buddy on leash.**

   When the bell rings and your dog goes through his antics, tell him to "Sit and Stay."

   To help make your helper's arrival as traditional as possible, have him or her ring the doorbell only once. Ask him or her to wait for you to open the door.

2. **Start to open the door and when he gets up, which he surely will, reinforce the Sit-Stay with a check.**

   If Buddy is an excitable soul, you may have to put him on the live ring of his training collar before he takes you seriously. Less excitable dogs catch on after two or three attempts.

3. **When Buddy stays, open the door and admit your accomplice.**

   At this point, Buddy will more than likely want to say hello. Again, reinforce the Stay, and have your helper approach him holding out the palm of his or her hand.

4. **Let Buddy sniff the palm, and then have your helper ignore him.**

   You may have to be right next to Buddy to reinforce the Sit-Stay.

5. **You need to repeat this procedure several times until Buddy is reliable and holds the Sit-Stay while you open the door.**

   Remember to release him. Successful training depends on who is more determined and persistent — you or your dog.

The procedure to teach Buddy not to jump on people is the same. Follow the same progressions as you did for the doorbell, and when Buddy wants to jump on your helper, reinforce the "Stay" command with a check. After several repetitions, Buddy should be steady enough to try him off leash. The key to your ability to control Buddy is a reliable Sit-Stay.

Having said that, you also need to remind your guests not to get Buddy all riled up with vigorous petting or active solicitations to play. The less excitement, the better. The proper way to greet a dog on a Sit-Stay is to let him sniff the palm of the hand and perhaps a little scratch under the chin. A dog doesn't like to have the top of his head patted anymore than kids do.

Paying attention to inflection

Give commands in a normal tone of voice. For example, when giving the "Sit" command, remember that it's "Sit!" — the command — and not "Sit?" — the question.

When releasing, say the release word in a more excited tone of voice, as in "That's it, you're all done!"

Unless impaired, a dog's sense of hearing is extremely acute, and when giving a command, there's absolutely no need to shout. In fact, the opposite is true — the more quietly you give your commands, the quicker your dog learns to pay attention to you.

When teaching a new command, you may have to repeat it several times during the initial introduction before your dog catches on. After the first session, teach him to respond to the first command. Give the command, and if nothing happens, show your dog exactly what you want by physically helping him. Consistency is the key to success.

Setting the Tone for Proper Table Manners

Teaching Buddy table manners is your responsibility, and you only have to remember one rule: Don't feed the dog from the table. This concept sounds a lot simpler than it is, especially in a multiperson household. Moreover, don't ever underestimate your dog's ability to train you.

Every time you reward your dog's efforts with a treat from the table, you're systematically teaching him not to take "no" for an answer.

When Buddy was a puppy, nobody thought much about occasionally slipping him something from the table. But now he is 6 months old, almost fully grown, and has started to beg at the table. Because his begging is no longer cute and is embarrassing when you have guests, the family resolves to put a stop to it.

At first, Buddy doesn't believe you're serious; after all, you were the one who started it in the first place. He digs a little deeper into his repertoire of begging routines. He may sit up, nudge you, paw you, or whine in the most pathetic tone as though he's near death's door from starvation. Sure enough, little Sally takes pity on him and slips him something.

As this scenario repeats itself, often with longer intervals before someone gives in, Buddy is systematically being trained to persevere at all cost and never give up. Looking at it from his point of view, you're rewarding, even encouraging, the very behavior you want to stop.

When you stop rewarding the undesired behavior (begging), your dog will stop begging at the table. As soon as you stop giving in to Buddy, his efforts will decrease, until over time, and provided you don't have a relapse, he'll stop begging altogether. In technical jargon, you have extinguished the undesired behavior by refusing to reward it.

You can also save yourself all this aggravation by teaching Buddy the "Go Lie Down" command so you can enjoy your meals in peace. (See "Go lie down, doggy!" earlier in this chapter.)

Chapter 8

Canine Cruise Control: Walking, Coming When Called, and Leaving Stuff Alone

*T*aking your dog for a nice, long walk is balm for the soul and good exercise for both of you, provided he doesn't drag you down the street. Teaching him to walk on a loose leash makes your strolls with Buddy a pleasure rather than a chore.

Most of you want to be able to take your dog for a walk on leash and have him remain within the length of his leash without pulling. A leisurely stroll is an important daily routine, and for many dogs, it's the only opportunity to get some fresh air.

Even better from the dog's perspective is a good run in the park or the woods. For this privilege Buddy has to learn to come when called. You can teach him to respond to the "Come" command by playing the Recall Game.

Another command you want Buddy to learn is "Leave it!" The command tells the dog to ignore whatever interests him at the time. The object of his interest can be a cat, another dog, a person, or something on the ground. "Leave it" is especially useful when Buddy discovers something disgusting he perceives as edible.

Walking Your Dog

Even if you don't ordinarily take him for walks, the well-trained dog knows how to walk on a leash without pulling your arms out. For example, at least once a year, you have to take him to the vet. If he has been trained to walk on leash, the visit will go much more smoothly than if he bounces off the end of the leash like a kangaroo. If your dog isn't already accustomed to a leash, see Chapter 7.

The reason dogs pull on a leash is that they're more interested in the sights and scents in their environment than in you. Your job is to teach Buddy to become aware of and respect your existence at the other end of the leash.

Born to pull

To teach Buddy not to pull, you need his training collar, his leash, and a few treats. Attach the leash to the live ring of the training collar. Take him to an area without too many distractions — you don't need other people and dogs (especially loose dogs) in the vicinity right now — and where you can walk in a straight line or in a circle (about 30 feet in diameter).

Perform these steps:

1. **Put the loop of the leash over the thumb of your right hand, and make a fist.**

2. **Place your left hand directly under your right.**

   Hold the leash in both hands as though it were a baseball bat. Plant both hands firmly against your belt buckle.

3. **Say "Let's go," and start walking.**

4. **Just before he gets to the end of the leash, say "Buddy, easy," make an about-turn to your right, and walk in the opposite direction.**

   Be sure you keep your hands firmly planted. As a safety precaution, don't put your entire hand through the loop of the leash or wrap it around your hand. If your dog catches you unaware and makes a dash, he could cause you to fall. By having the loop over your thumb, you can just let go, and it'll slide off.

5. **Step 2 produces a tug on Buddy's collar and turns him in the new direction.**

   As he scampers to catch up with you, tell him what a clever boy he is, and give him a treat. Before you know it, he'll be ahead of you again, and you'll have to repeat the procedure. When you make your turn, do it with determination. Be sure you keep your hands firmly planted against your belt buckle. Make your turn, and keep walking in the new direction. Don't look back, and don't worry about Buddy; he'll quickly catch up. Remember to praise and reward him when he does.

The first few times you try this, you'll be a little late — Buddy is already leaning into his collar. Try it again. Concentrate on Buddy, and learn to anticipate when you have to make the turn. Always give him a chance to respond by saying, "Buddy, easy" before you make the turn. You need to repeat this sequence several times over the course of a few training sessions until he understands that you don't want him to pull. Your goal is to teach him to walk within the perimeter of his leash without pulling.

Most dogs quickly learn to respect the leash, and, with an occasional reminder, they become a pleasure to take for a walk. Some, on the other hand, don't seem to get it. If Buddy seems particularly dense about this simple concept, you may need to use a *pinch collar.* Put Buddy in a position where you can praise him (see Chapter 6 for a story about situations where you may have to use of a pinch collar). The pinch collar, also called *prong collar,* is similar to a martingale in that it is self-limiting.

Remember, how readily your dog responds to his collar depends on

- ✔ How distracted he is by what's going on around him, including scents on the ground
- ✔ His size and weight in relation to your size and weight
- ✔ His Personality Profile (see Chapter 5)
- ✔ His touch sensitivity (see Chapter 9)

The pinch collar is an equalizer for these factors. It lets you enjoy training your dog without becoming frustrated or angry. Your dog, in turn, will thank you for maintaining a positive attitude and for praising him when he responds correctly.

Heeling on leash

Heeling and walking on a loose leash are two different exercises. When you take Buddy for a walk to give him exercise, or in order to do his business, he's on his own time. He can sniff, look around, or just aimlessly wander about, so long as he doesn't pull. For those times when you walk him on a busy sidewalk or in an area with traffic, Buddy needs to learn the "Heel" command.

Heeling means Buddy has to walk at your left side, the traditional position, while paying strict attention to you and staying with you as you change direction or pace. When your dog is heeling, he's now on your time. Buddy's responsibility is to focus on you, and you have to teach him to accept that responsibility. Buddy has to learn to heel whether you make a right turn, left turn, do an about-face turn, run, or slow walk. The key to teaching heeling is to get Buddy to pay attention to you.

Heeling is used for walking your dog in traffic — when you need absolute control — and for competitive obedience events. The American Kennel Club (AKC) definition of heeling is walking "close to the left side of the handler without swinging wide, lagging, forging, or crowding," either on a loose leash or off leash.

Teaching your dog to sit at heel

Before teaching Buddy to heel with both of you walking, you're going to teach him what to do when you stop, which is called the Automatic Sit at Heel:

1. **Attach your leash to the live ring of your dog's training collar and have him sit at your left side with both of you facing in the same direction while you put the leash over your right shoulder.**

2. **Say, "Buddy, heel."**

3. **Take a step forward on your right foot, and then a step with the left past the right; drop down on your right knee, put your right hand against your dog's chest, and fold him into a Sit at Heel position.**

   Use the same technique to sit your dog described in Chapter 2, and avoid the temptation to push down on his rear end. Keep your hands in place as you tell him how clever he is.

Buddy already knows the "Sit" command, but you're now showing him exactly where you want him to sit. Practice the Sit at Heel about five times or until both of you feel comfortable with this maneuver (see Figure 8-1).

Teaching heeling

To teach heeling, choose a location relatively free of distractions, preferably a confined area, such as your back yard, and follow these steps:

1. **Attach your leash to the live ring of your dog's training collar and have him sit at your left side with both of you facing in the same direction while you put the leash over your right shoulder.**

   You need to allow about four inches of slack so there's no tension on the leash when you start.

2. **Make a funnel with both hands around the leash.**

   Keep both hands about waist high and close to your body. The object is not to touch the leash until necessary.

Figure 8.1:
Preparing to
teach
heeling on
leash.

3. **In a pleasant, upbeat tone of voice, say "Buddy, heel" and start to walk.**

   Move out briskly, as though you're late for an appointment. Walk in a large, clockwise circle, or in a straight line.

4. **When your dog leaves your left side, close your hands around the leash, and bring him back to Heel position.**

   You'll notice that as soon as both of you are in motion, Buddy wants to get ahead of you. Close your hands on the leash, and firmly bring him back to your left side. Work on keeping his shoulder in line with your left hip. Anytime he gets out of position, bring him back and tell him how clever he is.

5. **After about ten steps, stop and place him into a Sit at Heel, and verbally praise him.**

   It'll take you a few tries to get the hang of it. At first, you'll be a little slow on the uptake. Buddy is joyfully bounding ahead of you, the leash has fallen off your shoulder, and you're scrambling to get it back. Just start over, and work on _anticipating_ what your dog is going to do.

When heeling your dog, walk briskly and with determination, as though you're trying to catch the next train home. The more energy you put into your pace, the easier it is to keep your dog's attention focused on you. If you dawdle, so does your dog. By paying attention to your dog, you'll discover when you need to bring him back to Heel. If you can see his tail, you've waited too long.

Your initial goal is to be able to heel Buddy for ten paces without having to touch the leash. How long it takes you depends on

- Your dog
- What your dog was bred to do
- His response to the training collar
- Your attitude

Generally, if you have a Shetland Sheepdog, you'll reach that goal in maybe five minutes; if you have a Fox Terrier, you'll work on it considerably longer.

When Buddy heels without you having to touch the leash for ten paces, gradually increase the number of steps before a halt. Bring him back to heel whenever necessary, and then praise him. After about five training sessions, he should be getting the idea, at least in an area relatively free from distractions.

Changing direction

After you and your dog have pretty much gotten the hang of heeling, your next step is to introduce your dog to changes of direction while heeling. In this section, you find out about the three essential turns — a right turn, an about-turn to the right, and a left turn.

Right turn

To stay with you when you're making a right turn, Buddy needs to speed up. And, at this stage in your training, Buddy isn't yet giving you 100 percent of his attention, and you're going to anticipate that he needs help with the right turn.

 If you want your dog to pay attention to you, you have to pay attention to your dog. Discovering how to anticipate what he's going to do is the first step to successful heeling. Just before you make the turn, enthusiastically say his name, make the turn, and keep moving. Using his name causes him to look up at you, and he notices that you're changing direction, which causes him to stay with you. Without giving him that cue, chances are that as you make the turn and go one way, he keeps going the other direction.

About-turn

An about-turn is a right turn times two. When you make your turn, keep your feet together so Buddy can keep up. As you did for the right turn, use his name just before you make the turn to encourage him to stay with you.

In the event Buddy has a particularly difficult time remaining at your side for the right or about-turn, you can use a treat or other object of interest to help guide him around. Hold the treat in your right hand as you're heeling. Before you make the turn, show it to your dog by bringing the treat directly in front of his nose and using it to guide him around the turn, and then give him the treat.

This approach has a potential drawback. Some dogs become overly stimulated when they know you have a treat in your hand. Make no mistake about it, Buddy knows. If you see that your dog becomes difficult to control under such circumstances, you may want to eliminate use of the treat. The hassle isn't worth the potential benefit.

Left turn

To make the left turn without bumping into him, Buddy needs to slow down as you make the turn and then resume normal speed after you make the turn. Just before you make the turn, slow down. With your left hand, draw back on the leash, make the turn, bring your hand back to position, and resume your normal brisk pace. Practice heeling and the turns for a few times as a regular part of your daily outings.

Changing pace

Next, you're going to teach your dog to change pace with you while heeling. He has to learn that whether you walk slowly or quickly, he has to stay in Heel position.

For the slow pace, cut the speed of your pace in half, but maintain the same length of stride. As you go into the slow pace, draw back on the leash to keep your dog in Heel position. For the fast pace, double the speed of your pace, again keeping the length of your stride the same. Just before you go into a fast pace, use your dog's name in an excited tone of voice to encourage him to stay with you.

You're still working with the leash over your shoulder. By now, you should also be able to tell whether Buddy is actually heeling. If heeling properly, Buddy doesn't swing wide on right and about-turns, bump into you on the left turn, fall behind you as you go into a fast pace, or get ahead of you as you go into a slow pace.

Winning the Game of Coming When Called

One of the greatest joys of owning a dog is going for a walk in a park or the woods and letting him run, knowing he'll come when called. A dog that doesn't come when called is a prisoner of his leash and, if he gets loose, is a danger to himself and others. This section offers some proven rules for helping you and your dog realize the benefits of coming when called.

Here are the basic rules you need to follow to encourage your dog to come to you when you call him:

✔ **Exercise, exercise, exercise.** Many dogs don't come when called because they don't get enough exercise. At every chance, they run off and make the most of this unexpected freedom by staying out for hours at a time.

Consider what your dog was bred to do, and that tells you how much exercise he needs. Just putting him out in the backyard isn't good enough. You have to participate. Think of it this way: Exercise is as good for you as it is for your dog. A good source for exercise requirements is *The Roger Caras Dog Book: The Complete Guide to Every AKC Breed,* 3rd Edition (M. Evans & Co.).

✔ **Whenever your dog comes to you, be nice to him.** One of the quickest ways to teach your dog not to come to you is to call him to punish him or to do something the dog perceives as unpleasant. Most dogs consider being called to be left alone in the house when you go out or to be given a pill unpleasant. In these circumstances, go and get Buddy instead of calling him to you.

Another example of teaching your dog not to come is to take him for a run in the park and call him to you when it's time to go home. Repeating this sequence several times teaches the dog that the party is over. Soon, he may become reluctant to return to you when called because he isn't ready to end the fun. You can prevent this kind of unintentional training by calling him to you several times during his outing, sometimes giving him a treat, sometimes just a word of praise. Then let him romp again.

✔ **Teach him to "Come" as soon as you get him.** Ideally, you acquired your dog as a puppy, which is the best time to teach him to come when called. Start right away. But remember, sometime between 4 and 8 months of age your puppy begins to realize there's a big, wide world out there (see Chapter 3). While he's going through this stage, keep him on leash so he doesn't learn that he can ignore you when you call him.

✔ **When in doubt, keep him on leash.** Learn to anticipate when your dog is likely not to come. You may be tempting fate by trying to call him after he has spotted a cat, another dog, or a jogger. Of course, there are times when you goof and let him go just as another dog appears out of nowhere.

Resist the urge to make a complete fool of yourself by bellowing "Come" a million times. The more often you holler "Come," the quicker he learns he can ignore you when he's off leash. Instead, patiently go to him and put him on leash. Don't get angry with him after you've caught him, or you'll make him afraid of you, and he'll run away from you when you try to catch him the next time.

✔ **Make sure your dog always comes to you and lets you touch his collar before you reward.** Touching his collar prevents the dog from developing the annoying habit of playing "catch" — coming toward you and then dancing around you, just out of reach. So teach him to let you touch his collar before you offer him a treat or praise.

Training Buddy to come when called

You need two people, one hungry dog, one six-foot leash, plenty of small treats, and two whistles (optional). Some people prefer to train their dog to come to a whistle rather than the verbal command "Come." Some people train their dog to do both.

What works best depends on the dog, and you may want to experiment. Consider trying the verbal command first, because there may be times when you need to call your dog but don't have your whistle. You can then repeat the steps, using a whistle, which goes very quickly because Buddy already has some understanding of what he's supposed to do.

For this exercise, you need to be inside the house, with your dog on a six-foot leash. You and your partner are sitting on the floor, six feet apart, facing each other, and your partner gently restrains the dog while you hold the end of the leash.

1. **Call your dog by saying "Buddy, come," and use the leash to guide him to you.**

   Avoid the temptation to reach for your dog.

2. **When Buddy comes to you, put your hand through his collar, give him a treat, pet him, and praise him enthusiastically.**

   Now you can and should pet Buddy so that he understands how happy you are that he came to you. This situation is different from the Sit or the Down in Chapter 7, where you want him to remain in place, and petting him would cause him to get up.

3. **Hold Buddy, and pass the leash to your partner, who says "Buddy, come," guides the dog in, puts his hand through the collar, gives him a treat, and praises the dog.**

   Keep working on this exercise until your dog responds on his own to being called and no longer needs to be guided in with the leash.

4. **Repeat the exercise with Buddy off leash, gradually increasing the distance between you and your partner to 12 feet.**

5. **Have your partner hold Buddy by the collar while you go into another room, and then call your dog.**

6. **When he finds you, put your hand through the collar, give him a treat, and praise him.**

   If he can't find you, *slowly* go to him, take him by the collar, and bring him to the spot where you called. Reward and praise.

7. **Have your partner go into another room and then call the dog.**

8. **Repeat the exercise until Buddy doesn't hesitate finding you or your partner in any room of the house.**

9. **Take Buddy outside to a confined area, such as a fenced yard, tennis court, park, or school yard, and repeat Steps 1, 2, and 3.**

Now you're ready to practice by yourself. With Buddy on leash, take him for a walk. Let him sniff around, and when he isn't paying any attention to you, call him. When he gets to you, give him a treat, and make a big fuss over him. If he doesn't come, firmly check him toward you (you may have to use the live ring of his training collar), and then reward and praise him. Repeat until he comes to you every time you call him. After Buddy is trained, you don't have to reward him with a treat every time, but do so randomly.

Adding distractions

Most dogs need to be trained to come in the face of distractions, such as other dogs, children, joggers, food, or friendly strangers. Think about the most irresistible situations for your dog, and then practice under those circumstances.

Put a 12-foot leash on your dog (you can tie two six-foot leashes together), and take him to an area where he's likely to encounter his favorite distraction. After he spots it (jogger, bicycle, other dog, whatever), let him become thoroughly engrossed, either by watching or straining at his leash, and then call him. More than likely, he'll ignore you. Give a sharp tug on the leash, and guide him back to you. Praise and pet him enthusiastically. Repeat three times per session until the dog turns and comes to you immediately when you call. If he doesn't, you may have to change your training equipment.

Some dogs quickly learn to avoid the distraction by staying close to you, which is fine. Tell him what a clever fellow he is, and then try with a different distraction at another time.

Repeat in different locations with as many different distractions as you can find. Try it with someone offering your dog a tidbit as a distraction (*don't* let the dog get the treat), someone petting the dog, and anything else that may distract him. Use your imagination. Your goal is to have Buddy respond reliably every time you call. Until he's steady on leash, he most certainly won't come off leash.

Advancing to off-leash distractions

How you approach adding off-leash distractions depends on your individual circumstances. For example, take your dog to an area where you aren't likely to encounter distractions in the form of other dogs or people. Let him off leash, and allow him to become involved in a smell in the grass or a tree. Keep the distance between you and him about ten feet. Call him, and if he responds, praise enthusiastically and reward. If he doesn't, avoid the temptation to call him again. Don't worry; he heard you but chose to ignore you. Instead, slowly walk up to him, firmly take him by his collar, under his chin, palm up, and trot backwards to the spot where you called him. Then praise and reward.

After he's reliable with this exercise, try him in an area with other distractions. If he doesn't respond, practice for the correct response with the 12-foot leash before you try him off leash again.

Can you now trust him to come to you in an unconfined area? That depends on how well you've done your homework and what your dog may encounter in the "real" world. Understanding your dog and what interests him helps you know when he's likely not to respond to the Come command.

Let common sense be your guide. For example, when you're traveling and have to let him out to relieve himself at a busy interstate rest stop, you'd be foolhardy to let him run loose. When in doubt, keep him on leash.

Mastering the "Leave It" Command

When we take our dogs for their daily walk in the fields, we aren't too thrilled when one or the other wants to ingest horse manure or geese droppings. Nor are we fond of having to extricate such delicacies from a dog's mouth. To tell the truth, we'd prefer if they didn't pick up *anything* from the ground they perceive as potentially edible. At a dog park in our area, several dogs became seriously ill after ingesting chunks of poison-laced hot dogs. This command is a good start for such situations.

Teaching this command is a wonderful opportunity to find out more about how your dog's thought processes work. You can truly see the wheels turning. Depending on how quickly Buddy catches on, you may want to practice this exercise over the course of several sessions. Keep the sessions short — no more than five minutes at a time, and follow these steps:

1. **Hold a treat between your thumb and index finger.**

2. **With your palm facing up, show the treat to your dog.**

   He'll try to pry it loose. Say "Leave it," close your hand into a fist, and turn it so that your palm now faces down. (See Figure 8-2.)

3. **Observe your dog's reaction.**

   He may stare fixedly at the back of your hand, he may try to get to the treat by nuzzling or nibbling your hand, or he may start barking. Ignore all these behaviors. You're looking for the first break in his attention away from your hand. He may make eye contact with you or look away.

4. **The instant he breaks his attention away from your hand, say "Good," and give him the treat.**

5. **Repeat until your dog looks at you or away from your hand when you give the command and turn your hand over.**

   You're teaching Buddy that looking at you and not at your hand is rewarded with a treat.

6. **To find out whether Buddy is responding to the command or to the turning of your hand, repeat Step 1 without turning your hand.**

   If he responds, praise and reward. If he doesn't, close your hand into a fist and wait for the break in attention. Repeat until he responds to the command.

7. **Make yourself comfortable on the floor, and show your dog a treat; put it on the floor, and cover it with your hand.**

   When his attention is on your hand or he tries to get to the treat, say "Leave it."

Figure 8-2:
Working
on the
"Leave it"
command.

8. **Wait for the break in attention, and then praise and reward.**

9. **Repeat Steps 6 and 7, but cover the treat with just your index finger. Then try it when placing the treat between your index and middle finger.**

10. **When successful, place the treat one inch in front of your hand, and repeat Steps 6 and 7.**

   Here you need to be watchful: He may be faster at getting to the treat than you can cover it.

11. **Put Buddy on leash and stand next to him (Heel position), neatly fold the leash into your left hand, and hold your hand as close to his collar as is comfortable without any tension on the leash.**

   You need to make sure that the amount of slack in the leash isn't so much that his mouth can reach the floor.

12. **Hold the treat in your right hand and show it to Buddy, and then casually drop the treat.**

   When he tries to get to the treat, say "Leave it." If he responds, praise him, pick up the treat, and give it to him. If he doesn't, check straight up. Repeat until he obeys the command.

   Test his response by taking the leash off and dropping a treat. If he makes a dive for it, don't attempt to beat him to it or yell "No." He's telling you he needs more work on leash.

Now, go outside, but first you need to do some preparation. Select a food item that's readily visible to you in the grass or the ground, such as some crackers or a few kernels of popcorn. Drop four or five pieces of food in the area where you're taking Buddy for the big test. Put some of your regular treats in your pocket, and take Buddy for a walk on leash in the area where you left the food. As soon as his nose goes to the food, say, "Leave it." If he responds, praise enthusiastically and give him a treat. If he doesn't, check straight up.

If he manages to snag a cracker or kernel of popcorn, you're too slow on the uptake. Practice walking around the food-contaminated area until he ignores the food on command.

Buddy should now know and obey the "Leave it" command. Test him off leash, and his response will tell you if he needs more work. Still, like any other command, you need to review it with him periodically on leash.

Part II
Giving Your Dog's Training Its Best Shot

The 5th Wave   By Rich Tennant

"Okay, this is getting ridiculous! Either teach your dog not to run away, or name him something other than 'Fire'."

In this part . . .

Of course you want your dog to succeed at training, because a well-trained dog is a happy dog, and happy dogs have happy owners. You can take several steps to ensure training success, and we focus on those steps in this part. For example, you need to understand what comes with your dog and the impact your dog's environment has on his behavior. Patience and understanding come in handy. You also need to know how to deal with some of the not-so-pleasant behaviors your dog may exhibit from time to time.

We also include in the part how to train your dog to become a Canine Good Citizen — a dog who has mastered the respectable behaviors that you expect of him at home and in public — the enormously popular American Kennel Club (AKC) program.

Chapter 9

Developing Training Savvy

Your dog's ability — just like your ability — to learn and retain information is directly related to what goes on around him and how he feels. A noisy and distraction-filled environment makes it difficult for Buddy to concentrate on learning new commands. Strife in the household may cause Buddy to become irritable, even aggressive — feelings that impede the learning process. Even what you feed your dog has an effect on his ability to learn.

Similarly, how Buddy feels, both mentally and physically, influences his ability to learn. If he feels anxious, depressed, or stressed, learning and retention decrease in direct proportion to the degree of the dog's distress. If he is physically ill or in pain, he can't learn what you're trying to teach him.

These observations are stating the obvious — just think how you'd react under similar circumstances — and yet we need to point them out in this chapter because dog owners seem to be oblivious to their effect on the dog's ability to learn.

Managing Your Dog's Environment

Your dog has a keen perception of his environment. Continuous or frequent strife or friction in your household can have a negative impact on your dog's ability to learn. Many dogs are also adversely affected by excessive noise and activity and may develop behavior problems.

Look for the following signs that your dog has a negative perception of his environment:

- ✔ Aggression
- ✔ Aloofness
- ✔ Hyperactivity
- ✔ Irritability
- ✔ Lethargy

Under these circumstances, learning is reduced — if it takes place at all — or the lesson won't be retained. However, if you also have a keen perception of how your dog responds to his environment, your training goals will be more easily attained. This section provides some tips on creating for your dog the best possible environment for learning.

Starting on the right foot

You've heard the saying "You don't get a second chance to make a first impression." You also know that the first impression leaves the most lasting impact. The stronger that impression, the longer it lasts.

Introductions to new experiences need to be as pleasant as possible. For example, Buddy's first visit to the vet needs to be a pleasant experience, or he'll have an unpleasant association with going to the vet. Have the doctor give him a dog treat before his examination and another treat at the end of the visit.

The importance of making a good first impression applies to your dog's training as well. A particularly traumatic or unpleasant first experience can literally ruin a dog for life. The object is to make your dog's first impression of training as pleasant as you can.

Recognizing your dog's social needs

Dogs are social animals that don't do well being isolated. For example, if you work, you likely have to leave your dog alone at home. Then when you get home, your dog is terribly excited and wants to play and be with you. But you may also go out in the evening, leaving your dog alone again.

Sometimes, your dog retaliates. In our younger (and more socially active) days, we had a lovely, well-trained Collie named Duke. Both of us worked, and we frequently went out in the evening. If we went out three days in a row, Duke would urinate on our bed. It took us a while to figure out this pattern; we solved the problem by not going out three days in a row, or by taking Duke with us.

Daycare centers for dogs are being established in many communities. You can leave your dog for the day without having to feel guilty about not giving him time to socialize. If you simply don't have the time to give your dog the attention he craves, consider finding a daycare center for your dog. Their popularity is proof of the need for these services. Your dog will spend his day playing and interacting with other dogs and having a good time. Perhaps the best feature, depending on your perspective, is that when you pick up Buddy on your way home, he'll be too tired to make many demands on you. In addition to keeping Buddy entertained and amused, many dog daycare facilities provide other services such as bathing, grooming, and training.

A potential downside of doggie daycare is that Buddy may think it's playtime whenever he meets another dog, making him hard to control around other dogs. Other potential downsides are possible exposure to disease and parasites, trauma due to inexperienced handling by daycare personnel, and personal liability for Buddy's actions.

Just like with any behavior, when it comes to exercise, your dog has a certain amount of energy. After Buddy has expended that energy, he is tired, and tired dogs have happy owners. If that energy isn't expended, it may redirect itself into barking, chewing, digging, house soiling, self-mutilation, and similar behaviors — clearly not what you have in mind for the well-trained pet.

Identifying your dog's emotional needs

Whether dogs have emotional needs depends on whether you accept that dogs have emotions. We believe they do, and here are some of them:

- Anger
- Apprehension
- Depression
- Fear
- Happiness
- Joy
- Sadness

You can see your dog exhibit some of these emotions, such as joy and happiness, on a daily basis, but what about sadness and depression? Dogs react with the same emotions that people have with the loss of a loved one, be it a member of the family or another dog.

For the last 30 years, we've always had more than one dog, at times as many as ten. When one of them passed on, there's no question that those closest to that dog experienced grief. We had a brother and sister pair of Landseers named Cato and Cassandra. When Cassandra died, Cato showed all the signs of clinical depression.

Cassandra died when Cato was 7 years old and had been retired from a very successful dog-show career. Because Cato really enjoyed pre-show training and going to dog shows, we started showing him all over in Canada to get him out of his depression. And it worked. He competed for another three years and finally retired for good at the age of 10.

How can you tell whether your dog is experiencing any of these negative emotions? Pretty much the way you can tell with a person. If your dog mopes around the house, doesn't seem to enjoy activities he previously enjoyed, is lethargic, isn't particularly interested in food, and sleeps a lot, chances are he's depressed. Under those circumstances, he may not feel much like training.

We sometimes see dogs with anxiety, apprehension, and fear — behaviors that can be hereditary, situational, or caused by some physical ailment. Whatever the cause, to train such a dog requires a great deal of patience and an understanding of how difficult it is for him to learn. On the other hand, the rewards are significant because through the structure of training, the dog's confidence is increased, sometimes to the point where these behaviors disappear altogether.

Feeding your dog's nutritional needs

The most important influence on your dog's ability to learn, and the one under your most immediate control, is what you feed him. Because feeding is so important, we devote a separate chapter to this topic (see Chapter 18).

For the well-trained dog, you need to become familiar with what foods are available and what's best for your dog. So many dog foods are on the market today that making the correct choice for Buddy can be a bewildering task. Just as you do when buying food for yourself or your family, you need to look at the ingredients. Dogs are carnivores and need animal protein. Select a food that lists an animal protein, such as chicken, beef, or lamb, in the first three ingredients. Avoid foods containing a lot of filler. When it seems that more comes out of your dog's rear end than went into the front end, you can safely bet the food contains more filler than protein.

Managing the Dog Within

Besides the principal influences on your dog's ability to learn that are *under your control,* there are influences that come *with* your dog, such as

- Breed-specific behaviors
- Temperament
- Mental sensitivity
- Responses to visual stimuli
- Sound sensitivity
- Touch sensitivity

All these things affect how the dog learns, what he finds difficult, and what comes almost naturally.

Breed-specific behaviors

Whether you have a designer dog — a dog of mixed origin — or a purebred, he comes with breed-specific behaviors, such as hunting or herding, among others. These behaviors, in turn, have been further refined. Some dogs hunt large game, others hunt small game, and yet others hunt birds. Some hunt close by, and others hunt far away. Some herd and guard, and others just herd; some were developed to herd cows, and others, sheep. You get the picture.

There are many different breeds of dogs. The American Kennel Club (AKC), the main governing body of dogdom, recognizes 153 different breeds, but many others aren't recognized.

These breeds are divided into seven groups, largely based on behavioral similarities. Some of these breeds are fairly close cousins, whereas others are as different as night and day. (There's also a Miscellaneous Class for newly accepted breeds.)

For example, Group VII, the Herding Group, includes the Belgian Malinois, the Belgian Sheepdog, and the Belgian Tervuren, which are closely related. It also includes the two Welsh Corgis, the Cardigan, and the Pembroke, which have no resemblance to any of the other dogs in that group but in turn are related to one another. The most obvious difference between the two is that the

Cardigan has a tail, and the Pembroke's tail is docked. Appearance aside, what all the dogs in that group share in common is the instinct to herd. In addition, many of them share the instinct to guard. The German Shepherd, for example, is a member of that group.

Table 9-1 shows the various groups.

Table 9-1	American Kennel Club Dog Groups
Group	*Type of Dog*
Group I	Sporting dogs — Pointers, Retrievers, Setters, and Spaniels
Group II	Hounds
Group III	Working dogs — includes sled and draft dogs, water dogs, and guard dogs
Group IV	Terriers
Group V	Toys — from Affenpinscher to Yorkshire Terrier
Group VI	Nonsporting dogs — sort of a catchall category for those that don't fit into any of the other groups
Group VII	Herding dogs — those that herd, some of which also guard

Because the dogs in a given group, with the exception of Group VI, are there because of common behavioral traits, you can get a pretty good idea of what's going to be easy for your dog and what's going to be hard. Most terriers, for example, are lively little dogs because they were bred to go after little furry things that live in holes in the ground. (See Figure 9-1.) Shetland Sheepdogs like to round up kids, because they were bred to herd. Pointers are bred to finger the game, Retrievers to bring it back, Spaniels to flush it, and so on, each one with its own special talents.

Because dogs were bred to work with or under the direction of man, these talents help with your training efforts. But sometimes the dog's instinct to do what he was bred for is what gets him into trouble today. Put another way, you may not want him hunting or herding or whatever. So some of your training efforts are spent in redirecting these behaviors. Whenever you run into a roadblock in your training, ask yourself, "Is that what this dog was bred to do?" If not, it will take him more time to learn that particular exercise, and you have to be patient.

Figure 9-1:
The Parson
Russell
Terrier is
a small,
lively dog.

Temperament

Most people readily agree that good temperament is the most important quality for pets. Unfortunately, the explanation of exactly what good temperament means is often vague and elusive, and sometimes contradictory. The official breed standard of most breeds makes a statement to the effect that the dog you're considering is loyal, loving, intelligent, good with children, and easy to train. If only it were true!

Simply defined, *temperament* is having the personality traits suitable for the job you want the dog to do. If you want your dog to be good with children, and your dog has that personality trait, then he has good temperament. He may not do so well in other areas, such as guarding or herding, but that may not have been what you were looking for.

Similarly vague and elusive have been attempts to define the dog's intelligence. Again, it goes back to function. We define a dog's *intelligence* as the ease with which he can be trained for the function the dog was bred for. For example, teaching a Labrador Retriever to retrieve is very easy. After all, that's what he was bred to do. On the other hand, you'd be dead wrong to think that an Afghan Hound is stupid just because he has no interest in that task. That's not what he was bred to do; it's not his job.

You need to recognize and be aware of your dog's strengths and limitations. They have a profound influence on the ease or difficulty of teaching your dog a particular task. Circus trainers have an old saying: "Get the dog for the trick and not the trick for the dog." Exploit your dog's strengths.

Mental sensitivity

Dogs, like people, vary in their ability to deal with negative emotions. Most dogs, however, are keenly aware of your emotions. Moreover, the more you work with Buddy, the greater the bond that develops. It seems as though he can read your mind. Okay, he may not be able to read your mind, but he certainly senses your emotions. If you're feeling frustration, disappointment, or anger, Buddy senses it.

Because dogs are ill equipped to deal with these emotions, they tend to become anxious and confused, which in turn slows down or even prevents the learning process. Your job in training Buddy is to maintain an upbeat and patient attitude. As your dog's trainer, your job is to teach him what you want and don't want him to do. Without your guidance, your dog simply does what comes naturally to him — he's a dog!

Blaming Buddy for what you perceive to be a shortcoming on his part doesn't help and undermines the very relationship you're trying to build. Remember, Buddy only does what comes naturally, and it's your responsibility to teach him what's acceptable and what's not.

You're the trainer, and Buddy is the student. He responds only to the commands you've taught him.

Responses to visual stimuli

How a dog responds to *visual stimuli* is a fancy way of saying how a dog responds to moving objects. For purposes of training, it relates to the dog's distractibility when faced with something that moves. This, too, varies from breed to breed and depends on the nature of the moving object. The following are a few examples:

 ✔ Terriers are notoriously distractible. Our Yorkshire Terrier, although technically a member of the Toy Group, was convinced that every moving leaf or blade of grass had to be investigated. Although this made perfect sense to him, it made training him to pay attention a real challenge.

✔ In the Hound Group, some breeds, such as Afghan Hounds, Borzois, or Salukis, called *sight hounds,* aren't much interested in objects close by and, instead, focus on those far away. Others, such as the Basset Hound, Beagle, or Bloodhound, are more stimulated by scents on the ground or in the air than by moving objects. Training a Beagle to *heel* — that is, walk on a loose leash while paying attention to you and not sniffing the ground — becomes a Herculean task.

✔ The guarding breeds, such as the German Shepherd, Doberman Pinscher, and Rottweiler, were bred to survey their surroundings — to keep everything in sight, as it were. They, too, find it difficult to focus exclusively on you in the presence of distractions. Remember, their job is to be alert to what's going on around them.

✔ The weavers of the Canton of Berne used the Bernese Mountain Dog as a draft dog, drawing small wagons loaded with baskets to the marketplace. As a breed, moving objects don't usually excite these dogs. After all, it would hardly do for the little fellow to chase a cat with his wagon bouncing behind him.

✔ The Newfoundland, an ordinarily sedate companion (see Figure 9-2), becomes a raving maniac near water with his instinctive desire to rescue any and all swimmers, totally disregarding that they may not want to be rescued.

Figure 9-2:
The New-
foundland,
a large
breed, is a
laid-back
dog except
around
water.

Sound sensitivity

Some dogs have a keener sense of hearing than others, to the point where loud noises literally hurt their ears. One of our Landseers would leave the room anytime the TV was turned on. Fear of thunder can be the result of sound sensitivity.

Under ordinary circumstances, sound sensitivity isn't a problem, but it can affect the dog's ability to concentrate in the presence of moderate to loud noises. A car backfiring causes this dog to jump out of his hide, whereas it only elicits a curious expression from another dog.

Touch sensitivity

A dog's threshold of discomfort depends on two things:

- His touch sensitivity
- What he's doing at the particular time

For purposes of training and for knowing what equipment to use, you need to have some idea of Buddy's touch sensitivity. For example, when a dog doesn't readily respond to the training collar, he's all too quickly labeled as stubborn or stupid. But nothing could be farther from the truth. It's the trainer's responsibility to select the right training equipment so that the dog does respond.

Discomfort thresholds tend to be breed-specific. For example, we'd expect that a Labrador Retriever, who's supposed to be able to cover all manner of terrain, as well as retrieve in ice-cold water, would have a high discomfort threshold. Shetland Sheepdogs tend to be quite touch sensitive and respond promptly to the training collar. What one dog hardly notices makes another one change his behavior. And therein lies the secret of which piece of training equipment to use.

Touch sensitivity isn't size-related. Our Yorkshire Terrier had a very high discomfort threshold. That, plus his sight sensitivity, made training him a real challenge. Neither is it age related. A puppy doesn't start out as touch sensitive and become insensitive as he grows older. There may be some increase in insensitivity, but it's insignificant. A dog's touch sensitivity, however, is affected by what he's doing. In hot pursuit of a rabbit, his discomfort threshold goes up, as it would during a fight.

After you have an idea of Buddy's discomfort threshold, you know how to handle him and the type of training equipment you need.

Stressing the Stressful Effects of Stress

Stress is a byproduct of daily life. If it isn't one thing, it's another — health, family, job, state of the economy, state of the country, state of the world. Even pleasurable experiences, such as taking a vacation, are a source of stress.

In order to deal with all these stresses, you may get one or more of the following (check the appropriate response):

❏ Boat

❏ Cabin in the woods

❏ Dog

❏ Motor home

❏ _____ (fill in the blank)

Now *it* becomes a source of stress, and so it goes.

Stress is a physiological, genetically predetermined reaction over which the individual, be it a dog or person, has no control. Stress is a natural part of everyone's daily lives and affects each person in different ways. Dogs are no different. Just like people, they experience stress. As your dog's teacher, you must recognize the circumstances that produce stress and its manifestations, and you need to know how to manage it.

Your personal experiences with stress help you relate to what your dog is experiencing. Learning the signs and symptoms isn't difficult after you know what you're looking for.

Understanding stress

Stress is defined as the body's response to any physical or mental demand. The response prepares the body either to fight or flee. Stress increases blood pressure, heart rate, breathing, and metabolism, and it triggers a marked increase in the blood supply to the arms and legs.

When stressed, the body becomes chemically unbalanced. To deal with this imbalance, the body releases chemicals into the bloodstream in an attempt to re-balance itself. The reserve of these chemicals is limited. You can dip into it only so many times before it runs dry and the body loses its ability to rebalance. Prolonged periods of imbalance result in neurotic behavior and the inability to function. Stress takes its toll on the body, be it a person's or a dog's. When the body's ability to counteract stress has been maxed out, the stress is expressed behaviorally and physically. This is as true for your dog as it is for you.

Mental or physical stress ranges from tolerable all the way to intolerable — that is, the inability to function. Your interest here lies with the stress experienced during training, whether you're teaching a new exercise or practicing a familiar one, or during a test, like the Canine Good Citizen test (see Chapter 12). You need to be able to recognize the signs of stress and what you can do to manage the stress your dog may experience.

Positive and negative stress — manifestations

Stress is characterized as *positive* — manifesting itself in increased activity — and *negative* — manifesting itself in decreased activity.

Picture yourself returning home after a hard day at work. A mess on the brand-new white living room carpet welcomes you. What's your response? Do you explode, scream at poor Buddy, your spouse, and the children, and then storm through the house slamming doors? Or do you look at the mess in horror, shake your head in resignation, feel drained of energy, ignore the dog, the spouse, and the children, and retire to your room?

In the first sample response, the chemicals released into the bloodstream energized your body. In the second sample response, your body was debilitated. Dogs react in a similar manner.

Help, I'm hyperactive

So-called positive stress results in hyperactivity, such as running around, not being able to stay still, not being able to slow down, not paying attention, bouncing up and down, jumping on you, whining, barking, mouthing, getting in front of you, anticipating commands, or not being able to learn. You may think your dog is just being silly and tiresome, but he's actually exhibiting coping behaviors.

Why am I so depressed?

So-called negative stress causes lethargy, such as a lack of energy, being afraid, freezing, slinking behind you, running away, responding slowly to commands, showing little interest in exercise or training, or displaying an inability to learn. In new situations, Buddy either gets behind you, seems tired and wants to lie down, or seems sluggish and disinterested. These aren't signs of relaxation but are the coping behaviors for negative stress.

Recognizing the symptoms of stress

In dogs, signs of either form of stress — positive or negative — are muscle tremors; excessive panting and drooling; sweaty feet that leave tracks on dry, hard surfaces; dilated pupils; and, in extreme cases, urination; defecation (usually in the form of diarrhea); self-mutilation; and anxiety.

Anxiety is a state of apprehension and uneasiness. When anxiety is prolonged, two things happen:

✔ The ability to learn and think is clearly diminished and ultimately stops. It can also cause a panic attack.

✔ It depresses the immune system, thereby increasing your chances of becoming physically ill. It affects your dog in the same way. The weakest link in the chain is attacked first. If the dog has structural flaws, such as weak *pasterns* (the region of foreleg between the wrist and digits), he may begin to limp or show signs of pain. Digestive upsets are another common reaction to stress.

Stress, in and of itself, isn't bad or undesirable. A certain level of stress is vital for the development and healthy functioning of the body and its immune system. It's only when stress has no behavioral outlet — when the dog is put in a no-win situation — that the burden of coping is born by the body, and the immune system starts to break down.

Origins of stress — intrinsic and extrinsic

Intrinsic sources of stress are inherited and come from within the dog, and they include structure and health. Dogs vary in coping abilities and stress thresholds. Realistically, you can't do much to change your dog, such as training him to deal better with stress. But you can use stress-management techniques to mitigate its impact (see the section "Managing Stress," later in this chapter).

Extrinsic sources of stress come from outside the dog and are introduced externally. They range from the diet you feed your dog to the relationship you have with him. Extrinsic sources include the following:

✔ Appropriateness of the training method being used

✔ Frustration and indecision on your part

✔ Lack of adequate socialization

>   🖝 How the dog perceives his environment
>   🖝 Training location

Fortunately, all these sources of stress are under your control (see the section "Managing Stress").

Relating stress to learning

All learning is stressful. For many people, us included, one of the most recent stress-inducing learning experiences was brought on by the computer revolution. In our case, plenty of times during the learning process we were tempted to throw the agonizing contraption out the window. At that moment, learning, and the ability to think rationally, had stopped. There was no point in trying to go on until the body had the chance to rebalance itself.

When you train Buddy, you can't prevent him from experiencing some stress, but you can keep it at a level where he can still learn. If you find that your dog is overly stressed during a training session, stop the session. At that point, your dog's ability to learn is diminished, and neither of you will benefit from continuing.

Instances are going to occur when Buddy just doesn't seem to get the message. They can happen at any time, especially when you're working with distractions. Nothing you do works, and you feel that you're not making progress.

"What can I do?" we're often asked. "If I stop, Buddy will think he has won and he will never do it for me." This line of thinking presumes that you and Buddy are adversaries, in some kind of a contest, such as, "you'll do it no matter what." If you approach training with this attitude, you're doomed to failure; at best, you'll have an unrewarding relationship with your dog.

Training Buddy has nothing to do with winning, but with teaching. You can walk away from a training session at any time, whether or not you think you've been successful. When you see that no further learning is taking place, stop! If you don't, and you insist on forcing the issue, you'll undermine both your dog's trust in you and the relationship you're trying to build.

Let Buddy rest for four hours and try again. You'll find that the light bulb suddenly seems to turn on. By having taken a break at that point, you give *latent learning* — the process of getting the point through time — a chance to work. Our advice is to quit training when you find yourself becoming irritable or when Buddy starts to show signs of stress.

Konrad Most, considered to be the "father" of modern dog training, recognized the importance of maintaining the dog's equilibrium. In his 1910 training manual, he wrote, "Good training needs a kind heart as well as a cool and well-informed head . . . ." Anyone can dominate a dog by physical or mental pressure, but only through the building of confidence by positive reinforcement can reliability and enjoyment of performance be achieved. Buddy must perceive you as trustworthy, or he'll begin to exhibit neurotic behaviors.

A stressful first impression

Making a good first impression is so important. A classic example of the impact of the first impression is the following incident: Pinny had entered her 1-year-old Landseer Newfoundland, Immy, in a Newfoundland Club of America Water Test. These events test the dog's rescue abilities and, when found satisfactory, result in a Water Dog title, attesting the fact the dog is a water rescue dog.

The Newfoundland Club of America conducts Water Tests where the dogs can demonstrate their water rescue abilities. Two levels exist: Water Dog and Water Rescue Dog. The Club also conducts Draft Dog tests.

The first part of this test is on land, where the dogs are expected to demonstrate a passing familiarity with basic obedience commands, such as "Heel," "Come," and "Stay." Immy was very well trained to do these tasks.

When Pinny and Immy approached the area in which they were to be tested, which had been roped off into a large square with yellow tape, she noticed that Immy was becoming extremely agitated. He outright refused to get close to, much less into, the roped-off enclosure. His eyes rolled back in his head, he wanted to bolt, and he became almost uncontrollable.

Pinny walked away from the area, calmed him down, and tried again. No way was Immy going close to the yellow tape that was flapping in the wind. Pinny didn't push the issue, but Immy went on and did the water part of the trial with great success.

Driving home, Pinny tried to think why Immy was so frightened of the yellow tape. And then she remembered. When Immy first came to her, he was already 6 months old. He was a tall and gangly puppy with lots of energy and a propensity for jumping straight up in the air. It wasn't long before he took this great talent and experimented with jumping the fence in the back garden. He took himself for a nice walk around the neighborhood and found visiting other dogs lots of fun.

Living on a rather busy street, Pinny was worried that he would get run over. So she came to the conclusion that an electric fence was the best solution to her problem. When the salesperson installed the fence, he asked Pinny if she'd ever trained a dog to the fence before. She answered that she had not. "Don't worry, I'll show you how to do it," said the salesman. He took Immy on a leash, went up to the fence, which had yellow flags on it, and as Immy approached curiously, he yanked him back as hard as he could, and screamed "no." Immy fell to the ground in shock, and Pinny was horrified.

Looking back, Immy clearly associated this most unpleasant experience with the yellow tape, and when he encountered it again at the Water Test, he wanted nothing to do with it.

Stress and distraction training

When distractions are introduced in training, your dog may not respond as you expect. As a result, you may become a little frustrated, taking the attitude, "How could you do this to me?" Buddy senses your feelings and becomes apprehensive and anxious. He only understands that you're upset, but he doesn't understand why. Unless you now calm him and yourself, and you reassure him that he's a good boy and should keep trying, your training session will deteriorate to the point where all learning stops.

Prepare to be patient when you first introduce your dog to training with distractions. Naturally, Buddy is going to be distracted (that's the point!), but over time, he'll learn to respond the way you want. If you feel yourself becoming distraught, it's time to take five.

When you take your Canine Good Citizen test (see Chapter 12), remain calm and control any nervousness you may experience. Your dog is acutely aware of your emotions, which are likely to interfere with his performance. Remember, the object of training and of the test is to make a positive experience for both you and your dog.

Most of the tests for the Canine Good Citizen involve some form of distraction. You need to monitor your dog's reaction to these distractions so that you can help him cope. One test requires you be out of your dog's sight for three minutes, which can be a source of significant stress to your dog. You need to introduce him to and condition him for this exercise in such a way that any stress he may experience is minimized.

Try to make every new exercise or distraction a positive experience for your dog. A favorable introduction will have a positive long-term impact. The first impression leaves the most lasting impact. Whenever you introduce your dog to a new exercise or distraction, make it as pleasant and as stress free as possible so that it leaves a neutral, if not favorable, impression.

Managing Stress

Become aware of how Buddy reacts to stress, positively or negatively, and the circumstances under which he stresses. Something you're doing, or even a location, may cause him stress.

Understand that Buddy has no control over his response to stress — he inherited this behavior — and that it's your job to manage it as best as you can. Through proper management, Buddy will become accustomed, with every successful repetition, to coping with new situations and handling them like an old trooper.

Managing positive stress

For example, say that Buddy stresses in a "positive" way, which means he gets overexcited and bouncy. In the case of a person, you may say that he or she is hysterical. In the old movies, when someone started screaming uncontrollably, this was handled by slapping the person on the cheek. (For Buddy, a check on the collar to settle him down would be the same thing.) However, we advise that you keep your hands still and off your dog and keep your voice quiet, or you'll excite him even more. Instead, give him the "Down" command and enforce it.

Every behavior has a timeframe, and experience tells you how long Buddy takes to calm down under different circumstances. During times of severe stress, Buddy is unable to learn or respond to commands, even those he knows well, until his body rebalances itself. Your goal is to restore your dog's breathing pattern and body posture to normal. With the right management on your part, Buddy will become comfortable with any new situation.

Managing negative stress

If Buddy stresses in a "negative" way, take him for a walk to get the circulation going and redistribute the chemicals that have been released so his breathing can return to normal. Massage the top of his shoulders to relax him — just because he's quiet doesn't mean he's calm. Try to get him excited with an object or food. Don't, under any circumstances, use a check to get him "out of it." A check will just produce even greater lethargy.

Stress manifests itself in so many ways, and it's up to you, the owner, to know your dog. Remember, the dog has no control over his response. It's also up to you to play detective to find out what triggers the stress behavior.

Other remedies for managing stress

Some dogs get unduly stressed during thunderstorms. Others, perhaps because of lack of socialization, get stressed when they're away from home, left in a kennel, taken to a class for the first time, riding in the car, and the like.

A successful outcome to a physical problem

Perhaps the strangest case we've had to deal with was that of one of our own dogs. D.J. is an extremely handsome black Briard. When D.J. was a young dog, he got stressed by almost everything. If we put him in the car, he'd throw up and turn in circles in his crate. When he got out, he'd be wet from drooling and would want to pace and pace. Around other dogs, he was anxious and wanted nothing to do with them. If they came too close, he'd lunge out at the end of the leash, teeth flashing — a frightening sight for any dog or person that happened to be close.

Knowing that D.J. was on the very best diet he could be on, we ruled out food-related problems. He went through every medical test in the book to try to find out the cause of his stressful behavior. Nothing was found, and so we lived with him, always seeking some kind of answer. The answer came when he was nearly 3 years old.

We learned that a veterinarian and Certified Animal Chiropractor was giving a clinic for dogs and horses in our area. The chiropractor was in a horse barn, working on some dogs when we arrived. She instructed us to bring in D.J. and just let him sit and watch what was going on for a while so he could get the feeling of his surroundings.

In the barn were horses, goats, and chickens. D.J. was fascinated by the smells and was fine so long as nothing or no one came close to him. We carefully inched him closer and closer to the doctor, who was sitting on a small stool. D.J. stood with his back to her, and all of a sudden, decided to back into her. She talked to him for a while, without touching his body. When she touched him, he jumped, and we all jumped.

She was a model of patience with D.J. and started again. While his attention was glued on a chicken, she was able to feel up and down his back. As she felt his back and then his tail, she told us that many vertebrae were out of alignment, and there'd been some kind of break in his tail. We surmised that this break must've happened during the birthing process, which apparently isn't uncommon. She very gently manipulated his back into position. But she really felt the problem was his neck.

Slowly, slowly, she moved up his body, and he was motionless. Thank goodness the chicken was obliging and stayed within a nose length of D.J., who was still staring at it. The doctor finally was able to feel his neck and with two rather quick movements, adjusted the vertebrae. He stood up and shook himself, sat down suddenly, and then just lay down.

She told us that his neck was such a mess that the nerves connected to his eyes were severely displaced. She felt that he'd never been able to see properly — either his vision was so distorted he couldn't make out shapes, or he was seeing upside down.

This of course explained all his behavior and the stress that he felt. If his vision was poor, naturally he always felt threatened when away from home. Because he was never off leash when we took him out, and couldn't run away as he wanted to do, he would then be forced into a defensive posture, hence the teeth and the growling.

After his adjustment, D.J. became a very cuddly and sweet dog. Most visitors pick out D.J. as our most friendly dog.

So the moral of this story is that when your dog is stressing, there's a reason for it. You just have to work at it until you find the answers.

Products now exist that make dealing with stress so much easier. Homeopathic remedies and Bach Flower Remedies are excellent to use for this purpose. You can address the following conditions with these specific products:

- ✔ **For fear of thunderstorms:** We recommend Aconite 30c. This remedy comes in liquid or pellet form. Usually one dose gives the dog a feeling of being able to cope with the storm.

- ✔ **Going to the doctor:** When taking a dog to a place where he experiences fear, such as the animal hospital, we use a product called Calm Stress. It's a liquid homeopathic that you can put it into your dog's mouth just before you enter. It lasts about 20 minutes. After your dog understands that he need not be afraid, and he has coped well with the environment, further dosing is unnecessary.

- ✔ **Carsickness:** A simple remedy for carsick dogs is a ginger cookie. Ginger has a wonderful way of settling the stomach, and if you give your dog a ginger cookie just as he gets into the car, the car becomes a good place to be in. If the trip is a long one, you can give him a ginger cookie period-ically. Dogs can get quite stressed in a car, not only because of the move-ment but also because of objects flashing by the windows. Using a crate for such a dog is a good idea, because you can cover the crate so the dog isn't constantly exposed to visual stimuli. (We also recommend you crate your dog for safety reasons — just like you use your seatbelt — anytime you take him in a car.) Rescue Remedy, together with Calm Stress, also works well to combat carsickness.

We also use the Calm Stress remedy to rehabilitate rescue dogs with great success, as well as another one called Rescue Remedy. A Bach Flower Remedy is used when the dog gets so stressed that he's in danger of shock. This remedy can be dropped directly into the dog's mouth (about four drops) or put into his water bowl.

Chapter 10

Dealing with Doggie Don'ts

• •

• •

Does your dog have what you think is a behavior problem? Does Buddy bark too much, but otherwise behave like a model dog? Does he jump on people when he first meets them, but is perfectly well behaved the rest of the time? Does Buddy have occasional accidents in the house, pull your arms out when you walk him on leash, or chew on your favorite possessions when left unattended?

Dogs can exhibit one or two irritating habits that aren't necessarily "behavior" problems. Some can be solved with very little training; others require more time and effort on your part. Whatever your situation, any training starts with convincing Buddy that you're the boss. Dogs are pack animals that come into the world with the expectation that someone has to be in charge of the pack. They need a leader, and that leader has to be you.

Without making the effort to become Buddy's leader, your attempts at training are going to be haphazard at best. The method we recommend to best establish your authority is an exercise called the *Long Down*. The Long Down is nonviolent and nonthreatening, and it's one exercise Buddy readily understands because it mimics behaviors used in a pack to maintain rank order. You can find details on this exercise in Chapter 2.

In addition, establish a line of communication with Buddy by teaching him the basic obedience commands in Chapters 7 and 8. You'll find addressing undesired behaviors much easier when Buddy has some understanding of what you expect than when you're trying to deal with a particular behavior in isolation.

The majority of "doggy don'ts" is a relationship problem rather than a behavior problem. These doggy don'ts are the result of insufficient training and insufficient time spent with the dog.

Figuring Out the Cause of Behavior Problems

Many dog behavior problems have a common cause or a combination of causes. In order of importance, they include the following:

- ✔ Boredom and frustration due to insufficient exercise
- ✔ Mental stagnation due to insufficient quality time with you
- ✔ Loneliness caused by too much isolation from human companionship
- ✔ Nutrition and health-related problems

Loneliness is perhaps the most difficult problem to overcome. By necessity, many dogs are left alone at home anywhere from eight to ten hours a day with absolutely nothing to do except get into mischief. Fortunately, there are some things you can do in addition to spending quality time with him when you're together. If Buddy is really unhappy, take him to doggie daycare or get another dog as his companion.

Before addressing behavior problems specifically, we give you our general prescription for good behavior in this section.

Exercise

You notice that exercise is at the top of the list. Exercise needs vary, depending on the size and energy level of your dog. Many dogs need a great deal more exercise than their owners realize. Bull Terriers are a good example. If the owner of an English Bull Terrier lives in an apartment in a large city, and the dog doesn't get enough free-running exercise, he's bound to develop behavior problems. These problems can range from tail spinning, which is a neurotic behavior, to ripping up furniture. This kind of dog would show none of these behaviors if he were living in a household where adequate exercise, both mental and physical, was provided.

Dog trainers have a maxim: "Tired dogs are happy dogs." Dogs that have adequate exercise and can expend their energy through running, retrieving, playing, and training rarely show objectionable behaviors. Dogs denied those simple needs frequently redirect their energy into unacceptable behaviors.

When your dog engages in behaviors that you consider objectionable, it can be a vexing problem. Sometimes the behavior is instinctive, such as digging. Sometimes it occurs out of boredom, but never because the dog is ornery. Before you attempt to deal with the behavior, you need to find out the cause.

The easiest way to stop a behavior is by addressing the need that brought it about in the first place rather than by trying to correct the behavior itself. If there's one single cause for behavior problems, it's the lack of adequate exercise.

Good company

Many years ago, we labeled a set of behaviors we used to see in our obedience classes as *single-dog syndrome*. These dogs would run away from their owners more frequently than those dogs living in multidog households. They'd growl around their food bowls, be picky eaters, be possessive about toys, and be much more unruly than dogs living in homes with other dogs.

Good company means not only that you act as a companion to your dog but also that your dog shares the company of other dogs as frequently as possible. Some possibilities include taking regular walks in parks where he can meet other dogs, joining a dog club where dog activities are offered, or putting your puppy into daycare several days a week. Dogs are pack animals and thrive in the company of other dogs. Socialization of your pet is a continuing process. For more information on doggie activities, see Chapter 21.

Good health

Keeping Buddy in good health isn't nearly as easy as it was 50 years ago. It seems that with the advance of science in so many dog-related fields, dogs should be healthier than ever. This isn't the case. Too often through poor breeding practices, poor nutrition, and overvaccination, a dog's health has been threatened as never before.

Having a dog that has constant health problems — from minor conditions, like skin irritations, picking up fleas, smelling, ear infections, and the like, to more serious conditions that affect his internal organs, such as kidneys, the heart, liver, and thyroid, is no fun! Not feeling well can cause your dog many behavior problems, from aggression to timidity, and health-related conditions are often confused with behavior problems. Buddy may have eaten something that upset his stomach, causing a house-soiling accident. He may have a musculoskeletal disorder making changes of position painful and causing irritability and sometimes snapping. These concerns are obviously not amenable to training solutions, and certainly not to discipline. For more on your dog's health, see Chapter 19.

Good nutrition

You are what you eat equally applies to dogs as it does to people. Properly feeding your dog makes the difference between sickness and health and has a profound effect on his behavior. And with the abundance of dog foods on the market, figuring out what's best for your pet can be difficult.

There are several ways to correctly feed your dog. One way is to select a commercial kibble that has two animal proteins in the first three ingredients. You can add some fresh, raw foods to the kibble. Another way is to buy a dehydrated version of a natural diet dog food, to which you add some yogurt and meat. A third way is to make your own dog food. Your choice depends on your level of comfort and the time you have to devote to your dog. For more on your dog's nutritional needs, see Chapter 18.

Good training

Behavior problems don't arise because your dog is ornery or spiteful, and discipline is rarely the answer. Mental stagnation can also be a cause of unwanted behavior. Training your dog on a regular basis, or having him doing something for you, makes your dog feel useful and provides the mental stimulation he needs (see Chapter 7).

Use your imagination to get your dog to help around the house, and you'll be surprised by how useful he can become.

Dealing with Your Dog's Objectionable Behavior

Like beauty, objectionable behavior is in the eye of the beholder. Playful nipping or biting may be acceptable to some and not to others. Moreover, there are degrees of objectionable behavior. Getting on the couch in your absence isn't nearly as serious an offense as destroying the couch in your absence.

Having worked with dogs for a lifetime, we're perhaps more tolerant of irritating behaviors than most. We know that dogs like to please and that most behaviors can be changed with a little good training. What we do find objectionable, however, is, when we visit friends, and their untrained dogs jump up at us and scratch us in the process. Other critical negative behavior patterns include dogs that don't come when called, which can be dangerous, and dogs that don't stay when they're told.

A dog's home is his crate

One tool that aids in dealing with any kind of inappropriate behavior is a crate. Leaving Buddy in a crate when you're at work saves you from worrying about housetraining, chewing, and digging. Properly trained to a crate, Buddy will think of it as his "den." He'll always be safe in his crate. He can go anywhere with you, from the car to a friend's house. You can take him on holiday with you. He'll be comfortable any time you have to leave him at the vet, where dogs are kept in crates during treatment. (See Chapter 4 for more on training with a crate.)

All these irritating behaviors can be trained away by the investment of a mere ten minutes a day, five times a week for about four weeks. It's such a small amount of time and energy to have a wonderful dog to be proud of. Trained dogs are free dogs — you can take them anywhere, and they're always welcome.

When you believe your dog has a behavior problem, you have several options:

- ✔ You can tolerate the behavior.
- ✔ You can train your dog in an effort to change the behavior.
- ✔ You can find a new home for the dog.
- ✔ You can take your dog for a one-way trip to the shelter or veterinarian.

Tolerating your dog's behavior problems

Considering the amount of time and energy that may be required to turn Buddy into the pet you always wanted, you may decide it's easier to live with his annoying antics than to try to change him. You tolerate him the way he is, because you don't have the time, the energy, or the inclination to put in the required effort to change him.

Time is a factor everyone has to consider. Can you be disciplined enough to put aside ten minutes five times a week to work with Buddy in a place with no distractions, just concentrating on him? If so, you may be able to solve those annoying habits.

Behaviors you shouldn't tolerate are those that threaten your safety or the safety of others, such as biting people or aggression. True aggression is defined as unpredictable — without warning — and unprovoked biting (see Chapter 11 for more on aggression). You also shouldn't tolerate behaviors that threaten the safety of your dog, such as chasing cars (see Chapter 7).

Trying to solve your dog's behavior problems

You've decided that you can't live with your dog's irritating behaviors and that you're going to work with him to be the pet you expected and always wanted. You understand doing so will require an investment of time, effort, and perhaps even expert help. But you're willing to work to achieve your goal — a long-lasting, mutually rewarding relationship. Good for you! This book can help you.

Obedience training, in and of itself, isn't necessarily the answer. Still, when you train your dog, you're spending meaningful time with him, which in many cases is half the battle. Much depends on the cause of the problem.

For most people, dog ownership is a compromise between tolerating and working with our dogs. We find certain behaviors objectionable but realistically can't do anything about them. As long as the joys of dog ownership outweigh the headaches, people usually put up with these behaviors.

Finding a new home for your dog

Your dog's temperament may be unsuitable to your lifestyle. A shy dog, or a dog with physical limitations, may never develop into a great playmate for

Going directly to the source

The easiest way to stop a behavior is by dealing with the need that brought it about in the first place rather than trying to correct the behavior itself. When your dog goes through teething, for example, you need to provide him with suitable chew toys. When your dog has an accident in the house, first ask yourself whether you've left him inside too long, or whether the dog is ill, and a trip to the vet is in order. If your dog is left alone in the yard and continuously barks out of boredom, don't leave him out there. Your neighbors will thank you. When your dog needs more exercise than you can give him, consider a dog-walker or daycare.

Every behavior has a timeframe and a certain amount of energy attached to it. This energy needs to be expended in a normal and natural way. By trying to suppress this energy, or not giving it enough time to dissipate, you help cause a majority of behavior problems. Remember, a tired dog is a happy dog.

By using the Personality Profile in Chapter 5, you can easily find out where the dog's energies lie. For example, is he high in prey drive? These dogs need more exercise than dogs in other drives. They're attracted to anything that moves quickly and want to chase it. Finding an outlet for these behaviors, such as playing ball, throwing sticks, or hiding toys and having Buddy find them, goes a long way to exhausting the energies of this drive.

active children. A dog that doesn't like to be left alone too long wouldn't be suitable for someone who's gone all day. Although some behaviors can be modified with training, others can't, or the effort required would simply be too stressful for the dog.

In some instances, the dog and the owner are mismatched, and they need to divorce. The dog may require a great deal more exercise than the owner is able to give him and as a result is developing behavior problems. Whatever the reason, under some circumstances, placement into a new home where the dog's needs can be met is advisable and in the best interest of both dog and owner.

We recall an incident involving an English Bull Terrier who was left alone too much and who started tail spinning. The behavior escalated to the point that the dog became a complete neurotic. At that point, we suggested a new home and found one for the dog on a farm. The dog now had unlimited daily exercise and within a few weeks, the tail-spinning behavior had completely disappeared.

Taking a one-way trip to the pound

If all reclamation efforts have failed — you can't live with this dog, and he can't be placed because he's dangerous or for some other reason — your final option is to put him to sleep. This option isn't something to be considered lightly, and you should only follow through if you've really tried to work it out and truly have no other alternatives.

Incidentally, don't kid yourself about taking your dog to a shelter. Most are overwhelmed by the number of unwanted dogs and are able to find new homes for only a small percentage of these orphans. The sad fact is that we live in a throwaway society. Far too often, when the dog outgrows that cute puppy stage, out he goes.

Digging the Scene

One of the favorite pastimes of our Dachshunds is digging, or "landscaping" as we call it. They engage in this activity at every opportunity and with great zest. Because Dachshunds were bred to go after badgers, this behavior is instinctive. Does that mean we have to put up with a yard that looks like a minefield? Not at all, but we do have to assume the responsibility for

 ✔ Expending the digging energy

 ✔ Providing an outlet for it

 ✔ Supervising the little darlings to make sure they don't get into trouble

---

Understanding the reasons for digging

Although some breeds, such as the small terriers, have a true propensity for digging, all dogs do it to some extent at one time or another. Take a look at some of the more common and sometimes comical reasons for digging:

- *Allelomimetic behavior,* or mimicking. In training, this practice is useful, but it may spell trouble for your gardening efforts. You plant, your dog digs up. Maybe you should do your gardening in secret and out of sight of your dog.

- To make nests for real or imaginary puppies (this one applies to female dogs).

- To bury or dig up a bone.

- To see what's there, because it's fun, or to find a cool spot to lie down.

- Boredom, isolation, or frustration.

Expenditure of the energy involves exercise, and providing an outlet means taking them for walks in the woods where they can dig to their little hearts' content. Of course, you can always cover your yard with Astroturf or green cement!

The good news is that most so-called behavior problems are under your direct control; the bad news is that you have to get involved. The cure to digging is rather simple: Don't leave your dog unattended in the yard for lengthy periods.

In order to eliminate digging before it becomes an issue for Buddy and you, recognize that this behavior is part of prey drive. So all the tips we give you about exhausting the behavior apply here. You can't make a dog dig until he's exhausted, but you can tire out your dog by playing ball or running with him so that he's too tired to dig!

Or, if you have Wirehaired Dachshunds, like we have, you can provide a place where it's safe for them to dig and where they don't excavate craters in the lawn. Put up a small fenced area for them where they can dig. In our case, we walk them in the woods and allow them to dig there. Interestingly, our little guys dig under specific grasses to get at the roots and dirt. It obviously satisfies some nutritional need, and we attribute the fact that they've never had worms to this daily intake of earth.

Barking Up Any Tree

On the one hand, few things are more reassuring than knowing the dog will sound the alarm when a stranger approaches. On the other hand, few things are more nerve racking than a dog's incessant barking. Dogs bark in response to a stimulus or because they're bored and want attention, any attention, even if it involves the owner being nasty to the dog. Therein lies the dilemma: You want the dog to bark, but only when you think he should.

Barking as a response

Your dog is outside in the yard, and some people walk by, so he barks. Barking is a natural response of defending his territory. After the potential intruders have passed, he's quiet again. People passing are the stimulus that causes barking, and after it has been removed, your dog stops.

If the people had stopped by the fence for a conversation, your dog would've continued to bark. To get him to stop, you have to remove your dog, or the people have to leave. Remove the stimulus from the dog or the dog from the stimulus. If you live in a busy area where this happens frequently, you may have to change your dog's environment. You may not be able to leave him in the yard for prolonged periods.

Your dog also barks when he's in the house and someone comes to the door. After he has alerted you, tell your dog "thank you, that's enough," and have him sit at your side as you answer the door. If necessary, put him on leash so that you can control him.

He may also rush to the window and stand there and bark because he sees or hears something. Again, thank him for letting you know what's going on and tell him "that's enough." If he doesn't stop, go to him, take him away from the window, and have him lie down in his corner.

Barking for no apparent reason

Your dog has a reason for barking, but it isn't apparent to you. It can be due to any or all of the following:

- ✔ Anxiety
- ✔ Boredom
- ✔ Seeking attention because he's lonely

Theoretically, none of these reasons is difficult to overcome if you work to eliminate the potential causes. Spend more time exercising your dog. Spend more time training your dog. Don't leave your dog alone so long, and don't leave him alone so often.

As a practical matter, it's not that easy. Most people work for a living and leave their dog at home alone for prolonged periods. If you live in an apartment, your

Knowing a dog's motivation

Whatever you may think, Buddy does what he does for a reason. Although the behavior may be unacceptable to you, to him, it's the only way he can express his unhappiness and frustration. Excessive barking is often attention-seeking behavior, even if the consequences of the attention are unpleasant. For example, when you scold your dog for barking or, worse yet, physically punish him, he's still getting attention.

dog certainly can't bark all day. The stress on the dog is horrendous, not to mention your neighbors' reactions. (See the section, "Coping with Separation Anxiety," later in the chapter.)

One way to stop a barking dog is an electronic bark collar, which causes a slight electric shock every time he barks. Another way is a citronella collar, which sprays some citronella in the direction of the dog's nose when he barks. These tools work well in a single-dog household. (See Chapter 6 for more info on these collars.)

Chewing — The Nonfood Variety

The principal reasons that dogs chew are physiological and psychological. The first passes, the second doesn't, and both are a nuisance.

The physiological need to chew

As part of the teething process, puppies need to chew. They can't help it. To get through this period, provide your dog with both a soft and a hard chew toy, such as a hard rubber bone or a real bone, as well as a canvas field dummy. Hard rubber Kong toys (www.kongcompany.com) with some peanut butter inserted can keep a dog amused for a long time. Don't give him anything he can destroy or ingest, except food items. Carrots, apples, dog biscuits, or ice cubes are great to relieve the monotony; otherwise, he'll be impelled to find more interesting things to chew on, such as those new shoes you left lying around.

Make sure your dog doesn't have access to personal articles, such as shoes, socks, and towels. Think of it as good training for you not to leave things lying around the house. A lonely dog may chew up anything in his path. Make sure your dog gets enough attention from you — and that he gets some strong chew toys!

The psychological need to chew

Chewing that takes place after the dog has gone through teething is usually a manifestation of anxiety, boredom, or loneliness. This oral habit has nothing to do with being spiteful. Should your dog attack the furniture, baseboards, and walls, tip over the garbage can, or engage in other destructive chewing activities, use a crate to confine him when you can't supervise him. Confining him saves you lots of money, and you won't lose your temper and get mad at the poor fellow. Even more important, he can't get into things that are a potential danger to him.

Instead of becoming angry at your dog for chewing up your prized possessions, give him some good solid chew toys. Use a crate or other means of confinement when you need to limit access to your personal items.

We want to emphasize that confinement is a problem-solving approach of last resort. Ideally, the dog isn't left alone so long and so often that he feels the need to chew in order to relieve his boredom. Your dog doesn't need you to entertain him all the time, but extended periods of being alone can make your pet neurotic. All the problems in this chapter fall under the category of too much isolation.

Coping with Separation Anxiety

With *separation related behaviors* (SRB), also called *separation anxiety,* your dog becomes anxious and stressed when you leave him. He's emotionally responding to being physically separated from the person he's attached to. Dogs that experience separation anxiety are usually high in pack drive and low in defense (fight) drive (see Chapter 5).

One solution to Buddy's boredom and loneliness is to get another dog. They can keep each other amused, and two dogs are more than twice the fun of one dog. But be warned that two dogs can also mean double trouble.

Separation anxiety isn't uncommon, especially among rescue dogs. In some cases, having an overly solicitous owner causes it. As the owner prepares to leave the house, he or she makes a big fuss over the dog: "Now don't worry, mommy/daddy will be back soon, but I have to go to work. You be a good boy while I'm gone and I'll bring you a nice treat." Such reassurances serve to increase the dog's anxiety at the expectation of being left alone. The owner then makes an equally big fuss upon his or her return: "Poor boy. Did you miss me while I was gone? I missed you too. Were you a good boy?" These utterances increase the dog's excitement in anticipation of the owner's return. Small wonder the dog becomes anxious.

The most typical and obvious signs of separation anxiety are destructive behaviors (chewing or scratching), vocalizations (whining, barking, or howling), house soiling, pacing, and excessive drooling.

The desensitizing approach

People are just as much creatures of habit as dogs are and tend to follow a specific pattern before leaving the house. This pattern becomes the dog's cue that you're about to depart. Make a list of your customary routine before you leave the house. For example, putting on makeup, picking up your bag or briefcase, picking up the car keys, putting on your coat, turning off the lights, and reassuring and petting the dog.

At odd intervals, several times during the day, go through your routine exactly as you would prior to leaving, and then sit in a chair and read the paper or watch TV, or just putter around the house. By following this procedure, you'll begin to desensitize the dog to the cues that you're about to leave.

When your dog ignores the cues, leave the house, without paying any attention to the dog, for about five minutes. Return, and again, don't pay any attention to him. Repeat this process, staying out for progressively longer periods. Turning on the radio or TV and providing suitable toys for your dog may also help. Whatever you do, make sure to ignore the dog for five minutes after your return. What you want to accomplish is to take the emotional element out of your going and coming so your dog will view the separation as a normal part of a day and not as reason to get excited.

The D.A.P. approach

Another way to cope with separation anxiety is to use D.A.P. — Dog Appeasing Pheromone — a product developed by vets that mimics the properties of the natural pheromones of the lactating female. After giving birth, a mother dog generates pheromones that give her puppies a sense of well being and reassurance.

D.A.P. is an electrical plug-in diffuser that dispenses the pheromone, which the dog's sense of smell detects. The pheromone reminds the dog of the well being he felt as a puppy. (D.A.P. is odorless to people.) In clinical trials, D.A.P. was effective in about 75 percent of cases in improving separation-related behaviors. To be effective, the diffuser must be left plugged in 24 hours a day. D.A.P. is available at pet stores and from pet product catalogs.

Soiling the House

House soiling that occurs after you've housetrained your dog and that isn't marking behavior (see Chapter 4) can have a variety of causes, other than separation anxiety. Its usual causes are one or more of the following:

✔ You've left your dog too long without giving him a chance to relieve himself. As the saying goes, accidents happen, and that's just what it was — an accident. You know your dog's endurance and schedule, so don't blame the dog when for some reason you were unable to adhere to it. You may have had to work late, or some other unforeseen event prevented you from getting home on time. As long as it doesn't become a regular occurrence on your part, the behavior won't be a continuing problem.

✔ Your dog may have eaten something that disagreed with him, and he has an upset stomach. Abrupt dietary changes, such as changing dog foods, are the most common cause for an upset tummy. Any time you change your dog's diet, do it gradually, over a period of several days, so his system can get used to the new food.

✔ Giving treats at holiday times that your dog ordinarily doesn't get, such as turkey and gravy or pizza, can create havoc with his digestive system.

✔ *Cystitis,* a bladder infection, is more common among female dogs than male dogs and may cause dribbling. You need to consult your vet.

Cystitis is an inflammation of the bladder wall that can be caused by a bacterial infection. It makes Buddy feel as if there's constant pressure on his bladder, and he'll think he has to urinate all the time, even after just relieving himself. When he does urinate, it can burn, which in turn causes him to spend a lot of time washing himself.

Although not very dangerous in and of itself, cystitis can cause all sorts of problems if left unattended, because the bacteria can spread up into the kidneys. If you see any of the preceding symptoms, a trip to your vet is a must. A short course of the appropriate antibiotics cures this inflammation quickly.

✔ As your dog ages, urinary incontinence may develop, and it can be treated with medication and homeopathic remedies.

The slackening of the sphincter muscles that holds the urine in the bladder often causes incontinence, which often happens as your dog ages. So many dogs are put to sleep for this perceived problem, which although not easy to live with, can be solved in several ways. Acupuncture is probably the best treatment and is very effective (see Chapter 19 for more on acupuncture). If you can find a vet trained in acupuncture, then have a series of treatments to solve the problem. Many vets today are trained in acupuncture, and finding one who can help isn't very difficult. A change in diet to a more natural diet (see Chapter 18) can often solve this problem. You can find many herbal and homeopathic remedies on the market specifically targeted at the kidney and bladder of older dogs. A good holistic vet can help you make the best choice for your dog.

✔ Chocolate can make your dog really sick. Although it contains several chemical agents that make it so good and tasty to us, these agents can be poisonous to Buddy. Be very careful to keep chocolate out of the way of your best friend.

While you're finding a vet to help you, you still have to live with the soiling problem. Put a tablecloth that's plastic on one side and has a soft backing on it under your dog's blanket. Doing so saves the furniture or floor, and both are easy to wash and keep clean. You can consider diapers, but only as a last resort. Don't give up on that old friend — explore the alternatives and see how you can support Buddy in his old age.

Dribbling, or Submissive Wetting

Dogs that are high in defense flight and low in defense fight drives are notorious for submissive wetting behavior. (See Chapter 5 for more on your dog's drives.) This behavior usually occurs upon first greeting the dog. He will either squat or roll over on his back and dribble, dating back to his days as a puppy, when his mother cleaned him.

When Buddy dribbles, don't scold your dog, because it only reinforces the behavior and actually makes it worse. By scolding him, you only make him act even more submissive, which brings on the wetting. Also, don't stand or lean over your dog or try to pick him up, because that, too, makes him act submissive and causes wetting.

Fortunately, submissive wetting isn't difficult to solve. Follow these steps:

1. **When you come home, ignore your dog.**

   Don't approach your dog; let him come to you instead.

2. **Greet your dog without making eye contact and by offering the palm of your hand.**

   This step is important. The back of the hand transmits negative energy, and the palm of the hand transmits positive energy.

3. **Keep your mouth shut, and let him sniff your palm.**

4. **Gently pet him under the chin, not on top of the head.**

5. **Don't reach or try to grab for the dog.**

When friends visit you, they can help you manage your dog's wetting behavior. Tell your visitors when they arrive to ignore the dog and let him come to them. Instruct them about offering the palm of the hand and about not grabbing for the dog.

If you follow this routine, your dog will stop dribbling.

Suffering from Carsickness

Carsickness, which manifests itself in excessive drooling or vomiting, can be attributed to

✔ True motion sickness

✔ A negative association with riding in a car

For obvious reasons, dogs that have a tendency to get carsick usually aren't taken for rides very often. And when they are, it's to the vet. You can compare his reaction to that of a child who, every time it gets in the car, goes to the doctor for a shot. It doesn't take many repetitions before your dog makes an unpleasant association with your car.

Some dogs get sick in vans because they *can't* see out of the window, and others get sick in cars because they *can* see out of the window. Whatever the reason for the dog's reaction, you can create a pleasant association with the car. When working with your dog to make car rides a positive experience, you can tell how well he's taking to the car and how much time you need to spend at each sequence.

Throughout this remedial exercise, maintain a light and happy attitude. Avoid a solicitous tone of voice and phrases such as, "It's all right. Don't worry. Nothing is going to happen to you." These reassurances validate the dog's concerns and reinforce his phobia about the car.

1. **Open all the doors and, with the engine off, coax your dog into the car.**

   If he doesn't want to go in, pick him up and put him in the car. After he's in the car (no matter how he got there), give him a treat, tell him how proud you are of him, and immediately let him out again. Repeat this step until he's comfortable getting into the car on his own.

2. **After your dog is comfortable getting into the car willingly, close the doors on one side of the car, keep the engine shut off, and coax your dog into the car again.**

3. **When he's comfortable with Step 2, tell your dog to get in the car, give him a treat, and close the doors.**

   Let him out again, and give him a treat. Repeat until he readily goes into the car, and you can close the doors for up to one minute.

4. **Tell your dog to get into the car, get in with him, close all the doors, and start the engine.**

   Give your dog a treat. Turn off the engine, and let him out.

5. **Now it's time for a short drive, no more than once around the block.**

   Increase the length of the rides, always starting and ending with a treat.

Give Buddy a ginger cookie. Ginger cookies are an excellent treat. Ginger calms your dog's stomach.

Chapter 11

Dealing with Aggression

. . . .

. . . .

*T*he term *aggression* means different things to different people. For example, a dog that runs along the fence in his yard barking and snarling furiously at a passerby may well be considered aggressive. But if he's your dog, you may consider the behavior to be a perfectly normal reaction: The dog is defending his territory, which is what you expect from him.

Many dog owners want a certain amount of protectiveness, or "aggression," from their companions — but only at the right time and under the right circumstances. For the dog, determining the right time and right circumstances can be a tough call. This chapter helps you sort out how to manage the aggression issue in a variety of situations.

What Is Aggressive Behavior?

The terms *aggression* and *vicious* are often used incorrectly for behaviors that aren't true aggression. Eberhard Trumler, the noted German behaviorist, defines true aggression as "unpredictable and unprovoked biting — without warning — with the intent to draw blood." By far, the greatest majority of so-called aggressive incidents are predictable, provoked, or both.

For example, you're walking your dog when a stranger approaches, and your dog starts to growl, maybe because he's afraid (defense flight; see Chapter 5) or maybe because he wants to protect you (defense fight; see Chapter 5). In either case, it isn't true aggression, because the dog is giving you ample warning of his intentions. It's now your job to manage the situation correctly.

A good reason to be aggressive

A good friend of ours, who was raised on a large farm, recalls an incident involving two of her younger brothers, ages 10 and 8. One morning, the boys announced they were going down to the pond to fish. Off they went with the family dog, Lucy, in tow. A short time later, they returned crying and sobbing: "Lucy won't let us dig for worms. She growled at us and showed her teeth." Because this behavior was uncharacteristic for Lucy, their mother decided to investigate. She found Lucy sitting at the edge of the pond where the boys had tried to dig for worms, intently staring at a rock. As the mother approached, Lucy became agitated and started barking. The mother then called one of the farm hands. With the aid of a rake, he turned over the rock, and they discovered a nest of copperheads.

You can cross the street; you can turn around and go the other way; or you can tell your dog to heel and pass the stranger, keeping yourself between the stranger and your dog. Under no circumstances should you make any effort to calm your dog by reassuringly petting him and telling him in a soothing voice, "There, there, it's perfectly okay, blah, blah, blah." Buddy will interpret your soothing as, "That's a good boy. I want you to growl." Well, perhaps you do, but if you don't, these kinds of reassurances reinforce the behavior.

Aggressive behavior can be directed toward any or all of the following:

✔ Owner

✔ Family

✔ Strangers and other dogs and animals

Signs of aggression include the following:

✔ Low-toned, deep growling

✔ Showing of teeth and staring

✔ Ears and whiskers pointing forward with the dog standing tall with his hackles up from his shoulders forward and his tail straight up

✔ Actual biting

When this behavior is directed toward you, ask yourself whether the question of who is Number One has been resolved. Usually it hasn't been, and the dog is convinced that he's Number One or thinks that he can become Numero Uno. He's not a bad dog; he's just a pack animal and is looking desperately for leadership. If that leadership isn't forthcoming on your part, he'll fill the vacuum. Dogs are quite happy and content when they know their rank order (see Chapter 2).

Looking at the Causes of Aggression

Aggressive behavior can be hereditary, can be caused by poor health, or can be the result of the dog's environment. Hereditary aggression, unless selectively bred for, is relatively rare, because it contradicts the whole concept of domestication. Aggressive behavior is more frequently the result of the dog feeling bad or being in discomfort, or even pain (see Chapter 19). In these cases, the dog's action isn't a behavior problem, but a health problem. The most common cause for dog bites is environmental — the result of a misunderstanding or outright mismanagement.

A misunderstanding can occur when the puppy nips at the owner's hand during play or when the puppy/dog is playing retrieve and accidentally bites the hand when he tries to get the stick. And some dogs, like our Newfoundlands for example, gently take our arms and try to guide us to the play area when they want to play. Most dog owners can recognize when a bite occurred due to a misunderstanding — the dog will be as horrified as the owner.

Bites occurring because of mismanagement are a different matter. For example, the kids are playing with Buddy, when Buddy has had enough and retreats under the bed. When one of the children crawls after Buddy and tries to drag him out, Buddy snaps at the child's hand and may even make contact. Not an uncommon scenario and certainly not aggression, even though there was no warning. Or was there? The fact that Buddy retreated should've told the children he'd had enough.

Aggression is a natural and even necessary phenomenon. In the case of unwanted aggression, human mistakes or misunderstandings are the usual cause. The owner may be unintentionally rewarding the undesired behavior, causing it to occur again and again, or the owner may not have socialized the dog properly. Only when you're unable to manage aggression, or don't understand its origin, does it become a problem.

A few years ago, it was brought to our attention that a number of Rottweilers had bitten the veterinarian when taken for their six-month checkups. Apparently, the situation had gotten so bad that many vets didn't want these dogs as clients anymore. At that point, the Rottweiler Club of England consulted us. We found that the same veterinary community that didn't want these dogs as clients anymore had advised the dogs' owners *not* to let the dogs out in public before they had all their vaccinations — that is, until they were 6 months of age. Those owners who followed this advice ended up with completely unsocialized dogs.

This example is a classic case of aggression on a grand scale caused by a lack of understanding of behavior. Socialization is a continuing necessity throughout your dog's life. If you don't socialize Buddy, you *will* have problems as he grows up. Take this advice seriously, and get Buddy into a good puppy class as soon as you can. And continue to take him out so that he can mix with other dogs as he continues to mature. (Check out Chapter 3 for more about puppies.)

Keeping your dog at home until he has had all his vaccinations at 6 months of age prevents proper socialization with people and other dogs, which can be a cause for aggression.

Managing Your Dog's Aggression — Prey, Pack, Fight, and Flight Drives

This section examines the triggers of aggression in the context of the three drives — prey, pack, and defense. The triggers are different in each drive, and so is the *management*, or cure. Your dog's Personality Profile (see Chapter 5) will tell what the likely triggers are going to be so that you can predict what Buddy will do under certain circumstances.

Discovering how to anticipate your dog's reaction under certain situations is part of managing his behavior.

Other than ignoring or putting up with the behavior, you have three basic options:

- **Expending the energy:** Each behavior has a *timeframe,* or energy, and it can be managed by expending that energy, which means exercise specifically focused on that energy. The exercise can be playing ball, jogging, playing tug-of-war games, or whatever. Training is always a good idea.

- **Suppressing the energy:** This option means that the dog isn't given an outlet for the energy. Suppression can be an effective *temporary* solution, provided that the dog has periodic opportunities to expend the energy. Absolute or long-term suppression isn't a good idea. The energy only redirects itself into another undesirable behavior.

- **Switching the drive:** When Buddy growls at another dog, for example, he's in defense drive. To manage the situation, switch him into pack drive. Cheerfully say something like "You must be joking" and walk away in the opposite direction.

Depending on the situation, you're going to use a combination of the three options in your management program.

Aggression from dogs high in prey drive

You shouldn't be surprised that *prey behaviors,* those associated with chasing and killing prey, are one of the leading causes for aggression. In a sense, aggression coming from this drive is the most dangerous, because so many different stimuli can trigger it. Dogs high in prey drive are stimulated by sounds, smells, and moving objects.

Triggers

Anything that moves triggers prey behaviors. Dogs high in prey drive chase cars, bicycles, joggers, cats, other dogs, squirrels, bunnies, you name it. And if they catch up with whatever they're chasing, that's when the problem starts.

Management

Play retrieve games on a regular basis, and make sure the dog gets plenty of exercise. When you take him for a walk and he spots a cat or squirrel, distract him, redirect his attention on you, and go in the opposite direction. The "Leave it" command may be sufficient, or you may have to give him a check on the leash to refocus his attention on you.

If he doesn't reliably respond to the "Come" command, don't let him loose in situations where he may take off. Better yet, train him to come reliably on command. Whatever you do, don't let Buddy chase cars, joggers, or cyclists.

Aggression from dogs high in fight drive

Survival and self-preservation govern defense drive, which consists of both fight and flight behaviors. Defense drive is more complex than pack or prey because the same stimulus that can cause aggression (fight), can also elicit avoidance (flight) behaviors.

After they understand who's in charge, these dogs are terrific companions and protectors, great competition and show dogs, and a joy to own. As young dogs, they may start bucking for a promotion. You may see signs of aggression toward you when you want the dog to get off the furniture or in similar situations — when he doesn't want to do what you tell him.

If a puppy is allowed to grow up doing anything he likes and isn't given parameters for what he can and can't do, he'll assume that you're not strong enough to be the pack leader.

If you don't give your puppy strong, consistent guidance as to what he may and may not do, he'll develop a sense that you're a pushover. He'll try to take over. Full-fledged signs of aggression don't just suddenly occur. He'll give many warnings, from growling to lip lifting to staring at you. If you condone these behaviors and don't deal with them, your dog is on his way to becoming aggressive.

Buddy may also be aggressive toward other dogs. When meeting another dog, he'll try to dominate the other dog. The classic sign is putting his head over the shoulder of the other dog. The dog of lesser rank lowers his body posture, signaling that he recognizes the other dog's rank.

But when two dogs perceive each other as equal in rank, a fight may ensue. Left to their own devices, though, both dogs most often decide that discretion is the better part of valor. Both know that there are no percentages to fighting. They slowly separate and go their own way.

A true dogfight is a harrowing and horrifying experience, and most people prefer not to take the chance that it'll occur. Discover how to read the signs and take the necessary precautions by keeping the dogs apart. Dogs are no different from people: Not all of them get along.

Some owners inadvertently cause dogfights by maintaining a tight leash on the dog. A tight leash alters your dog's body posture, thereby giving an unintended aggression signal to the other dog. Maintain a loose leash when meeting another dog so you don't distort Buddy's body posture. And at the slightest sign of trouble, such as a hard stare from the other dog, a growl, or a snarl, happily call your dog to you and walk away. *Happily* calling is important because you want to defuse the situation and not aggravate it by getting excited. You want to switch the dog from fight drive into pack drive.

A female dog is entitled to tell off a male dog that's making unwanted advances. She may lift her lip, a signal for the male dog to back off. If the male doesn't take the hint, she may growl or snap at him. This behavior isn't aggression but perfectly normal dog behavior.

Triggers

There can be a variety of triggers for aggression. Some of the more common ones are

- Approaching the dog in a threatening manner
- Hovering or looming over the dog
- Staring at the dog
- Teasing the dog
- Telling him to get off the couch
- Trying to take something out of his mouth (see the sidebar, "Taking something out of Buddy's mouth")

Taking something out of Buddy's mouth

Sometimes you'll have to take something out of Buddy's mouth. It could be a chicken bone from the garbage or anything else inappropriate. Don't yell at him or chase him. He'll redouble his efforts to eat whatever it is. Try the "Leave it" command (see Chapter 8). If that doesn't work, try a trade. Offer him a fair trade, such as a piece of cheese or raw meat. As he reaches for it, of course, the chicken bone will drop out.

Remember: Never chase Buddy and corner him. Doing so destroys the very relationship you've been working so hard to achieve.

You can avoid some of these triggers altogether — like teasing him, staring at him, or hovering over him. Just don't do them. Other triggers, though, you need to deal with.

Management

You have four ways to manage aggression triggered by fight drive.

Provide exercise and training

One way is to provide plenty of exercise and training. Exercise physically tires the body, and training tires the brain. In this situation, lack of mental stimulation gets the dog into trouble. Aim for two training sessions a day, each at least ten minutes long. If you keep to the same time schedule, you'll have a happy puppy.

Play tug of war

Another way is to expend the energy in this drive by playing a good game of tug of war. This game allows the dog to use up his timeframe of wanting to growl, tug, and bite. Instead of trying to suppress the behavior, dissipate its energy. The absence of an outlet for that energy, or efforts to suppress it, only makes matters worse.

Put aside ten minutes several times a week to play tug of war at the same time every day. Here's what you do:

1. **Get a pull toy, a piece of sacking, or a knotted sock to use for the game.**

2. **Allow your dog to growl and bite the object and shake it.**

3. **Let him bring the object back to you to play again.**

4. **Be sure to let him win each and every time.**

5. **When he's had enough, or the ten minutes are up, walk away from this session with the dog in possession of the toy.**

The game effectively discharges the energy and the timeframe in that drive. The game should be removed from regular training sessions and done when you and your dog are alone with no distractions. It's his time and his only. You'll be amazed at how satisfying the game is to your dog and at the calming effect it has on him.

Practice the Long Down

A third way to manage this type of aggression is with the Long Down (see Chapter 2). We can't emphasize enough the importance of this exercise. It's a benign exercise and establishes quite clearly who's in charge in a nonpunitive way. For dogs that express any kind of aggressive behavior, go back to this exercise and do a 30-minute Down, last thing at night, two or three times a week. It reinforces in your dog's mind that you're in charge. The Long Down and the tug-of-war game are simple solutions for the good dog that gets too pushy.

Use a muzzle

If your situation has reached the point where you're afraid of your dog, he tries to bite you, or you can't get him into the Down position, use a muzzle. You may also require professional help (see Chapter 20).

When you're nervous or anxious about what your dog may do if he encounters another dog or person, your emotions go straight down the leash, which can cause your dog to react in an aggressive manner. In a sense, your worries become a self-fulfilling prophecy. You can solve this dilemma with the use of a muzzle.

A muzzle allows you to go out in public with your dog without having to worry about him. A strange thing happens to a dog while wearing a muzzle. After you've taken away his option to bite, he doesn't even try. It's almost as if he's relieved that the decision has been taken away from him. Even better,

A tug-of-war case in point

When we came up with this *tug-of-war-is-good* concept, we were teaching a class of students who were very advanced in their training. Many of them were training their second or third dog, and all were experienced competitors. They'd chosen dogs with a relatively high fight drive because they knew how well those dogs trained and how good the dogs looked in the show ring — bold and beautiful. But they had to live with the dogs' tendency toward aggressive behavior and always had to be careful in a class or dog show situation — when the dog was around other dogs.

For the entire eight-week session, they were told to put time aside daily to play tug of war with their dogs. By the third week, we already noticed a big difference in the dogs' temperaments. When together in class, the dogs became friendly toward each other, played more, and trained better, and they were perfectly well behaved when away from home.

it allows you to relax. On the other hand, although your dog acts differently, so will people you encounter. A muzzle should be a last resort and isn't a substitute for seeking professional help.

Using a muzzle is a simple solution to a complex problem. It takes the decision about whether or not to bite away from your dog and gives you peace of mind.

Training to a muzzle should be done slowly and gently because, at first, many dogs panic from having something around their faces. But with diligence, common sense, and some compassion for the dog, you can train him quite easily to accept it. Here's what you need to do:

1. **Put the muzzle on your dog for a few minutes, and then take it off again.**

2. **Give him a treat, and tell him what a good boy he is.**

3. **Repeat Steps 1 and 2 over the course of several days, gradually increasing the length of time your dog wears the muzzle.**

4. **When he's comfortable wearing the muzzle at home, you can use it when you take him out in public.**

In some European cities, ordinances have been passed that require certain breeds to wear muzzles in public. We've seen many of these dogs happily accompanying their owners on walks. They were well behaved and seemed to be quite comfortable with their muzzles.

Many owners are reluctant to use a muzzle because of the perceived stigma attached to it. You have to make a choice — stigma or peace of mind. Something else to think about: Suppose that your dog actually bites someone. When you have such a simple solution, why take the chance?

Aggression from dogs high in pack drive

Pack drive consists of behaviors associated with reproduction and being part of a group. Believing that a dog high in pack behaviors could be aggressive may be difficult to grasp, but this dog may

✔ Show signs of aggression toward people

✔ Attack other dogs with no apparent reason

✔ Not stop the attack when the other dog submits

Triggers

The problem with this kind of aggression is that there don't seem to be many obvious triggers. It's frequently observed in dogs that are taken away from their litter and mother before 7 weeks of age. Between 5 and 7 weeks of age, a puppy learns to inhibit his biting (see Chapter 3). He also learns canine body language at this time. In short, your puppy learns he's a dog. Puppies that haven't learned these lessons tend to be overly protective of their owners and may be aggressive to other people and dogs. They can't interpret body language and haven't learned bite inhibition.

In a household with more than one dog, while one dog is being petted and the other is seeking your attention at the same time, the dog being petted may aggress toward the other dog. This overpossessiveness isn't uncommon from adopted older dogs and rescued dogs.

Lack of adequate socialization with people and other dogs prior to 6 months of age can cause subsequent aggressive behaviors. We can think of several instances when a female owner has come to us because her dog was aggressive toward men. The cause in each case was lack of socialization or exposure to men. As long as the dog didn't come in close proximity with men, there wasn't a problem. A change of circumstances, such as a boyfriend, however, made it a problem.

Management

You can solve a lack of socialization with other people by gradually getting the dog used to accepting another person. Take the case of a man-aggressive dog, for example. As always, the job is made easier when the dog has some basic training and knows simple commands like "Sit" and "Stay." Here's what you need to do:

1. **Begin with Buddy sitting at Heel position, in Control Position (no tension on the leash and only ½ inch of slack).**

2. **Have the person walk past the dog from a distance of six feet, without looking at the dog.**

3. **Just before he passes the dog, have the person throw Buddy a small piece of a hot dog or another treat.**

4. **Repeat Steps 1 through 3 five times per session — but no more.**

5. **When Buddy shows no signs of aggression at six feet, decrease the distance.**

6. **Keep decreasing the distance until Buddy will take a treat, open palm, from the person.**

   The person shouldn't look at the dog. He should pause just long enough to give the dog the treat and then pass.

7. **After you've gotten to this point, follow the procedure outlined for submissive wetting (see Chapter 10).**

Aggression toward other dogs, especially if the aggressor has had a few successes in his career, isn't so simple to resolve. Prevention here is the best cure: Keep your dog on leash, and don't give him a chance to bite another dog when you're away from home.

To calm dogs with aggressive tendencies, get some essential oil of lavender from a health food store. Put just a couple drops on a small cloth, and wipe it onto your dog's muzzle and around his nose. Lavender has a calming effect, and we've had great success with it in class situations, where one dog aggresses at another dog. It enables the dog to concentrate on his work.

We've also used it in a spray bottle (four drops of oil to eight ounces of water) and sprayed the room before the dogs come in. It really works wonders with the dogs and even calms the owners. Some of our students who've been in agility competition, and have dogs that couldn't concentrate because of the number of dogs and people around them have found that wiping their dog's muzzles and noses with the oil has made a dramatic improvement in their performances.

Feeding and Aggression

Your dog may growl when you get close to his food bowl. From his point of view, he's guarding his food — an instinctive and not uncommon reaction. The question is this: Should you try to do anything about it? And if so, what?

We've never been particularly concerned by food possessiveness in a dog, provided that it's the only time we see him act aggressively. However, some owners unwittingly exacerbate the behavior by trying to take the dog's food bowl from him while he's eating. Doing so definitely isn't a good idea. Why create unnecessary problems? Don't attempt the practice of taking food away from him and then putting it back. Imagine how you'd feel if someone kept taking away your dinner plate and putting it back. In no time at all, you'd become paranoid at the dinner table. That sort of thing creates apprehension and makes the guarding and growling worse.

In order to change the behavior, you need to change the environment. Make sure Buddy is fed in a place where the children or other dogs can't get to his food. A good place to feed him is in his crate. Give him his bone in his crate, and give him peace and quiet. And make sure that when he's in there, everyone leaves him alone.

Dealing with Fear-Biters — Dogs High in Flight Drive

The term *aggression* for fear-biters is actually a misnomer. They don't aggress — they only defend themselves. When they do bite, it's out of fear. And hence they're called *fear-biters*. Anytime this type of dog feels that he's cornered and unable to escape, he may bite. Biting to him is an act of last resort. He'd much rather get away from the situation.

Avoid putting this dog in a position where he thinks he has to bite. Use a similar approach to the one described in Chapter 10 for submissive wetting. Fear-biters are most comfortable when they know what's expected of them, as in training. Timid behavior can resurface when they're left to their own devices and not given clear instructions on how to behave.

Dogs high in *flight drive* can appear shy around strangers, other dogs, or new situations. They may hide behind their owners and need space. Keep them a good distance away from people and other dogs, and don't corner them for any reason. Use your body to reassure these dogs; bend down to their level, bending your knees and not hovering over them, and coax them to you with some food. Be patient to gain their confidence, and never, ever grab for them.

What this dog needs is confidence building. Training with quiet insistence and encouragement is one way to achieve a more comfortable dog. To get the dog used to people and other dogs, enroll him in an obedience class. You need to be patient with this dog and figure out how to go slowly. If you try to force an issue, you may wipe out whatever advances you've made.

This dog needs a structured and predictable environment. Walk, feed, and play at certain times of the day so the dog knows what's coming. Dogs have a phenomenal biological clock, and deviations from the time of walking and feeding can make undesirable behaviors resurface.

Rescued dogs — in particular, those that have gone through several homes — often have large numbers of flight behaviors. A tightly controlled schedule greatly helps in their rehabilitation.

Getting Attacked by Another Dog

What do you do when you're walking your dog down the street on leash and another dog comes out of nowhere and attacks your dog? You do this:

- ✔ No matter what, *don't* yell or scream. Remember, prey drive is stimulated by sound — especially high-pitched sounds.

  Screaming just escalates the intensity of a dogfight. Try to keep calm at all times.

- ✔ While you have hold of the leash, your dog is at the mercy of the other dog. Let go so he can either retreat or fend for himself.

> ✔ For your own safety, don't try to separate the dogs, or you may get bitten. In the vast majority of incidents like this, one dog gives up, and the other one walks away.
>
> ✔ Find out who the loose dog belongs to so you can take appropriate action.

When we trained and exhibited our Yorkshire Terrier, Ty, we got into the habit of being ever vigilant about the intentions of other dogs. We learned to position ourselves between Ty and other dogs so that they couldn't make eye contact with each other. Fortunately, we never had any incidents with him.

Discovering the Truth about Electric Fences

Many housing developments have covenants against fences. That's a problem when you have a dog you want to keep confined. Tying a dog out on a line, except for brief periods, isn't a humane option.

Never fear, technology is here, and the electric fence is the answer. A wire is buried around the perimeter of the property, where a fence would normally be. The dog wears a collar, which serves as a receiver. If he tries to cross the invisible fence, he receives an electric shock. The dog figures this out very quickly and stays in the yard, well away from the fence.

Sounds too good to be true, and it is. In the heat of chasing a cat, a dog, or another animal, dogs high in prey with a high discomfort threshold sometimes don't honor the fence and break through. The dog is then faced with a dilemma: Now that his adrenaline has worn off, he can't get back into the fenced area for fear of getting shocked. Another potential drawback is that when the fence works as it's intended to, it keeps your dog in the yard, but it doesn't keep other dogs or children out. It's no protection against bullies coming into your yard and picking on your dog, and it won't protect a female in season from unwanted suitors. Having an electric fence may make your dog fearful of other dogs or aggressive toward them. Keep an eye on him when he's out there, and don't leave him for prolonged periods without supervision.

Chapter 12

Preparing for Your Dog's Citizenship Test

. . . .

. . . .

*T*o demonstrate that Buddy has achieved the training level that you want for him, you may want to consider taking the Canine Good Citizen test. Many dog organizations offer it, and your local kennel club will know the particulars. You can locate the kennel club in the phonebook, or you can ask your vet, a dog groomer, or any obedience school.

The Canine Good Citizen test uses a series of exercises that checks the dog's ability to behave in an acceptable manner in public. Its purpose is to demonstrate that the dog, as a companion for all people, can be a respected community member and can be trained and conditioned to always behave in the home, in public places, and in the presence of other dogs in a manner that reflects credit on the dog.

The test is unique in that it is the only American Kennel Club–sponsored activity that includes mixed-breed dogs. The concept of a Canine Good Citizen is based on the premise that all dogs should be trained. It's also an outreach program — to motivate dog owners and encourage them to go further in training their dogs.

This chapter shows you what you and your dog can do to prepare for the Canine Good Citizen test. The Canine Good Citizen is a window of opportunity to a variety of dog sports. When you and your dog earn a Canine Good Citizen Certificate, you have accomplished more than millions of other dog owners. Are you ready for the challenge?

Becoming a Canine Good Citizen

Ideally, every dog should be trained to become a Canine Good Citizen and the more that are, the better the chances of counteracting the growing antidog sentiment in many communities. Irresponsible dog ownership has been the cause for this sentiment and only responsible pet ownership can reverse it. To become a Canine Good Citizen your dog must demonstrate, by means of a short test, that he meets these requirements.

Exercise requirements of the Canine Good Citizen test

To become a Canine Good Citizen, a dog must pass a test that demonstrates his ability to behave in an acceptable manner in public. The test consists of the following ten exercises, all of which are scored on a pass/fail system:

- Accepting a friendly stranger
- Sitting politely for petting
- Appearance and grooming
- Walking on a loose leash
- Walking through a crowd
- Sitting, downing, and staying in place
- Coming when called
- Reaction to another dog
- Reaction to distractions
- Supervised separation

These are practical exercises that determine the amount of control you have over your dog. During the test, you can repeat commands several times, encourage, and praise your dog. Repeating commands too often, however, demonstrates a lack of control and causes you to fail. You're also not permitted to give food to your dog during the test. All tests are done on leash and dogs need to wear a well-fitting buckle or slip collar made of leather, fabric, or chain. Other collars, head halters, or harnesses aren't permitted. The leash can be either fabric or leather.

We discuss each test briefly in the following sections, including what to expect during the test.

Test 1: Accepting a friendly stranger

This test demonstrates that the dog allows a friendly stranger to approach and speak to the handler in a natural, everyday situation.

The evaluator approaches the dog and handler and greets the handler in a friendly manner, ignoring the dog. The evaluator and handler shake hands and exchange pleasantries. The dog must show no sign of resentment, aggression, or shyness. The dog may not break position, jump on the evaluator, or try to go to the evaluator. If the handler has to hold the dog to control it, the dog fails the exercise.

Test 2: Sitting politely for petting

This test demonstrates that the dog allows a friendly stranger to touch him while he is out with the owner/handler (see Figure 12-1). With the dog sitting at the handler's side (either side is permissible) throughout the exercise, the evaluator pets the dog on the head and body only.

Figure 12-1:
Sitting politely for petting.

The handler may talk to the dog throughout the exercise.

After petting, the evaluator then circles the dog and handler, completing the test. The dog mustn't show shyness or resentment. The dog may stand while being petted, but must not struggle or pull away to avoid the petting, and shouldn't lunge at or jump on the evaluator.

Test 3: Appearance and grooming

This test demonstrates that the dog welcomes being groomed and examined and permits a stranger, such as a vet, groomer, or friend of the owner, to do so. It also demonstrates the owner's care, concern, and responsibility.

For the appearance and grooming test, make sure Buddy looks his best. If he needs a bath before the test, give him one.

The evaluator examines the dog to determine if he is clean and groomed. The dog must appear to be in healthy condition — proper weight, clean, healthy, and alert. Bring the comb or brush you commonly use on the dog. The evaluator easily combs or brushes the dog and, in a natural manner, lightly examines the ears and gently picks up each front foot.

The dog doesn't need to hold a specific position during the examination, and the handler may talk to the dog, praise, and give encouragement throughout. A dog that requires restraining during this examination fails the test.

Test 4: Out for a walk — walking on a loose leash

The fourth test demonstrates that the handler is in control. The dog may be on either side of the handler, whichever the handler prefers. The dog's position should leave no doubt that the dog is attentive to the handler and is responding to the handler's movements and changes of direction. The dog need not be perfectly aligned with the handler and need not sit when the handler stops.

An *occasional* tight leash is permissible, but constant straining or pulling on the leash is unacceptable. Similarly, excessive sniffing of the floor or ground, indicating that the dog isn't attentive to the handler, is also unacceptable.

During this test, you must make a left turn, a right turn, and an about-turn, with at least one stop in between and another at the end. The handler may talk to the dog along the way to praise or command him in a normal tone of voice. The handler may also sit the dog at the halt, if desired.

Test 5: Walking through a crowd

This test demonstrates that the dog can move about politely in pedestrian traffic and is under control in public places. The test is a great incentive to train Buddy around distractions.

The dog and handler walk around and closely pass several people (at least three). The dog may show some interest in the strangers but must continue to walk with the handler, without evidence of overexuberance, shyness, or resentment. The handler may talk to the dog and encourage or praise the dog throughout the test. The dog shouldn't strain at the leash, jump on people in the crowd, or try to hide behind his handler.

Children may act as members of the crowd in this test, as well as in the reaction to distractions test, that we discuss later in this chapter. Another leashed, well-behaved dog may also be in the crowd.

Test 6: "Sit" and "Down" on command — staying in place

This test demonstrates that the dog responds to the handler's commands to "Sit" and "Down," and remains in the place commanded by the handler.

Prior to this test, the dog's leash is replaced with a 20-foot line. The handler may take a reasonable amount of time and use more than one command to make the dog sit and then down. The evaluator must determine if the dog has responded to the handler's commands. The handler may not force the dog into either position but may touch the dog to offer gentle guidance.

When instructed by the evaluator, the handler tells the dog to "Stay" and, with the 20-foot line in hand, walks forward the length of the line, turns, and returns to the dog at a natural pace (the 20-foot line isn't removed or dropped). The dog must remain in the place in which he was left (the dog may change position such as stand up), until the evaluator instructs the handler to release the dog. The dog may be released from the front or the side.

Test 7: Coming when called

This test demonstrates that the dog comes when the handler calls him. The dog remains on the 20-foot line that was used in the sixth test. The handler walks ten feet from the dog, turns to face the dog, and calls the dog. The handler may use body language and encouragement when calling the dog and may tell the dog to "Stay" or "Wait" or just walk away. The dog may be left in the Sit, Down, or Standing position. If the dog attempts to follow the handler, the evaluator may distract the dog (for example, by petting) until the handler is 10 feet away.

The point of the test is to determine whether the dog comes when called and whether he stays, and the exercise is completed when the dog comes to the handler and the handler attaches the dog's own leash.

Test 8: Reaction to another dog

This test demonstrates that the dog can behave politely around other dogs.

Two handlers and their dogs approach each other from a distance of about ten yards, stop, shake hands and exchange pleasantries, and continue on for about five yards.

The dogs should show no more than casual interest in each other. Neither dog should go to the other dog or its handler. See Figure 12-2.

Figure 12-2:
Reaction to
another dog.

Test 9: Reaction to distractions

This test demonstrates that the dog is confident at all times when faced with common distracting situations. The evaluator selects only two from the following list. (*Note:* Because some dogs are sensitive to sound and others to visual distractions, most tests involve one sound and one visual distraction.)

- ✔ A person using crutches, a wheelchair, or a walker.

- ✔ A sudden closing or opening of a door.

- ✔ Dropping a large book, pan, folded chair, or the like, no closer than five feet behind the dog.

- ✔ A jogger running in front of the dog.

- ✔ A person pushing a shopping cart or pulling a crate dolly passing five to ten feet away.

- ✔ A person on a bicycle passing at least ten feet away.

- ✔ For you cat lovers, you're in luck. Cats aren't used as a distraction.

The handler may talk to the dog and praise him during this test. In a similar situation in real life, you probably would talk in an encouraging way to your dog.

The dog may express a natural interest and curiosity and may appear slightly startled but shouldn't panic, try to run away, or show aggressiveness. An isolated bark (one) is acceptable, but continued barking causes the dog to fail. The handler may talk to the dog and encourage or praise her throughout the exercise.

Test 10: Supervised separation

This test demonstrates that the dog can be left with another person and maintain its training and good manners while the owner goes out of sight. Evaluators say something like, "Would you like me to watch your dog?"

The handler fastens the dog to a six-foot line, such as the dog's leash, gives the end of the leash to an evaluator, and goes to a place out of sight of the dog for three minutes. The dog shouldn't continually bark, whine, howl, pace unnecessarily, or show anything other than mild agitation or nervousness. This test isn't a Stay exercise; dogs may stand, sit, lie down, and change positions during this test.

Dogs are tested individually, not as a group, and more than one dog can be tested at a time.

Getting ready to take the exam

If you have done the basic training, you're already halfway to being ready for the Canine Good Citizen. The exercises you need to work on are those that add distractions. They are the following:

- ✔ Accepting a friendly stranger

- ✔ Sitting politely for petting

- ✔ Appearance and grooming

- ✔ Reaction to another dog

- ✔ Reaction to distractions

- ✔ Supervised separation

Because Buddy's ability to Sit-Stay is so critical to success on many of the tests, make sure that he has this exercise down pat.

Training for accepting a friendly stranger and sitting politely for petting

We suggest that you start by teaching your dog the Sit for Examination and build from there. You need a helper for these exercises.

If you have scored your dog for fight or flight (see Chapter 5), you remember that this score determines his response to the helper. For example, if the helper is a stranger and your dog is high in fight, he may show signs of protectiveness. On the other hand, if he is low in fight and high in flight behaviors, Buddy may try to hide behind you or show signs of shyness when the helper approaches. Because the Sit for Examination is the cornerstone for all the distraction tests, you need to condition your dog to perform this exercise correctly before you continue.

With Buddy in Heel position, begin as you do for the Sit-Stay. Say and signal "Stay" and have your helper approach your dog from six feet at a 45-degree angle to your left. Have the helper approach in a friendly and nonthreatening manner, without hovering over the dog. Have the helper show your dog the *palm* of a hand and continue to walk by. If Buddy stays, praise and release. If your dog wants to get up, check straight up with your left hand with "Stay" and immediately try again.

Buddy's response determines how close the helper gets in the beginning. If he becomes apprehensive about the helper's approach and tries to move, we suggest that he or she walk past the dog at a distance of two feet without making eye contact or looking at the dog, which Buddy may perceive as threatening. As the dog gets used to that maneuver, have the helper offer a treat to the dog, placed on the open palm, as he or she walks by, still without making eye contact with the dog. It doesn't matter whether the dog takes the treat or not — it's the gesture that counts. When your dog accepts the helper walking past and offering a treat, stop for this session.

At your next session, have the helper first offer a treat and then pet the dog on the head, still without making eye contact, as he or she continues past the dog. Next, the helper can attempt to look at the dog as he or she touches the dog and goes past. For this particular test, the eye contact in connection with the examination is the hard part of the exercise, and it may require several sessions before the dog is steady.

The aim of this exercise is for the dog to allow the approach of a stranger who also then pets the dog. For the majority of dogs, this exercise isn't particularly difficult, but it does require a little practice.

Training for appearance and grooming

Appearance and grooming is a similar test that you can introduce as soon as your dog accepts petting by a stranger. Have your helper lightly comb or brush Buddy with you at his side or directly in front. The helper examines the ears and picks up each front foot. If your dog finds this difficult, have the helper give the dog a treat as he or she touches a foot. Condition the dog with praise and treats to accept having the feet handled.

The appearance and grooming test is one of the most frequently failed tests, and mainly because the dog won't permit the evaluator to handle his feet. If you make a point of handling your dog's feet when he is a puppy (and have your friends do it too), he won't be upset by this action as an adult.

Training for reaction to another dog

Your dog may stand or sit for this test. He is less likely, however, to try to initiate contact with the other dog from a Sit. Practice this exercise with someone else who also has a well-trained dog. With your dogs at Heel position, approach each other from a distance of about 20 feet and stop close enough to each other so you can just shake hands. As you stop, tell Buddy to "Sit" and "Stay."

Should he want to say hello to the other dog, reinforce the "Stay" command. Be sure you instruct your training partner not to let his or her dog come to say hello to Buddy.

Training for reaction to distractions

Take another look at the list of distractions in the section, "Reaction to distractions," earlier in this chapter. If you think that your dog may be unduly startled by any one of them, you need to practice and condition him to ignore that distraction.

Because your dog's Personality Profile (see Chapter 5) determines how he reacts to a particular distraction, expose him to different distractions to see how he deals with them. Some dogs take it all in stride and others require several exposures to become accustomed to the distraction. The best foundation is a solid Sit-Stay.

Training for supervised separation

Although this test doesn't directly deal with distractions, it does evaluate a dog's response to the unforeseen, and so resembles the other tests. It shows that the dog can be left with someone else, which demonstrates training and good manners. You hand your leash to an evaluator who watches your dog, and in some cases, other dogs may be in the vicinity that are also doing this test or just being walked. The dog shouldn't bark, whine, howl, or pace unnecessarily, or register anything other than mild agitation or nervousness.

You can leave your dog in either the Sit or the Down position; he doesn't need to hold that position until you return, only that he doesn't vocalize or pace unnecessarily. Still, by having Buddy focus on staying in place, you reduce the likelihood that he will bark or howl, or become overly agitated. You can develop this skill as a simple Down-Stay exercise, which is what we recommend.

Passing the Test

Organizations offering the Canine Good Citizen test have considerable leeway in making up the order in which to give the tests. The most common order is the one in which we list them in "Exercise requirements of the Canine Good Citizen test" earlier in this chapter. The supervised separation test may take place in the presence of other dogs that are also doing this test.

Usually three evaluators conduct the test. The first evaluator conducts tests one through three, the second one tests four through nine, and the third one test ten. The test is scored on a pass/fail basis and in order to qualify for a Canine Good Citizen certificate, the dog must pass each of the ten tests.

An automatic failure results when a dog eliminates (poops or pees) during testing, except during test ten, provided it's held outdoors. Any dog that growls, snaps, bites, attacks, or attempts to attack a person or another dog isn't a good citizen and must be dismissed from the test.

Do's and Don'ts of Taking the Test

The following few hints can help you prepare for and participate in the Canine Good Citizen test.

Your attitude and state of mind are the most important influence on the test's outcome. If you're excessively nervous, your dog will become nervous, too. Handlers under stress sometimes behave in ways they would never dream of doing any other time. If you do act differently, your dog will notice and be confused to the point where she might fail. Maintain a positive outlook and rely on your training.

Do:

✔ Practice the entire test with a helper and friends before you actually enter a test. Doing so is more for your benefit than Buddy's. As you become familiar with the test, you'll lose some of your nervousness. It also can identify Buddy's weak areas and give you additional time to work on them.

✔ Give your dog a bath and thoroughly groom him before the test.

✔ Use the correct equipment for the test — a well-fitting buckle or slip collar of leather, fabric, or chain, and a leather or fabric leash (see Chapter 6 for more on leashes).

✔ Exercise Buddy before you take the test. If your dog eliminates at any time during testing, he fails.

✔ Warm up your dog before taking the test so that both of you are as relaxed as possible under the circumstances.

✔ Use a second command for any exercise, if necessary.

✔ Talk to your dog during an exercise to keep attention on you, if necessary.

✔ Ask the evaluator for an explanation if you don't understand a procedure or an instruction.

✔ Maintain a loose leash throughout the entire test, even between exercises, to the extent possible. Although an occasional tightening of the leash generally isn't considered a failure, it does become a judgment call for the evaluator in assessing your control over your dog. Don't put yourself or the evaluator in that position.

✔ Understand that your attitude and state of mind are the most important influences on the test's outcome. If you're excessively nervous, your dog will become nervous, too. Maintain a positive outlook and rely on your training.

✔ Conduct yourself in a sportsmanlike manner at all times.

✔ Keep in mind the purpose of the Canine Good Citizen and become an ambassador of goodwill and good manners for all dogs.

Of course, if you take the time to participate in the Canine Good Citizen test, you obviously want Buddy to pass. Even if he doesn't, you can still feel good about yourself and Buddy. You're making an effort to train your dog to be a model member of the community. In that small way, you're doing a service to all dogs and their owners.

Don't:

✔ Lose your temper or attitude if your dog fails an exercise. If you berate your dog, you sour him on the entire experience. You may feel a certain amount of disappointment and frustration, but you need to control those feelings. The more you work with your dog, the more attuned he is to your feelings. He'll associate them with the circumstances and not the failure of an exercise.

✔ Change your attitude toward your dog after he has failed an exercise. Your remedy isn't to make the dog feel anxious, but to review your training, work on the difficult exercise, and try again. If you undermine your dog's confidence, training will take longer and become a less rewarding experience than if you realize that your job is to support and encourage your dog at every step of the way.

Part III
Training for Competition

"You got an 'F' in Internal Medicine, an 'F' in Clinical Diagnosis, and you ate the liver out of a cadaver in your Gross Anatomy class?! Shoot, I told everyone you'd never learn to heal."

In this part . . .

This part introduces you to the world of American Kennel Club (AKC) obedience events. We take you from firming up your dog's understanding of basic exercises to teaching him advanced obedience. You and your dog can strive for several titles awarded by the AKC, and we show you how to train for them. Or, you may just want your dog to learn how to retrieve. We include a chapter so you can teach him this exercise.

Chapter 13

Getting Ready to Compete

· ·

In This Chapter

▶ Introducing your dog to competition

▶ Preparing for the Pre-Novice and Novice classes

▶ Getting your dog's attention

▶ Heeling and doing the Figure 8

▶ Participating in the Rally class

▶ Reinforcing your dog's training

· ·

*I*f you and Buddy enjoy working together, the sky is the limit. You can participate in obedience competitions and earn obedience titles. Doing so is a lot of fun, and you meet lots of nice people. We must warn you, though, that after you get started, you can become addicted. And your life will never be the same.

Almost every weekend of the year, you can go to a dog show and show off what the two of you have accomplished. Dog shows are either conformation shows, where your dog is judged on his appearance, or obedience trials, where your dog and you are judged on his and your ability. The shows can be held together or separately.

If you've already been to a dog show and watched the obedience trial, you were probably amazed at the training and maybe thought to yourself, "My dog could never do that." Well, not necessarily. It all depends on his Personality Profile and whether the two of you enjoy spending quality time with each other (see Chapter 5 for more about Personality Profiles).

Training for Competitive Dog Titles

Different organizations have licensed shows, including those in which designer dogs can participate. In this book, we concentrate on the shows held under the auspices of the American Kennel Club (AKC), the oldest and largest organization to license such events.

More information on dog organizations

Check out these Web sites for more information on the American Kennel Club (AKC) and the United Kennel Club (UKC):

✔ The official Web page of the American Kennel Club (www.akc.com) offers information on almost everything to do with dogs. You can get the profiles of different breeds, find out how to register your dog, or get answers to questions about registration. You can find out about dogs in competition and what titles dogs can earn. This Web page tells you about pedigrees and, if you have a purebred dog, how to get a three-generation pedigree from the AKC. It offers reproductions from the Dog Museum, where many famous pieces of art and old books are housed, and it has archives of articles that have appeared recently, together with information about how the AKC works.

✔ The United Kennel Club (www.ukcdogs.com) is the second oldest and second largest all-breed dog registry in the United States. Founded in 1898 by Chauncey Z. Bennett, the registry has always supported the idea of the "total dog," meaning a dog that looks and performs equally well. With 250,000 registrations annually, the performance programs of UKC include conformation shows; obedience trials; agility trials; coonhound field trials; water races; night hunts and bench shows; hunting tests for the retrieving breeds; beagle events, including hunts and bench shows; cur, feist, squirrel, and coon events; plus bench shows. The UKC world of dogs is a working world. That's the way Bennett designed it, and that's the way it remains today.

The AKC awards three basic obedience titles:

✔ Companion Dog, or C.D., from the Novice class

✔ Companion Dog Excellent, or C.D.X., from the Open class

✔ Utility Dog, or U.D., from the Utility class

The level of difficulty increases with each class, from no more than basic control to retrieving and jumping to responding to signals and direction. The classes are designed so that any dog can participate successfully and earn titles. After your dog has earned a Utility Dog title, you're then eligible to compete for the special obedience titles of Obedience Trial Champion and Utility Dog Excellent. All three classes and all levels of competition have one exercise in common: heeling. This means that you and Buddy need a firm foundation and have to practice, practice, practice.

Understanding the system

You and Buddy can enter either the Pre-Novice or the Novice class. The required exercises for both classes demonstrate the usefulness of the purebred dog as a companion. You can also enter the Rally class (see the section, "The Rally Class," later in the chapter).

The Pre-Novice is a nonregular class that, like the Canine Good Citizen (see Chapter 12), serves as an introduction to the world of obedience events. Seven nonregular classes — Graduate Novice, Graduate Open, Brace (two dogs handled by one person), Veterans (for dogs at least 7 years of age), Versatility, Team (four dogs and four handlers), and Pre-Novice — are available. Participation in nonregular classes doesn't earn AKC titles.

For the Pre-Novice class, no minimum point score is required for a qualifying score, and whoever has the highest score wins the class. Pre-Novice is ideal for people or dogs who've never participated in a dog show before.

The cornerstones of the Pre-Novice class, and of all the other obedience classes, are having a dog that does the following:

✔ Pays attention to you

✔ Knows how to heel

Later in this chapter, we concentrate on these two concepts.

Requirements for Pre-Novice

The Pre-Novice class consists of six exercises, each with a specific point value. Your dog should respond to the first command, and you'll be penalized for additional commands. All the exercises are performed on leash. Before each exercise, the judge asks, "Are you ready?" You say that you are, and the judge then gives the command, such as "Forward" for the Heel On Leash (see the section "Exercise 1's Heel On Leash: 'Let's Dance, Buddy,'" later in the chapter) and Figure 8 exercises (see the section, "Exercise 1's Figure 8: 'Buddy, Do the Twist,'" later in the chapter), or "Stand your dog and leave when ready" for the Stand for Examination (see Chapter 14). These exercises are always done in the order in which they're listed in Table 13-1.

Table 13-1	The Pre-Novice Class
Required Exercises	*Available Points*
Heel On Leash	45
Figure 8	25
Stand for Examination	30
Recall	40

(continued)

Table 13-1 *(continued)*

Required Exercises	Available Points
Long Sit (1 minute)	30
Long Down (3 minutes)	30
Maximum Total Score	200

The exercises listed in Table 13-1 are an extension of those required for the Canine Good Citizen and are a preview of those required for the Novice class.

Prelude to Exercise 1: Teaching the "Ready!" Command

The first exercise in either the Pre-Novice or the Novice class is the Heel On Leash, and we like to teach our dogs a command that tells them that the two of us are going to heel together. The command we've chosen is "Ready!" Notice that the command includes an exclamation mark and not a question mark. You say it in a quiet and yet excited tone of voice — almost a whisper. The reason we've chosen this command is simple: In an obedience trial, the judge asks, "Are you ready?" before he or she gives the order "Forward."

When the judge asks you the question, naturally, you're expected to give some indication that the two of you are ready to go. We use the answer "Ready!" and Buddy snaps to attention and is all set to go. The judge then says "Forward," at which point you give Buddy the command, "Buddy, heel!" and start to move.

Dog show tidbits

To participate in a dog show, you need to enter about three weeks ahead of time. To participate in an AKC-licensed event, your dog must be a purebred and must be registered with the AKC.

If you have a dog that looks like a purebred, but you don't have papers for him, you may be able to get an Indefinite Listing Privilege (ILP) number from the AKC that permits you to participate in obedience trials.

At a dog show, the dogs are exhibited in a clearly defined enclosure, often made of baby gates, called a *ring,* which is a rectangular area no less than 30 feet by 40 feet.

No doubt you're wondering why all this is necessary when Buddy is supposed to respond to the "Heel" command and move with you when you do. The reason is that when you give the "Heel" command, you want to make sure that Buddy's attention is on you and not something else that may have attracted his attention. Otherwise, he may just sit there like a bump on a log, totally engrossed in what's going on in the next ring, and when you start to walk, he has to play catch-up.

To avoid this scenario, teach Buddy the "Ready!" command. In addition, you need to decide on your leadoff leg — the one that tells the dog when he's expected to go with you. If you're right-handed, you'll be more comfortable making your leadoff leg your right one, but you can start on either leg as long as you're consistent. We suggest you experiment and make your leadoff leg the one that helps your dog stay in Heel position when you start.

Using Control Position

In practice, you're also going to graduate from leash over the shoulder to *Control Position,* which makes it easier for you to remind Buddy of his responsibility to pay attention to you and stay in Heel position when he permits himself to become distracted. Control Position (see Figure 13-1) is used whenever you want to practice attention and precision heeling.

Figure 13-1:
Using the
Control
Position.

To hold the leash in Control Position,

1. **Attach the leash to your dog's training collar.**
2. **Position both rings of the collar under his chin.**
3. **Put the loop of the leash over the thumb of your right hand.**
4. **Neatly fold the leash, accordion-style, into your right hand, with the part going to the dog coming out from under your little finger.**
5. **Place your right hand against the front of your leg, palm facing your leg.**
6. **With your left hand, grasp the leash in front of your left leg, palm facing your leg.**

Keep both hands below your waist at all times and your elbows relaxed and close to your body. Take up enough slack in the leash so that the leash snap is parallel with the ground.

Focusing Buddy's attention on you

The purpose of the following training sequences is to systematically teach your dog a command, which means "Pay attention."

1. **Attach the leash to the training collar and sit your dog at Heel position.**
2. **Hold the leash in Control Position and look at your dog, keeping your left shoulder absolutely straight.**

   Don't forget to smile and relax.
3. **Say your dog's name, release with an enthusiastic "Okay," and take five steps forward at a trot, keeping your hands in Control Position.**

   Don't worry about what Buddy is doing; just concentrate on your part.
4. **Repeat ten times.**

Introducing Buddy to the "Ready!" command

Now for your Sequence 2 goal — to introduce your dog to the "Ready!" command.

When teaching "Ready!" hold your hands in Control Position, and keep your shoulders absolutely straight. You want to use body language to communicate forward motion to your dog. Dropping your left shoulder or pointing it back communicates just the opposite.

1. **Attach the leash to the training collar, and sit your dog at Heel position.**

2. **Hold the leash in Control Position and look at your dog, keeping your left shoulder absolutely straight.**

3. **Quietly and in an excited tone of voice, say "Ready!"**

4. **Say "Buddy, heel," move out briskly for five paces, and release.**

   Wait until you finish giving the command before you move. Otherwise, you're teaching your dog to move on his name or your motion — not a good idea.

5. **Repeat ten times.**

Ignore what Buddy is doing in this exercise. Concentrate on your part — which is making it exciting and fun for your dog — of keeping your hands in position and starting and releasing on the leadoff leg.

Getting Buddy to respond to "Ready!"

The goal of Sequence 3 is to teach your dog to respond to the "Ready!" command:

1. **Attach the leash to the training collar, and sit your dog at Heel position.**

2. **Hold the leash in Control Position and look at your dog, keeping your left shoulder absolutely straight.**

3. **Quietly and in an excited tone of voice, say, "Ready!"**

4. **Say "Buddy, heel," start at a fast pace as quickly as you can for ten paces, and release.**

5. **Repeat ten times.**

Here are a couple helpful hints for you as you do this sequence the first few times:

   ✔ Wait until you've finished the command before you start to run. It would hardly be fair to your dog to take off without having told him what you want. You may feel a little tension on the leash before Buddy understands that you want him to move with you.

✔ Resist the temptation to let your left hand trail out behind you when you feel a little tension on the leash, and resist the urge to let your left shoulder drop. Hook the thumb of your left hand under your waistband and lock it in place, and concentrate on keeping that left shoulder straight.

After four to five tries, you'll notice that Buddy is actually responding when you say "Ready!" and is outrunning you.

Rewarding Buddy's response

Sequence 4 rewards dogs that respond to the "Ready!" command and helps those that are a little slow to pick up on it:

1. **With your dog sitting at a Heel position, neatly fold the leash into your left hand, which should be placed at your belt buckle.**

2. **Hold a treat in your right hand, placing your hand at your right side.**

3. **Look at your dog, smile, and say "Ready!"**

4. **Do one of the following:**

   • **If he looks at you, tell him how clever he is, give him the treat, and release.**

   • **If he doesn't look at you, put the treat in front of his nose, and move the treat in the direction of your face. When he follows the treat, tell him how clever he is, give him the treat, and release.**

5. **Repeat until your dog responds without hesitation to the "Ready!" command.**

Reinforcing the "Ready!" command

Sometimes Buddy will be distracted to such an extent that he won't respond to the treat, much less the command. For those occasions, you need to be able to reinforce the command so that he'll learn that when you say the magic word, he has to pay attention no matter what's out there. Perform the following steps to reinforce the "Ready!" command, Sequence 5's goal:

1. **Attach the leash to the training collar, and sit your dog at Heel position.**

2. **Hold the leash in Control Position and look at your dog, keeping your left shoulder absolutely straight.**

3. **Give the "Ready!" command.**

4. **Do one of the following:**

   • **If Buddy looks up at you expectantly, praise and then release.**

   • **If he does not look up at you, check in the direction you want him to focus — usually, your face. When he looks up, praise and release.**

Nagging your dog with ineffective checks isn't a good training technique. Get a response the first time so you can praise and release him. If you repeatedly don't get a response, review the prior sequences.

5. **Repeat until your dog is rock solid on responding to the "Ready!" command.**

Getting Buddy to ignore distractions

Sequence 6's goal is to ignore distractions. This sequence is the review progression for the entire "Ready!" exercise.

You can now start working with a helper who will try to distract your dog. Your helper can be a friend or family member. The three main distractions are

- ✔ **Visual, or first degree:** Helper approaches and just stands there.

- ✔ **Auditory, or second degree:** Helper approaches and tries to distract Buddy with "Hello, puppy! Want to come and visit?" or whatever else comes to mind. Note that the name of the dog isn't used.

- ✔ **Object of attraction, or third degree:** Helper approaches and offers Buddy a toy or a treat.

When doing the following steps, practice with first degree until your dog ignores the distracter. Then move on to second degree and third degree, respectively.

1. **Neatly fold the leash into your right hand, and place your left hand around the leash directly under your right hand, as though you are holding a baseball bat.**

   Allow about two inches of slack in the leash and place both hands against your belt buckle.

2. **Give the "Ready!" command.**

3. **Have the helper approach in a nonthreatening manner.**

When you're working on distraction training, have the helper approach your dog at a 45-degree angle and not straight on from the front or the side. The helper starts to approach the dog from ten feet away and stops two feet from the dog.

4. **Do one of the following:**

   • **If your dog keeps his attention focused on you, praise and release.**

   • **If he permits himself to become distracted, reinforce, praise, and release.**

You need to review this exercise with Buddy on a regular basis.

Heeling with Distractions

Now that you've taught Buddy to pay attention to you on command and while he's sitting at the Heel position, you have to teach him to pay attention during heeling. Up to now, most of your heeling has probably been done in areas relatively free of distractions, perhaps even in the same location (see Chapter 8). The time has come to expand your and Buddy's horizons. You need to get him out to new places.

For Buddy, any new location is a form of distraction training. Everything looks different, and more important, there are new smells. When you take him to a new place, let him acclimate himself first — take in the sights and smells. Give him a chance to relieve himself.

When you participate in an obedience trial, defecating in the ring is an automatic nonqualification (NQ), so you need to teach Buddy that when he's working it's not the time or place for bathroom breaks.

Heeling in new places

In a location new to your dog, and after he has had a chance to look around a bit and relieve himself, do some heeling with particular emphasis on having your dog paying attention to you. Anytime his attention wanders — he may want to sniff the ground or just look around — remind him with a little check that he has to pay attention to you. When he does, tell him what a good boy he is, and then release him.

Check in the direction you want your dog to focus — somewhere on you. Depending on his size, this can be your ankle, lower leg, upper leg, torso, or face. Focusing on your face would be ideal, and some dogs learn it quickly; others are structurally unable to.

When you release him with "Okay," take five steps straight forward at a trot. Keep both hands on the leash. You want to get him excited about heeling with you. If he gets too excited, release him with somewhat less enthusiasm. After a check to refocus the dog's attention on you, release him. Make it fun for your dog to watch you.

Heeling with a distracter

The purpose of heeling with distractions is for your dog to ignore them, concentrate on what he's supposed to do, and learn to pay attention to you. Exactly how he accomplishes this goal isn't important, so long as he does. Dogs have excellent peripheral vision and can heel perfectly well without directly looking at you.

You now need a helper to assist you. Heel your dog past your helper, who can be standing, sitting, or squatting, while smiling invitingly at your dog. If your dog permits himself to become distracted, check him to refocus his attention on you. When he does, praise and release. Repeat until your dog ignores your helper and instead pays attention to you as you pass the distracter.

Next, have your helper talk to your dog (the helper does *not* use the dog's name), and then have your helper offer your dog a treat. You want to teach your dog to ignore such distractions and remain attentive to you. When he does, be sure to praise and release him.

After Buddy has caught on to the concept that he has to pay attention to you no matter what, use the release less frequently until you can eliminate it altogether.

Responsibilities during heeling

Both you and your dog have specific responsibilities for heeling (see Table 13-2). Notably, yours are far more numerous than your dog's.

Table 13-2	Responsibilities for Heeling
Yours	*Your Dog's*
Leash handling	Paying attention to you
Body posture	Staying in position
Pace and rhythm	
Concentrating on dog	
Use of the leash	
Anticipating when to check	
Direction of check	
When and how to reward	

The Novice Class: What's Expected from You and Buddy

The Novice class consists of six exercises, each with a specific point value (see Table 13-3). For a qualifying score, you and Buddy have to earn more than 50 percent of the available points for each exercise and a final score of more than 170 out of a possible 200.

A qualifying score at an obedience trial is called a *leg*. Your dog needs three legs under three different judges to earn the AKC title, Companion Dog.

Table 13-3	The Novice Class
Required Exercises	*Available Points*
Exercise 1: Heel On Leash and Figure 8	40
Exercise 2: Stand for Examination	30
Exercise 3: Heel Free	40
Exercise 4: Recall	30
Exercise 5: Long Sit	30
Exercise 6: Long Down	30
Maximum Total Score	200

The six exercises are always done in the order listed in Table 13-3, and they're all pack behavior exercises.

"So where do I get those Obedience Regulations thingies?"

You can get your own copy of the Obedience Regulations by contacting the American Kennel Club at 5580 Centerview Drive, Suite 200, Raleigh, NC 27606-3390 (919-233-9767 or www.akc.org).

Getting your own copy of the regulations is a piece o' cake, so go ahead and get them. Knowing the rules is a good idea so you know what's expected from you and your dog.

Like the Pre-Novice class, the Novice class exercises are an extension of those required for the Canine Good Citizen test (see Chapter 12). The Stand for Examination exercise, for example, is a form of temperament test similar to Accepting a Friendly Stranger and Sitting Politely for Petting in the Canine Good Citizen test.

There are, however, some important differences and additions in the Novice class exercises:

- ✔ Buddy has to respond to the first command.

- ✔ Walking on a loose leash (see Chapter 12) is now called Heeling and consists of both heeling on leash and off leash and includes a Figure 8 on leash (see "Exercise 1's Figure 8: 'Buddy, Do the Twist,'" later in the chapter). It's also more exacting.

- ✔ The temperament test requires the dog to stand and is done off leash with you standing six feet in front of your dog. When you're in position, the judge will approach your dog from in front and touch Buddy's head, body, and hindquarters with the fingers and palm of one hand.

- ✔ In addition to the Heel On Leash, there's Heeling Off Leash (see Chapter 14).

- ✔ The Come When Called (see Chapter 8) is now called the Recall (see Chapter 14). It's done off leash and requires Buddy to come on command, sit in front of you, and then go to Heel position on command.

- ✔ The Sit and Down-Stay (see Chapter 14) are done off leash for one and three minutes, respectively.

The Novice class is tailor-made for the dog that's highest in pack drive behaviors. For the dog that's highest in prey drive behaviors, this class is a little more difficult because of his distractibility around sights, sounds, and smells. (See Chapter 5 to see what the different behaviors mean.)

When you look at the Novice class exercises, you see that 120 points depend on your dog being able to *stay* — for the Stand for Examination (see Chapter 14), the Recall (see Chapter 14), the one-minute Sit, and the three-minute Down-Stay (see Chapter 14). So you can see how important the "Stay" exercise is.

Exercise 1's Heel On Leash: "Let's Dance, Buddy"

Heeling is like dancing with your dog. And *you* have to be the leader. If you know anything about dancing, then you know that you have the tougher job.

The dog will follow only your lead, and you need to give him the necessary cues to change direction or pace.

Heeling is a pack drive exercise (see Chapter 5). Before giving the command to heel, put your dog into pack drive by smiling at him and gently touching him on the side of his face.

In the section, "Heeling with Distractions," earlier in the chapter, you teach Buddy to heel around distractions, and you need to review that exercise on a frequent basis. In addition, you need to work on perfecting those turns and changes of pace.

Under the AKC Obedience Regulations (see the sidebar, "'So where do I get those Obedience Regulations thingies?'" for more info), the judge will call a heeling pattern for you. The pattern has to include — in addition to normal pace — a fast pace, a slow pace, and a right, left, and about-turn. That pattern is the bare minimum. A simple heeling pattern may look something like this: forward, fast, normal, left turn, about-turn, halt, forward, right turn, slow, normal, about-turn, halt.

If you have your dog's attention, and if you don't accidentally confuse him with incorrect cues, everything should go reasonably well. Still, you need to look at each of the maneuvers as a separate exercise that you and Buddy have to practice — sort of like the steps of a particular dance.

Table 13-4 sets up how to practice the different component parts of heeling. (The following two sections get into the specifics.) The column "Responses You May See" alerts you about what to watch for so you can work on it in your training. If you need to check your dog, release after the check. When your dog is doing something correctly, or is trying, be sure to reward him with a treat or praise.

Table 13-4	**Practicing the Components of Heeling**		
Component	*Dog's Responsibility*	*What You Need to Practice*	*Responses You May See*
Start	Accelerate	Fast starts	Slow start, lags behind
Normal pace	Normal pace	Straight line or large circle. If the dog is distracted, check and release.	Lags or forges, crowds or goes wide, sniffs or becomes distracted (Prey drive)
Halt	Decelerate	Check into sit and then release	Forges ahead, sits crooked

Component	Dog's Responsibility	What You Need to Practice	Responses You May See
Normal to slow Fast to normal	Decelerate	Draw back on the leash as you slow down	Crowds, forges ahead as you slow down
Slow to normal Normal to fast Right turn About-turn	Accelerate	Alternate between release, treat, and check	Lags, goes wide
Left turn	Decelerate	Draw back on the leash	Forges or crowds, then lags, goes wide
Left turn	Accelerate	Alternate between release, treat, and check	Forges or crowds, then lags, goes wide

The halt

When you *halt,* Buddy is expected to sit at Heel position without any command or signal from you. This maneuver is called the Automatic Sit, because the cue for the dog to sit is when you stop. Under the Obedience Regulations, you're penalized if you use a command or signal to get the dog to sit. The dog has to do it on his own.

To teach Buddy the Automatic Sit, put the rings of the training collar on top of your dog's neck. As you come to a halt, check with your left hand straight up. Be careful that you don't inadvertently check toward or across your body, because doing so will cause your dog to sit with his rear end away from you and not in a straight line. Practice two or three Automatic Sits with a check, and then try one without a check. Your dog will immediately tell you where you stand with that exercise.

Changes of pace and turns

For the changes of pace and turns, we train dogs to take their cue from the leadoff leg. We use three techniques to teach this concept:

- ✓ The release
- ✓ An object of attraction, which can be a treat or favorite toy
- ✓ A check

Changing pace

This section contains a changing pace example: Suppose that you want to teach the dog to stay with you as you change pace from slow to normal. Perform these steps:

1. **Release your dog from a slow pace on your leadoff leg.**

   The idea is to get your dog all excited about accelerating with you from slow to normal.

2. **As you go from slow to normal, use a treat to draw the dog forward as the leadoff leg makes the transition.**

   Hold the leash in your left hand and the treat in your right. Show the dog the treat just as you're about to make the change, and draw him forward with your right hand as the leadoff leg accelerates into normal pace.

3. **Hold the leash in Control Position (see the section, "Using Control Position," earlier in the chapter) and occasionally, and only when necessary, give a little check straight forward at the same time the leadoff leg makes the transition.**

   The check teaches your dog that ultimately it's his responsibility, on or off leash, to accelerate when you change pace.

Most of your repetitions of any of the heeling components should include the release or a treat.

Making turns

When making turns, try to keep your feet close together so your dog can keep up with you. For the right and about-turn, Buddy needs to learn to accelerate and stay close to your side as you make the turn. You can teach him by using

- ✔ The release as you come out of the turn
- ✔ A treat to guide him around the turn
- ✔ If necessary, a little check coming out of the turn

When you use a treat,

- ✔ Neatly fold the leash into your left hand, and place it against your right hip. Doing so keeps your shoulder facing in the right direction.
- ✔ Hold the treat in your right hand at your side.
- ✔ Just before you make the turn, show your dog the treat, and use it to guide him around the turn.
- ✔ Hold the treat as close to your left leg as you can so your dog learns to make nice, tight turns.

For the left turn, Buddy first needs to slow down so you don't trip over him and then accelerate again. Draw back on the leash just before you make the turn, and then use the same techniques as you use for the right and about-turns.

You don't have to practice these maneuvers in succession, so long as you do two or three of each during a training session.

Once a week, test your dog's understanding of heeling by doing a little pattern with him that's similar to what you'd perform in the ring. In the ring, you're not allowed to check your dog, and you can't have any tension on the leash. The only true test is when your dog is off leash, but using umbilical cord or Show position also gives you a good idea of what you need to practice. For Show position, neatly fold the leash into your left hand, and place it at your belt buckle, allowing anywhere from three to eight inches of slack, depending on the size of the dog.

The purpose of testing your dog's understanding of heeling is to see what you need to practice. Most of your time should be spent practicing. Test every fourth or fifth session.

Exercise 1's Figure 8: "Buddy, Do the Twist"

The *Figure 8* is a fun exercise. In the ring, it's done around two people, called *stewards,* who stand eight feet apart and act as posts. You and your dog start equidistant from the two posts and walk twice completely around and between them. In practice, you can use chairs as posts. In order to stay in Heel position, your dog has to speed up on the outside turn and slow down on the inside turn, while you maintain an even brisk pace throughout.

One lament we frequently hear is, "He does fine at home, but take him anywhere and forget it!" Make a point to seek out new locations, at first without distractions and then with distractions, to see how Buddy does.

Until your dog has learned this exercise, he'll have a tendency to forge or crowd on the inside turn and to lag or go wide on the outside turn. In teaching this exercise, use your body as your main communication tool. By rotating the upper part of your body back toward your dog, or forward away from your dog, you'll cause him to slow down or speed up, respectively. Your left shoulder will be the cue for your dog, indicating what you want him to do. When the left shoulder points back, your dog will slow down; when it points forward, he'll speed up. Just as dogs communicate with each other through body language, so can you.

Go ahead and try it. It's almost the same motion as the twist, only from the waist up. Rotate the upper part of your body first to the left and then to the right. You'll use this motion to control your dog's momentum.

Preparing Buddy for the Figure 8

Before you begin practicing going around posts, teach Buddy that he has to speed up his pace when you circle to the right and to slow down when you circle to the left.

For the inside turn,

1. **Start with your dog sitting at the Heel position, with your leash in Control Position.**

2. **Say "Buddy, heel," and walk a circle to the left, about four feet in diameter, at a slow pace.**

3. **Twist to the left as you walk.**

4. **Release your dog after you've completed the circle.**

After two or three tries, you'll notice how your dog responds to your body cues. If nothing happens, exaggerate your body motion.

For the outside turn,

1. **Start with your dog sitting at the Heel position, with the leash neatly folded into your left hand.**

2. **Put your left hand against your right hip.**

    Doing so keeps your left shoulder facing forward.

3. **Have a treat in your right hand.**

4. **Say "Buddy, heel," and walk in a circle to the right, about four feet in diameter, at your normal brisk pace.**

5. **Use the treat, which is held just in front of his nose, to guide your dog around, and give him the treat after you've completed the circle.**

The Obedience Regulations are quite specific about the position of your hands. For the Heel On Leash, you can hold the leash in either hand or in both, so long as they're in a natural position. For the Heel Free, your arms can swing naturally at your side, or you can swing your right arm naturally at your side and place your left hand against your belt buckle, which is the position we use.

You're looking for a visible effort on the part of your dog to accelerate. Repeat these steps several times so you become comfortable with the maneuver. Then try going at a trot.

Teaching Buddy the actual Figure 8

The Sequence 2 goal is to teach your dog the Figure 8. Following is the review progression for this exercise:

1. **Place two chairs about 12 feet apart.**

2. **Start with your dog sitting at the Heel position, two feet from the centerline, equidistant between the chairs.**

3. **Neatly fold the leash into your left hand, and place it against your belt buckle; hold a treat in your right hand.**

4. **Say "Buddy, heel," and start to walk at a slow pace around the chair on your left, rotating the upper part of your body to the left.**

5. **When you get to the center between the two chairs, show your dog the treat and guide him around the chair on your right at a trot, keeping your left shoulder facing forward.**

6. **Stop at the center, and sit your dog; then praise and release.**

Hold the treat at your right side and out of Buddy's sight until you get to the center and want him to speed up. Then hold it as close as you can to your left leg so he learns to stay close to your side. Don't show the treat to him on the inside turn, or he'll try to get to the treat instead of slowing down.

Your success in keeping Buddy at Heel position without crowding or lagging depends on how well you use your shoulders to communicate with him.

Doing the perfect Figure 8

Sequence 3's goal is the perfect Figure 8:

1. **Practice the review progression (see the preceding section), making two complete Figure 8s.**

2. **Start from the center and complete one Figure 8 at normal pace, using your shoulders to cue your dog.**

   Stop and sit your dog. Repeat the review progression often to maintain your dog's enthusiasm.

3. **Over the course of several sessions, put the chairs closer together in one-foot increments until they're eight feet apart.**

4. **Practice a Figure 8 with umbilical cord (see Chapter 14), concentrating on the direction of your shoulders.**

   Keep your left hand on your belt buckle.

5. **Try a Figure 8 off leash.**

   Although the Figure 8 is done on leash in the Novice class, practicing it off leash is a good test. You'll quickly see where your dog needs more practice.

At one point or another, you may have to use a little check going into the outside turn to impress on Buddy how important it is to you that he speed up.

The Rally Class

The name *rally* comes from the use of directional signs, similar to a Road Rally for cars. The AKC Rally Class provides a link from the Canine Good Citizen test to obedience and agility competition.

In the Rally Class the dog and handler complete a course following a series of 10 to 20 signs, depending on the level. Each sign, called a "station," instructs the handler on each exercise the dog has to perform. For example, the sign may say "Forward," "About-turn," or "Halt."

After the judge has given the first "Forward," the handler and dog team move continuously from one sign to the next on their own instead of waiting for the judge's command for each exercise as in all the other obedience classes. Unlimited communication from handler to dog is permitted, but the handler may not touch the dog and physical guidance is penalized.

This class is fun because you can give all the extra help your dog may need in the form of commands, encouragement, and praise. It's also fast paced, because you move from one sign to the next without any interruption, which makes it very exciting for the dog.

The starting score is 200, and deductions are made for any errors on the part of the dog performing the designated exercise at a station, or for not completing a required exercise. Scoring is more lenient than traditional obedience, although there should be a sense of teamwork between the dog and handler. You'll encounter approximately 40 different stations, representing all the basic obedience exercises and maneuvers.

There are three Rally classes:

- ✔ Novice
- ✔ Advanced
- ✔ Excellent

To earn an AKC Rally title, the dog must achieve three qualifying scores under at least two different judges.

In the Rally Novice class, all exercises are done on leash, and there are 10 to 15 stations. In the Rally Advanced class, all the exercises, which include one jump, are done off leash, and there are 12 to 17 stations. The Rally Excellent class is also done off leash and includes two jumps and 15 to 20 stations. Finally, the Rally Advanced Excellent title requires the dog to qualify ten times in both the Rally Advanced Class and the Rally Excellent Class at the same trial.

Your Dog Isn't an Elephant

True or false? After my dog is trained, I'll never have to practice his lessons again.

Answer: False.

Your dog doesn't have the memory of an elephant, so you need to review his lessons on a regular basis.

For example, if you've used the Recall Game (see Chapter 8) to teach Buddy to come when called, you need to reward him with a treat on a variable schedule when he responds to your call and comes to you. If you get lax, the association between the command and the reward will weaken. You can tell when this begins to happen: First, Buddy doesn't come immediately. He may take a detour or lift his leg just one more time. Then, you have to call him again. Finally, he ignores you when you implore him to come.

The principle of *successive nonreinforced repetitions* sounds more complicated than it is. These repetitions are responses to a command without any reinforcement, such as not giving your dog a treat when he comes to you after you've called him.

Every time your dog responds to a command without reinforcement, which can be a reward or a little check, depending on how you have taught the dog the command, it's a nonreinforced repetition. The number of these repetitions is finite and depends on the extent to which the behavior is in harmony with the dog's instincts or drives. After a Labrador Retriever has been trained to retrieve, he'll happily fetch almost indefinitely without any reinforcement. An Afghan Hound will probably retrieve only a few times without reinforcement. The Labrador was bred to retrieve; the Afghan wasn't.

Every command you've taught your dog needs to be reinforced on a random basis, or the association between the command and the reinforcement weakens.

Several years ago, we had a wonderful demonstration of this principle when we visited friends in Newfoundland, who have two delightful Whippets. Every morning, our friends take a short ride to the local park for their own daily walk and to let the dogs run. Naturally, we joined them.

The park covers about 100 acres, with wonderful walking trails, plenty of wildlife, and a large pond inhabited by a variety of fowl. After we were inside the park, much to our surprise, our friends let the dogs loose. When we say surprised, it's because Whippets are sight hounds, extremely high in prey drive that love to chase anything that moves. They're also incredibly fast and can cover great distances in seconds. We were wondering how our friends would get these dogs back.

To make a long story short, when the dogs ranged a little too far or started chasing something, our friends called them back. To our amazement, the dogs came instantly every time, and every time they got a treat. The response was reinforced!

Any taught response needs to be reinforced. You needn't worry about the exact number of nonreinforced repetitions your dog will retain of a given behavior. All you need to know is that they're finite. To keep him sharp, randomly reinforce — whether you think he needs it or not.`

Making excuses and blaming the dog is easy, but your dog isn't an elephant and needs occasional reminders.

Chapter 14

The Companion Dog Title

Chapter 13 introduces the American Kennel Club's (AKC) Novice class and its goal — the Companion Dog title. That chapter gives an overview of the six required exercises for the title and the points needed to earn that title, and it also provides the nitty-gritty details for completing the first exercise. This chapter covers the remainder of the exercises for the Companion Dog title:

✔ Stand for Examination

✔ Heeling Off Leash

✔ Recall

✔ Group Exercises

  • Long Sit

  • Long Down

During a training session, practice different exercises, and vary the order. Start with some brisk heeling as a warm-up, including fast starts and changes of pace. Keep training interesting and fun for both of you.

The Stand for Examination

The *Stand for Examination* is a requirement for the Novice class, but it's also a practical and useful command to teach your dog in general. Brushing, grooming, and wiping feet, as well as visiting the vet, are certainly a lot easier with a dog that's been trained to stand still than with one that's in perpetual motion.

In the ring, Stand for Examination looks something like this: You give your leash to the steward. Then the judge says, "Stand your dog and leave when ready." You stand your dog in Heel position (see Chapter 7), say "Stay," walk six feet straight forward in front of your dog, turn around, and stand facing the dog. The judge approaches your dog from in front and touches your dog's head, body, and hindquarters with one hand. The judge then says, "Back to your dog." You walk around behind your dog and return to the Heel position.

When you put Buddy into a Stand, watch his front feet. They must remain in place and not move forward. You can lock them in place by applying a little downward pressure with two fingers in his collar underneath his chin as you stand him.

When you begin teaching this exercise to your dog, you can stand, kneel on your right knee or both knees, or have the dog on a table, depending on his size. You want to avoid leaning over him, because if you do, he'll want to move away from you — especially if he's low in defense fight behaviors (see Chapter 5).

Teaching Buddy the "Stand" command

To prepare Buddy for the Stand for Examination exercise, you'll need to teach him a number of sequences. First, you need to teach him to stand on command. Then you need to teach him to stand still, and finally, the examination part of the exercise.

Your Sequence 1 goal is to teach your dog the "Stand" command:

1. **Start with Buddy sitting at your left side, off leash, with both of you facing the same direction**.

   Make sure your shoulders are square and not turned toward him.

2. **Put the thumb of your right hand in the collar under his chin, fingers pointing to the floor, palm open and flat against his chest.**

3. **Apply a little downward pressure on the collar, say "Stand," and at the same time, apply backward pressure on his *stifles* (the joint of the hind leg between the thigh and the second thigh — the dog's knees) with the back of your left hand.**

   (See Figure 14-1.)

4. **Keep both hands still and in place — the right hand through the collar and the left hand against his stifles, and count to 10.**

5. **Praise and release.**

Repeat this exercise three to five times per session over the course of several sessions.

Figure 14-1:
Placing your hands properly for the "Stand" command.

Teaching Buddy to stand still: The hands-on method

Sequence 2's goal is to teach Buddy to stand still:

1. **Place your dog into a Stand (see the preceding section).**

2. **With both hands on your dog, keep him standing still to the count of 30.**

3. **Over the course of several sessions, increase the time you keep him standing still to one minute.**

Teaching Buddy to stand still: The hands-off method

Your Sequence 3 goal is to get your dog to stand still without holding him in position:

1. **Place Buddy into a Stand (see "Teaching Buddy the 'Stand' command" earlier in this chapter).**

2. **Take away your left hand.**

3. **Count to 30.**

   Reposition him if he moves.

4. **Praise and then release.**

5. **When he's steady without you holding onto him with your left hand, take your right hand out of the collar.**

It will take Buddy several sessions to learn this sequence.

Praise is a verbal thing — not a petting thing. When you praise Buddy, be sure that he remains in position. Praise tells him he's doing something correctly and isn't an invitation to move. Don't confuse verbal praise with the release.

Teaching Buddy the "Stand-Stay" command

Sequence 4's goal is to teach Buddy the Stand and Stay:

1. **Stand your dog as described in "Teaching Buddy the 'Stand' command" earlier in this chapter.**

2. **Take both hands off your dog and stand up, keeping your shoulders square.**

3. **Signal and say "Stay."**

4. **Count to 30, praise, and release.**

5. **Practice until you can stand next to him for one minute without him moving.**

Learning the "Stand" command (or "Sit" or "Down-Stay") isn't exciting for your dog, so follow the exercise with something he enjoys. After the release, play ball or throw a stick. Give him something to look forward to.

Leaving Buddy in a Stand-Stay

Ready for Sequence 5? You're going to leave Buddy in a Stand-Stay position:

1. **Stand next to your sitting dog.**

2. **Put the thumb of your right hand through the collar as in Sequence 1 (see "Teaching Buddy the 'Stand' command" earlier in this chapter).**

   Depending on the size of your dog, you may have to bend at the knees to avoid leaning over him.

3. **With a little downward pressure on the collar, say "Stand."**

   He should now stand without you having to touch his stifles.

4. **Take your right hand out of the collar and stand up straight.**

5. **Say "Stay," and step directly in front of him.**

6. **Count to 30, step back to a Heel position, praise, and release.**

   Reposition him if he moves.

7. **Gradually increase the distance you leave him to six feet in front.**

8. **From now on when you leave him, go six feet straight forward, turn and face him (don't back away from him), count to 30, go back, praise, and release.**

Teaching Buddy the Return

Your Sequence 6 goal is to teach the Return behind your dog:

1. **Stand your dog (see "Teaching Buddy the 'Stand' command" earlier in this chapter), and go six feet in front (see the preceding section).**

2. **Go back to your dog, put two fingers of your left hand on his withers to steady him, and walk around behind him to the Heel position.**

3. **Pause, making sure he doesn't move, praise, and release.**

4. **When he understands that you're going to come around behind him, eliminate touching him as you return to the Heel position.**

Dog shows are held indoors and outdoors in all kinds of weather conditions. If the dog show you're attending is outdoors and it's raining, the judge will have on rain gear, which may include a big, floppy hat — something your dog may not have experienced before. Don't be caught unprepared: Practice under those unpleasant conditions.

Teaching Buddy the actual examination

Sequence 7's goal is to teach Buddy the examination part of the exercise. For this sequence, you need a helper. At this time, the helper can be a family member. Eventually, however, Buddy has to be examined by a stranger, and because the judge can be either male or female, you need to practice with both men and women.

To introduce your dog to this exercise, start with the Sit for Examination, which is almost identical to Sitting Politely for Petting in the Canine Good Citizen test (see Chapter 12). Do the following:

1. **Put the rings of the collar on top of the dog's neck.**

2. **Attach your leash to the collar.**

3. **Sit your dog at the Heel position.**

4. **Neatly fold the leash into your left hand, hold it above his head, and say "Stay."**

5. **Have your helper approach and offer your dog the palm of his or her hand.**

   If Buddy tries to say hello to the helper, reinforce the "Stay" command with a check straight up.

6. **Have your helper lightly touch Buddy's head and back.**

7. **Praise and release.**

8. **Repeat Steps 1 through 7 until he readily permits the examination.**

   Practice the examination over the course of several sessions.

9. **Repeat the steps off leash with your dog standing at heel, then with you standing directly in front, then three feet in front, and finally six feet in front.**

Before every exercise, the judge asks, "Are you ready?" We answer with "Ready!" for the heeling exercises and "Yes" for everything else. (Check out Chapter 13 for how to prepare your dog for the "Ready!" command.)

Transitioning to Heeling Off Leash

To make the transition from Heeling On Leash to Heeling Off Leash, we use a technique called *umbilical cord*. This maneuver lets you and your dog experience the feeling of Heeling Off Leash while he's still attached. Here's how it works:

1. **With your dog sitting in the Heel position and the leash attached to the collar, take the loop end of the leash in your right hand and pass it around behind you into your left hand.**

2. **With your right hand, unsnap the leash from the collar, pass the snap through the loop of the leash, and reattach it to the collar.**

3. **Pull on the leash to tighten the loop end around your waist at your left side.**

4. **Put your left hand against your belt buckle, and let your right hand swing naturally at your side.**

5. Say "Buddy, heel," and start to walk your normal brisk pace.

If your dog deviates from Heel position, *slowly* reach for the collar. Put two fingers of your left hand through the collar, palm facing you, at the side of his neck, and bring him back to Heel position. Keep walking, let go of the collar, and tell him what a good dog he is. If Buddy is a small dog or has long hair, use the leash snap to bring him back to Heel position.

Use slow, deliberate movements when training. When you reach for your dog, be sure you do it slowly so as not to frighten him. Remember, he's still on leash and can't go anywhere. If you start snatching at him, he'll become apprehensive and try to bolt.

For Buddy, this lesson is important. He learns to accept you reaching for the collar so that you can do it when he's actually off leash. Reaching slowly is so important so you don't inadvertently teach him to become apprehensive when you reach for his collar.

If you have difficulty getting two fingers through the collar — because your dog is small or has lots of hair around his neck — use the leash snap to bring him back to Heel position. When you get to the off-leash part, put a little hang tag on his collar that you can easily grasp.

The umbilical cord technique teaches your dog that it's his responsibility to remain in Heel position. Unless he learns to accept that responsibility, he won't be reliable off leash. You can help the process by being consistent in reminding him of that responsibility. Anytime you make a move to bring him back, you must follow through. If Buddy deviates and you reach for the collar, but he corrects himself and you do nothing, Buddy doesn't learn anything.

Keep the time and distance short, and you have a better chance of maintaining your dog's interest and attention.

Gradually increase the number of steps, make a right turn, take another ten steps and halt, praise, and release. Remember to say your dog's name before you make the turn. Start over and incorporate an about-turn, using his name before the turn. Also incorporate changes of pace. You get the picture.

As you and your dog's proficiency increase, add distractions in the order you did in Chapter 13. You also need to gradually increase the time and distance that you heel your dog before a halt. How much total time should you spend on this exercise? After a two-minute warm-up of heeling in *Control Position* (see Chapter 13) in a large circle or straight line with plenty of releases, you should spend no more than one to two minutes per training session.

Heeling Off Leash

Heeling Off Leash, although it's really only an extension of Heeling On Leash, isn't quite the same. Buddy knows when he's on leash and when he's off leash. When he's on leash, he may give you the impression that he's perfect. Then you take the leash off, and he acts as though he has no idea what the exercise is all about. The reason is simple — he knows he's off leash.

If this situation happens to you, review Heeling On Leash (refer to Chapter 13), and reinforce the "Heel" command with a treat or a check when he needs help. For normal pace, he usually doesn't need any reinforcement, but he probably does for changes of pace and turns.

You can remind your dog of his responsibility to remain in Heel position by taking him by the collar as you do when heeling with umbilical cord (see the preceding section).

Remember that Heeling Off Leash is the ultimate test of your training. With a little practice, Buddy will get the hang of it. To make sure he understands, 90 percent of your practicing should be done on leash so you can remind him what you expect from him.

You're now ready for Heeling Off Leash. If you have any doubt about what Buddy will do, practice in a safe area, such as your backyard.

1. **Start with a two-minute warm-up in Control Position (see Chapter 13).**

   Walk in a large circle or a straight line. Forget about turns, and concentrate on keeping his attention on you.

   Now is the time to remind him to pay attention to you. Check, if you have to, and then praise and release.

2. **Set up for umbilical cord (see the preceding section), and heel for 10 to 15 steps and release.**

   Set up again and heel for about the same distance and halt.

3. **Put your right hand against his chest, place him into a Sit, and stand up.**

4. **Unclip the leash from his collar, and put the snap into your left pocket so a loop dangles on your side.**

5. **Say "Buddy, heel," and start at a brisk pace.**

   If you need to reinforce, very slowly reach for his collar, bring him back, let go, and praise.

6. **Halt after ten steps, and sit your dog.**

7. **Put the leash back on your dog and release.**

8. **Go on to another exercise or end your session.**

Proficiency comes in small increments and not all at once. Add something new to your off-leash heeling each session, such as a turn (use his name) or a change of pace. Keep it short and snappy, and make it exciting and fun. Over the course of several sessions, both you and Buddy will become increasingly confident and begin to work as a team. Resist the temptation to go beyond his ability to be successful.

When you and your dog are comfortable doing this exercise in an area relatively free of distractions, you can go on to Heeling Off Leash with Distractions. Use the same order as you do when Heeling Off Leash — that is, making it incrementally more difficult as you progress. When you come to halt, put your right hand against Buddy's chest for the Sit.

The Recall

The *Recall* exercise is different from the traditional "Come" command, where you're only concerned about the dog coming to you. The Recall consists of four components:

- ✔ Stay
- ✔ Come
- ✔ Front
- ✔ Finish

The Recall is performed from one end of the ring to the other. The judge tells you to leave your dog in a Sit-Stay and to go to the other side of the ring. He or she then tells you to call your dog. You give the "Come" command, Buddy comes, and he's expected to sit directly in front of you. The judge then says "Finish," and you say "Buddy, heel," and Buddy goes to the Heel position.

Stay

Chapter 7 covers the basics of the "Stay" command. We cover training your dog to stay with distraction in "The Group Exercises" section later in this chapter. For the Recall exercise, the judge designates the starting point for the exercise, usually at the far end of the ring. He or she tells you to leave your dog. You say, "Stay" and leave your dog, going to the opposite end of the ring. The judge then tells you to call your dog. You call, Buddy comes, and he sits directly in front of you. The judge then says, "Finish," and you give the "Heel" command and Buddy goes to heel.

Come with distractions

Even though Buddy already knows the "Come" command, you still need to work on distraction training — for which you need a helper. Leave Buddy in a Sit-Stay, and go 20 feet in front. Have your helper position herself equidistant between you and Buddy — about two feet from Buddy's anticipated line of travel. Facing Buddy, the helper crouches and smiles.

Call your dog, and as he passes the distracter, release backward with an enthusiastic "Okay!" Then give him a treat when he gets to you. If he goes to the distracter, smile and very slowly approach Buddy. Put the leash on the dead ring of the training collar and, with a little tension on the leash, show him exactly what he should've done by trotting backward to the spot where you called him. Praise and release backward. You may have to show him a few times until he catches on. After he's successful, stop for that session.

Release backward any time you want to encourage the dog when he's coming toward you. Lean backward, throw up your hands invitingly, and take a few steps back with an enthusiastic "Okay!"

If your dog veers from the distracter, use two distracters, separated by about ten feet, and teach your dog to come between them. As Buddy progresses in his training, work your way through second and third degree distractions.

The purpose of distraction training is to build your and your dog's confidence that he can do it. It also teaches him to concentrate on what he's supposed to do. If at any time you feel the exercise is too much for him, stop. Come back to it at another session.

Front

The object of both the Front and the Finish (see the following section) is to teach the dog a position, and you can practice both exercises inside in the form of a game. The Front is similar to the Automatic Sit at Heel (see Chapter 13) in that the dog is supposed to come to you and sit in front without a command to sit. We like to use a chute to teach the dog exactly where we want him to sit when he comes to us. For a chute, we use plastic rain gutters, commensurate to the size of the dog. They should be about as long as your dog. Place them on the ground, just far enough apart so your dog can sit comfortably in between.

When practicing the Front, keep the upper part of your body erect. If you lean over or toward your dog, he won't come in close enough. If you need to get down to his level, bend at the knees.

Getting Buddy used to the chute

Sequence 1's goal is to get Buddy used to the chute:

1. **Place the chute on the ground.**
2. **Walk your dog through the chute a few times.**
3. **Heel your dog into the chute and have him sit in it.**
4. **Repeat Steps 1 through 3 until he readily sits in the chute.**

Teaching Buddy to come into the chute

Yep, Sequence 2's goal is indeed to teach your dog to come into the chute:

1. **Heel your dog up to the chute, and tell him to stay.**
2. **Walk through the chute and face your dog.**
3. **Hold a treat in both hands below your waist.**
4. **Call your dog and, as he comes, bring your hands to your waist — using the treat to make him sit.**
5. **Give him the treat, praise, and release backward.**

    (See the section "Come with distractions" earlier in this chapter for info on the release backward.)

6. **Practice Steps 1 through 5 about five times.**
7. **When your dog understands this part, leave him on a Stay three feet from the entrance of the chute and call him.**
8. **Increase in 2-foot increments the distance that you leave him facing the entrance of the chute, until he is 35 feet from the entrance.**

You want to teach Buddy to sit as close as possible in front of you without touching you. Using treats, you can practice this sequence inside without the chute. Call him to you and use your treat to make him sit. Only give him the treat when he sits straight. If he doesn't, try again.

In the ring, you're not allowed to carry food or give second commands. You can give either a command or a signal but not both. The exception is the "Stay" command, which can be accompanied by the "Stay" signal.

Ultimately, Buddy has to sit in front of you with your hands hanging naturally at your side, so you need to wean him from seeing you with your hands in front of you. You can still reward him in practice when he does the exercise correctly.

Finish

After your dog comes to you and sits in front, the judge says "Finish." You say "Buddy, heel," and your dog goes to the Heel position. He can either go directly to Heel position to the left, or go to the right and walk behind you to Heel position. We like to teach both, just to keep the dog guessing. For the Finish to the left, we use the "Heel" command and for the Finish to the right, we use the "Place" command (see Teaching a Finish to the right). Actually, we prefer giving a signal because the dog more readily understands a signal than a command — and it more clearly indicates to the dog the way we want him to go. For the Finish to the left, use your left hand to indicate the direction in which you want Buddy to go, and for the Finish to the right, use your right hand.

Teaching a Finish to the left

Your Sequence 1 goal is to introduce Buddy to the Finish to the left:

1. **Sit your dog at Heel position, say "Stay," and step directly in front of him.**

2. **Say "Buddy, heel," and then take a step back on your left leg, keeping the right leg firmly planted in place, as you guide him with a treat held in your left hand in a semicircle into Heel position.**

   Make the semicircle large enough so that he winds up in the correct position.

3. **Give him the treat, praise, and release.**

4. **Repeat Steps 1 through 3 until he enthusiastically and briskly goes to heel.**

You'll quickly see that the guidance of your left hand becomes his signal to go to heel.

Any time we want a dog to move, we use his name before the command — for example, "Buddy, come." Any time we don't want him to move, we eliminate the name — for example, "Stay." Using a dog's name makes him excited and ready to move, and not using his name on the stationary exercises helps him to focus on the exercise and stay still.

Teaching a Finish on command or signal

Your Sequence 2 goal is to teach Buddy to finish on command or signal:

1. **Put the leash on the training collar.**

2. **Neatly fold the leash into your left hand.**

3. **Step in front, say "Buddy, heel," and step back on your left leg, using the leash to guide him into Heel position.**

4. **Reward him with a treat, praise, and release.**

5. **Practice Steps 1 through 4 until he goes to heel without any tension on the leash.**

6. **Now eliminate the step back on the left leg, and experiment by using either the command or signal.**

   The signal is the same guiding motion you use in Sequence 1 (see the preceding section).

Teaching a Finish to the right

The Finish to the right uses the same progressions as the finish to the left, except that you step back on the right leg and guide Buddy around behind you into Heel position. When you're using a treat, you have to switch it behind your back from the right hand into the left. The same applies to the leash.

Your dog's response to the Finish to the right or left tells you which direction is better for him. As a general rule, a long-bodied dog does better going to the right.

The Group Exercises

The group exercises are the last part of the Novice class test. They consist of a Long Sit and a Long Down for one and three minutes, respectively, and they're done off leash in a group. The number of dog/handler teams in a group depends on the number of exhibitors competing in the class and the size of the ring. The judge tells the teams to line up on one side of the ring. He or she then instructs the handlers to sit their dogs and leave their dogs, whereupon the handlers go to the opposite side of the ring, turn, and face their dogs. After a minute the judge gives the order to return and the handlers go back to their dogs, walking around behind the dogs to Heel position. The same procedure is followed for the three-minute Down. A dog that lies down during the Long Sit, sits during the Long Down, or moves out of position, receives a nonqualifying score.

When you're training your dog, change only one variable at a time. When teaching a Stay, for example, change the distance or the time but not both together. Increase one, and increase the other when Buddy is steady.

Look at the Stay exercises from the perspective of time and distance. Teach Buddy to stay in place for a specific period of time with you about three feet in front. Then the first time you increase the distance from your dog, decrease the time you're away from him.

Although you can give a command and/or signal for any Stay exercise, your dog's Personality Profile (see Chapter 5) influences whether you want to use a signal. Any Stay is a pack drive exercise, so you want your dog in pack drive. For dogs low in defense fight behaviors, a "Stay" signal puts them into defense drive where they're uncomfortable. Using a "Stay" signal may cause the dog to break the Stay and come to you — or to whine and fidget.

Because he is competing for the Companion Dog title, Buddy already knows the basics of the Sit and Down-Stay. You just need to fill in the missing pieces, meaning you need to practice

✔ With distractions

✔ Off leash

✔ At the right distance

✔ For the requisite length of time plus one minute

✔ At different locations and on different surfaces

The review progression for any Stay is the Sit-Stay test (see Chapter 7).

Introducing self-generated distractions

To introduce self-generated distractions, put the leash on the collar, with the rings under his chin. Then say and signal "Stay," and step three feet in front. Place your left hand against your belt buckle and hold your right hand ready to reinforce. Jump to the right, the middle, the left, the middle, forward, and backward. Any time Buddy wants to move, reinforce the stay. How vigorously you do these distractions depends on Buddy's Personality Profile and your physical condition.

As he learns, add clapping and cheering. And periodically review these distractions in your training.

Increasing the level of difficulty

Practice with self-generated distractions off leash from about three feet and then six feet in front of Buddy to increase the level of difficulty. When Buddy is off leash, and you need to reinforce the Stay, slowly approach him and put him back by placing two fingers of each hand through the collar at the side of his neck. If he's coming to you, put him back from in front — that is, guide him back to the spot where you left him in such a way that you're facing him when you reinforce the Stay. Don't repeat the command.

You also need to practice the Down-Stay, using the same distractions you did for the Sit-Say, both on and off leash.

Whenever you approach your dog, do so in a nonthreatening manner so he doesn't become anxious. You never want your dog to become frightened when you approach him.

Gradually increase the time to two minutes for the Sit-Stay and four minutes for the Down-Stay. Although practical, these are boring exercises for both you and your dog. You usually don't need to practice them every session. Once or twice a week suffices. Afterward, reward your dog with something he enjoys, like throwing a Frisbee or a stick.

When Buddy stays for the requisite length of time, gradually increase the distance you're away from him to 35 feet. Increasing the distance should go quickly, because this exercise isn't new for him. Finally, you need to practice in different locations and on different surfaces.

Oops: Playing the yo-yo game

Some handlers have unintentionally taught their dogs, or vice versa, what we call the yo-yo game. The scenario goes something like this:

1. **Buddy is on a Sit-Stay with his handler standing 30 feet away.**

2. **Buddy lies down, and the handler approaches to reinforce the Stay.**

3. **Buddy sits up by himself, and the handler retreats.**

This scenario can, and often does, deteriorate into the yo-yo game. Buddy lies down, the handler approaches, Buddy sits up, and the handler retreats, with Buddy not having learned a blessed thing — except perhaps how many times he can play the game.

Moral of the story? When you make a move — any move — to reinforce a command — any command — you *must* follow through, even if Buddy corrects himself before you've had a chance to reinforce the command. But always do it with a smile.

Chapter 15

Retrieving

*M*ost of you aren't too thrilled about having Buddy lug your possessions about. You'd prefer he limited his retrieving instincts to his own things.

Many dogs like to retrieve, or at least chase, a variety of objects. For them, it's a self-rewarding activity. They do it because they enjoy it. Some of them actually bring back the ball, Frisbee, or stick just so you can throw it again. They continue so long as it's fun. When it's no longer fun, they stop. They also retrieve only articles they like. For example, your dog may happily retrieve a ball, but turn up his nose when you want him to pick up a glove.

The well-trained dog has been taught to retrieve and has learned to do it for you and not just himself. Of course, he can have fun in the process, so long as he understands that it's not a matter of choice.

In this chapter we take you through the necessary steps to make a reliable retriever out of Buddy. Most dogs, of course, already know many of the different component behaviors of retrieving, but few know them all. Even though Buddy may know how to retrieve, you still need to go through the progressions of teaching him this exercise, just to make sure he knows all of its parts.

Taking the Steps to Successful Retrieving

As a part of mastering how to retrieve on command, your dog learns to take, as well as to give, an equally important lesson. If it hasn't happened to you already, it will. Buddy has picked up something he thinks is edible, but which you don't think is a suitable dietary supplement. Having taught him to retrieve, you'll be able to convince him to give it up.

There is another practical side to teaching your dog to retrieve. One of our students wanted her Golden Retriever, Sunny, to bring in the morning paper, preferably in readable condition. So we first had her teach Sunny the formal retrieve. We then told her go out with Sunny, have him pick up the paper, bring it in the house, and reward him with a dog biscuit.

It only took Sunny two repetitions until he figured it out and from then on, every morning he dutifully brought in the paper. After several days we got a frantic phone call. It seems that Sunny was somewhat of an entrepreneur. In an effort to garner more biscuits he started retrieving the neighbors' papers as well. Fortunately, that problem was easily fixed — a biscuit only for the first paper. When he realized that, he stopped bringing home other papers.

The Retrieve sounds simple, but it consists of many separate behaviors, some or all of which the dog has to learn:

- Going to the object
- Picking it up
- Holding it
- Walking with and carrying the object
- Bringing it back
- Giving it up

For the dog that already retrieves on his own, teaching him to do it on command is a cinch. For those dogs who don't, you need to have a little more patience. Your dog's ability to learn to retrieve depends on what your dog was bred to do and how many prey drive behaviors he has (see Chapter 5).

The object we use for the Formal Retrieve is a wooden dumbbell. You can buy one at your local pet store or through catalogs. You need to get one that is commensurate to the size of your dog and the shape of his mouth. You want the bells to be big enough so your dog can pick it up off the ground without scraping his chin, and the diameter of the bar thick enough so he can comfortably carry it. The bar's length should be such that the bells just touch the sides of his face.

You can also purchase plastic dumbbells; they last a lot longer than wooden ones. In the teaching process, however, we have found that dogs take more readily to wooden dumbbells than to plastic ones.

To get started, you need the following equipment:

- Enthusiastic handler
- Hungry dog
- Small can of cat food

✔ Metal spoon

✔ Wooden dumbbell

✔ Chair

For some reason dogs can't resist cat food; it works well as a reward. Because many dogs aren't fond of retrieving metal objects, use a metal spoon to get them used to the feel of metal. We also let Buddy lick out and play with the empty can.

Retrieving on command

Although many dogs retrieve a variety of objects on their own, they don't necessarily do so on command. To teach them to retrieve on command we begin by creating an association with the command and what we want the dog to do — take an object in his mouth. The one object few dogs can resist is food, so that is how we start.

The ideal time to start teaching Buddy to retrieve is when he is hungry, before you feed him.

1. **Place the food, spoon, and dumbbell on a chair.**

2. **With Buddy sitting at your left side, face the chair.**

3. **Put a small portion of food on the spoon and offer it to him with the command "Take it!"**

4. **Give the command in an excited and enthusiastic tone of voice to elicit prey drive behavior.**

   (Check out Chapter 5 for information on the basic drive behaviors.)

5. **Repeat this exercise ten times or until Buddy readily opens his mouth to get the food.**

   Few dogs can resist this treat.

Introducing the object of retrieve

As soon as Buddy has an inkling of what the command "Take it" means, you're ready to introduce him to his dumbbell. But going from food to a dumbbell is quite a transition, so you need to be patient with him.

When you're teaching Buddy any of the behaviors associated with retrieving, your body posture is important. You want to be at his right side without hovering or leaning over him because that posture would put him into defense drive when you want him in prey drive.

You now also need bite-sized treats, such as TOTs (Training Opportunity Treats made by Kong [kongcompany.com]), Bribery Bits (thedog8it.com), or liver treats. You may have to experiment with different treats until you find one Buddy really likes. Put a dozen treats on the chair, and you're ready to start.

1. **With Buddy sitting at your left side, again facing the chair, put your left palm lightly on top of his muzzle and place your left index finger behind his left canine tooth. (See Figure 15-1.)**

Figure 15-1:
Gently
opening
your dog's
mouth.

2. **Gently open his mouth and with your right hand place the dumbbell in his mouth with the command "Take it."**

3. **Rest the thumb of your right hand on top of his muzzle, fingers under his chin, and cup his mouth shut. (See Figure 15-2).**

4. **Praise enthusiastically, immediately say, "Give," and take the dumbbell out of his mouth.**

Hold the dumbbell by the bell so you can easily put the bar in his mouth. After one second, take it out with "Give."

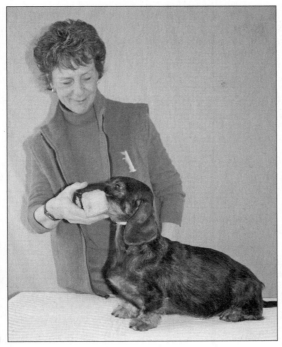

Figure 15-2:
Putting the
dumbbell in
your dog's
mouth.

The goal of this progression is for your dog to accept the dumbbell in his mouth voluntarily. It's only an introduction and you don't want to close his mouth over the dumbbell for longer than one second. When Buddy readily accepts the dumbbell consistently, you can go on to the next sequence.

5. **Reward with food.**

6. **Repeat this process ten times each for five sessions.**

When we teach one of our dogs to retrieve, we practice this exercise once a day on consecutive days. If you're the ambitious type, you can practice more frequently, as long as your dog remains interested and will actively work for the treat. What's not a good idea is to practice sporadically because your dog will forget what he has learned during the last session and you basically have to start all over.

Helping your dog retrieve

After Buddy has become accustomed to having the dumbbell in his mouth, you're ready to tackle the next step. The goal is for Buddy to take the dumbbell voluntarily in his mouth when you give the command.

1. **Have Buddy sit at your left side, have the chair with treats in place, and put two fingers of your left hand through his collar, back to front, palm facing you, at the side of his neck.**

2. **With your right hand, place the bar of the dumbbell directly in front of his mouth, touching the small whiskers.**

3. **Say, "Take it," and when he takes it, briefly cup his mouth shut and tell him how clever he is.**

4. **Say, "Give," take out the dumbbell, and reward with food.**

   At this point in the training, your dog may not yet take the dumbbell but will open his mouth. In that case, just put the dumbbell in, cup his mouth shut, and so on.

If he sits there like a bump on a log, watch for signs of intention behavior. *Intention behaviors* are those actions that tell you what the dog is thinking (see Chapter 1). They range from the subtle, such as bringing the whiskers forward, to the overt, such as sniffing the dowel, licking his lips, or intently staring at the dumbbell. Buddy is thinking about taking the dumbbell but isn't quite sure he can.

When you see intention behavior, take your hand out of the collar, open his mouth, put the dumbbell in, and briefly cup his mouth shut. Praise, remove the dumbbell from his mouth, and reward with food. Repeat until Buddy readily opens his mouth and accepts the dumbbell. Praising him while he has the dumbbell in his mouth is important.

Be patient. Sometimes it can take several minutes before the dog makes a move. If absolutely nothing happens and the little wheels have come to a grinding halt, review the preceding step five times and then try again. Some dogs appear to be particularly dense about taking the dumbbell voluntarily on command, but with enough repetitions, they'll get it.

Learning to hold on

Before you proceed with the retrieve part of this exercise, you need to teach Buddy what you want him to do with the dumbbell after he has it in his mouth. You want him to hold the dumbbell in his mouth and not spit it out before you give the "Give" command. You may think this concept is obvious, but it's not to Buddy until you teach it to him.

Your goal is to have Buddy firmly hold the dumbbell until you say "Give."

1. **Start in the usual position, with Buddy at your left side and the treats on the chair.**

2. **Put the dumbbell into his mouth and say, "Hold it."**

   Keep the upper part of your body straight so you don't hover or lean over him.

3. **Make a fist with your right hand and hold it under his chin. (See Figure 15-3.)**

   If you hold the palm of your hand under his chin, Buddy may construe it as an invitation to spit out the dumbbell.

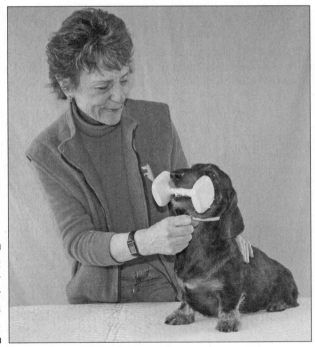

Figure 15-3:
Holding your hand under the dog's chin.

4. **Smile and count to five.**

5. **Praise, remove the dumbbell, and reward him with food.**

6. **Repeat 20 times, increasing gradually the time you have him hold the dumbbell in 5-second increments up to 30 seconds.**

If Buddy starts rolling the dumbbell around in his mouth or looks as though he will open his mouth to spit out the dumbbell, give him a *gentle* tap under the chin with "Hold it." Then remove the dumbbell with "Give," praise, and reward.

Learning to reach for the retrieve

As soon as Buddy understands that he has to hold the dumbbell, the next sequence is to teach him to reach for it.

1. **With two fingers of your left hand through his collar at the side of his neck, back to front, palm facing you, hold his dumbbell two inches in front of his mouth.**

2. **Say, "Take it."**

3. **If he does, cup his mouth shut with "Hold it," count to five, praise, remove dumbbell with "Give," and reward with food.**

4. **If he doesn't take the dumbbell, *lightly* twist his collar by rotating your left hand a quarter of a turn toward you, which will bring his head forward and toward the dumbbell, until he reaches for and takes it.**

5. **Cup his mouth shut with "Hold it," count to five, praise, remove the dumbbell with "Give," and reward with food.**

   Don't twist his collar for more than 30 seconds or try to increase pressure more than a quarter of a turn.

6. **Put the dumbbell in his mouth, cup shut with "Hold it," praise, remove, and reward.**

7. **Repeat until your dog voluntarily reaches for and takes the dumbbell.**

   Increase the distance Buddy has to reach for the dumbbell in two-inch increments to arm's length.

If your dog shows signs of noticeable stress during this sequence, the following will happen:

- If he is a negative stresser, he'll clamp his mouth shut and turn inward when you apply pressure on the collar. Pressure on the collar won't make him open his mouth. Stop, put the dumbbell in his mouth, praise, reward, and try again.

- If he stresses positively, he'll try different behaviors, one of which will be to grab the dumbbell, at which point you praise and reward.

Walking after retrieving

The next step in the retrieve progressions is teaching Buddy to hold onto the dumbbell while walking with it in his mouth. Okay, you're probably saying to yourself, "For Pete's sake, is all this really necessary?" The answer? It depends on the dog. At this point in the training, the majority of dogs understand the concept and are perfectly able to hold the dumbbell in their mouths and walk at the same time. (Hey, even some people have difficulty walking and chewing gum at the same time, so give your dog a break.) If your dog does it, you can skip this step. Still, we've seen dogs, including some of our own, that couldn't make this transition and had to be taught. So when we devised this approach to teaching retrieving, we included the walking-while-holding sequence just to make sure that all eventualities are covered.

1. **With Buddy sitting at your left side, facing the chair with the treats on it from about six feet away, put the dumbbell in his mouth with "Take it," followed by "Hold it."**

   Encourage him to walk toward the chair.

2. **To give Buddy confidence, put your right hand under his chin when he starts to move.**

3. **When he gets to the chair, praise, remove the dumbbell, and reward him.**

4. **Repeat until Buddy walks with the dumbbell without you holding your hand under his chin.**

   Then gradually increase the distance to 20 steps in 5-step increments.

Teaching the pick-up

You and Buddy have arrived at the final progression of teaching him to retrieve — the pick-up. Resist the temptation to just throw the dumbbell and expect Buddy to pick it up and bring it back. He may actually do it, but he also may not. He may just chase it and then stand over it, not knowing what to do next. In the long run, make sure that he knows what you expect by teaching him.

1. **Have Buddy sit at your left side and place the chair with the treats on it behind you.**

2. **With your fingers in his collar, hold the dumbbell about two inches from Buddy's mouth and say "Take it."**

3. **When he does, praise enthusiastically, say "Give," remove the dumbbell from his mouth, and reward him with a treat.**

   Your goal is to lower the dumbbell in two-inch increments toward the ground and have Buddy retrieve it from your hand.

4. **When you get to the ground, place the bell of the dumbbell on the ground and hold it at a 45-degree angle.**

5. **Say, "Take it," and when Buddy takes the dumbbell, take your hand out of the collar, say, "Hold it," and back up two steps.**

   He'll quickly come to you to get his reward.

6. Praise, remove, and reward.

7. Repeat until he is comfortable picking up the dumbbell with you holding it at that angle.

8. Place the dumbbell on the ground but keep your hand on it.

9. Have Buddy retrieve the dumbbell several times while you have your hand on it.

10. Hold your hand first 2 inches, and then 6 inches, and then 12 inches away from the dumbbell until you can place it on the ground and stand up straight.

11. Each time he retrieves the dumbbell, back up several steps, praise, remove, and reward.

12. If your dog doesn't pick up the dumbbell from the ground, lightly twist the collar until he picks it up.

    If this sequence becomes an issue and your dog continues to refuse to take the dumbbell, review the prior progressions. Make sure that you followed them religiously and that your dog has mastered each progression before you went on to the next.

13. Say, "Stay," and place the dumbbell one foot in front of your dog.

14. Say, "Take it," and when he brings it back, praise, remove, and reward.

15. Repeat by first placing it three feet and then six feet in front of your dog.

Your dog will tell you how many times in a row you can ask him to retrieve. If he has many prey drive behaviors, you can get in quite a few repetitions. If not, he'll quickly lose enthusiasm. You're better off stopping after five repetitions and picking the game up again at the next session.

For the dog, picking up a dumbbell that you placed on the ground isn't terribly exciting, and if it weren't for the reward, it would be an absolute bore. Still, this sequence is necessary because you want your dog to learn he has to do it for you and not for himself.

Chasing to retrieve

Now comes the fun part, where you get to throw the dumbbell and Buddy gets to chase it. Throw the dumbbell a few feet and at the same time send your dog with "Take it." As soon as he picks up, tell him how terrific he is. When he gets back to you, take the dumbbell with "Give" and reward him with a treat.

Sometimes dogs get carried away by the fun of it all and don't come right back with the dumbbell. They might make a detour, or just run around for the joy of it. If that happens, say, "Come," as soon as he picks up the dumbbell, and praise and reward him when he gets back to you.

Gradually increase the distance the dumbbell is thrown. As he gains confidence, introduce the Sit in front with "Hold it." When he gets back to you say, "Sit" and "Hold it." Because he hasn't done this task before, you may have to hold your hand under his chin to prevent him from dropping the dumbbell. Praise, remove, and reward. From now on make him sit and hold the dumbbell every time he gets back to you.

Testing your dog's patience

Buddy also has to learn to stay while you throw the dumbbell and until he is permitted to get it. Making him wait gets him all the more excited about getting to his dumbbell. Trying to teach your dog patience is almost like teaching your two-year-old child patience, but you can do it. Just follow these steps:

1. **Start with Buddy at your left side.**
2. **Put two fingers of your left hand through his collar, say, "Stay," and throw the dumbbell about 15 feet.**
3. **Very, very gingerly let go of his collar, count to five and say, "Take it."**
4. **When he returns, praise, remove, and reward.**
5. **Repeat until your dog holds the Stay without having to hold him by the collar.**

Remember to give the command in an excited and enthusiastic tone of voice to put the dog into prey drive. Never use a harsh or threatening tone of voice because your tone of voice may put the dog in the wrong drive and make it more difficult for him to learn. If at anytime your dog needs motivation, throw the dumbbell at the same time as you say, "Take it," letting him chase after it.

Congratulations. You now have a dog that retrieves on command — at least a dumbbell. To play the game of fetch, however, most people probably use a Frisbee, a ball, or a stick. Few dogs have any difficulty making the transition from the dumbbell to one of these objects. Usually, it's the other way around. The dog will happily retrieve a ball but will turn his nose up at the dumbbell.

You can also use the "Retrieve" command to have Buddy bring in the newspaper, carry his leash, and — size permitting — carry your handbag. We taught one of our dogs to open the refrigerator door and retrieve a can of pop. Unfortunately, we were unable to teach the dog to close the fridge door and had to abandon that trick.

Retrieving with Distractions

After Buddy knows how to retrieve, he's ready for distraction training.

Introduce your dog to distractions as follows:

1. **The distracter stands about two feet from the dumbbell.**

   He assumes a friendly posture, not threatening to the dog.

2. **Send Buddy and as soon as he picks up the dumbbell, enthusiastically praise.**

   Look at the exercise as having been completed as soon as your dog picks up his dumbbell.

3. **As the dog gains confidence, have the distracter stand a little closer, and then over the dumbbell.**

   The distracter also hides the dumbbell by standing directly in front of it with his back to the dog, and then lightly puts his foot on it. You can use a chair as a distraction by putting the dumbbell under the chair and then on the chair.

During distraction training, you see the following responses, or variations thereof:

- ✔ He starts going toward the dumbbell but then backs off and fails to retrieve, meaning, "I don't have the confidence to get close enough to the distracter to retrieve my dumbbell."

  Remedy: Without saying anything, slowly approach him, put two fingers of your left hand through the collar, back to front, palm facing you, at the side of his neck and take him to the dumbbell. If he picks up the dumbbell, praise, remove the dumbbell and reward; if he doesn't, put the dumbbell in his mouth, and then praise, remove, and reward. Don't repeat the command.

  Try again. Remember your dog's learning style and how many repetitions it takes before he understands. You may find that you have to help him several times before he has the confidence that he can do it by himself. As soon as he has done it on his own, stop for that session.

- ✔ He leaves altogether and doesn't retrieve, saying, in effect, "I can't cope with this."

  Remedy: Same.

- ✔ He does nothing, meaning, "If I don't do anything, maybe all of this will go away."

  Remedy: Same.

✔ He permits himself to be distracted, meaning, "I would rather visit than retrieve my dumbbell."

Remedy: Same.

✔ He takes the dumbbell to the distracter.

Remedy: Slowly approach your dog without saying anything, put the leash on the dead ring of the training collar and, with a little tension on the collar, show him exactly what he was supposed to do by guiding him to you. No extra command is given.

✔ He anticipates the Retrieve, meaning he is catching on and wants to show you how clever he is.

Remedy: Without saying anything, slowly approach him, take the dumbbell out of his mouth, put it down where he picked it up, go back to the starting point and then send him. Whatever you do, don't shout "no," or do anything else that would discourage him from retrieving after you have just worked so hard to get him to pick up the dumbbell.

✔ He does it correctly and that is when you stop for that session.

Continue to use food rewards for Buddy on a random basis, that is, not every time, and not in a predictable pattern but often enough to maintain his motivation.

When your dog confidently retrieves under these circumstances, introduce the next level of distractions. The distracter crouches close to the dumbbell and tries to distract him by saying "here puppy, come visit for some petting." The distracter doesn't use your dog's name.

After Buddy has successfully worked his way through that level, favorite object distractions are added, such as offering the dog food or a ball or toy. Of course, the distracter never lets the dog have the food.

Distractions add an extra dimension and take training to a higher level. Distraction training builds your dog's confidence and teaches him to concentrate on what he is doing. This type of training is especially important for the shy dog, providing the confidence he needs to respond correctly under different conditions.

During distraction training, keep in mind that anytime you change the complexity of the exercise, it becomes a new exercise for the dog. If Buddy goes for the food, you would treat his response the same way you did when you first introduced him to distraction training. No, your dog isn't defiant, stubborn, or stupid, just confused as to what he should do and has to be helped again.

You're now ready to work with different objects. When you do, you may have to review the first few sequences. Just because Buddy retrieves one object doesn't necessarily mean he'll retrieve others. He may need to get used to them first.

By challenging Buddy to use his head, you can increase the strength of his responses and increase his confidence in his ability to perform under almost all conditions.

When using distraction training, giving Buddy a chance to work it out for himself is important. Don't be too quick to try and help him. Be patient, and let him try to figure out on his own how to do it correctly. After he does, you'll be pleasantly surprised by the intensity and reliability with which he responds.

Chapter 16

The Companion Dog Excellent Title

A fter you obtain your Companion Dog title from the American Kennel Club's (AKC) Novice class, you're eligible to enter the AKC's Open class and compete for the Companion Dog Excellent title. The Novice class is tailor-made for the dog highest in pack behaviors, but the Open class is for the dog that also has many prey behaviors.

This chapter gets you up to speed on what's required in the Open class and what the point system is, and it provides the details for how to achieve your goal.

The Open Class: What's Expected from You and Buddy

The Open class consists of seven exercises, each with a specific point value (see Table 16-1). For a qualifying score, you and Buddy have to earn more than 50 percent of the available points for each exercise and a final score of at least 170 out of a possible 200. This class is ideal for the dog high in pack and prey behaviors.

Some Open class exercise trivia

The first obedience trials held under the auspices of the American Kennel Club (AKC) took place in 1936. The classes were the same as today, but the requirements varied somewhat. For example, the Open class included a Speak on Command exercise. But contrary to popular belief, not all dogs are instinctive barkers, and the exercise was subsequently eliminated.

The first obedience test was held in 1933 and consisted of what are now the Open class exercises. For the Retrieve on the Flat, the dumbbell weighed 2 pounds. The Retrieve Over High Jump was a 3-foot-6-inch obstacle, and the dumbbell weighed 8 to 10 ounces. The Broad Jump was 6 feet wide.

Table 16-1	The Open Class	
Required Exercises	*Available Points*	*Behavior/Drive*
Exercise 1: Heel Free and Figure 8	40	Pack
Exercise 2: Drop on Recall	30	Pack
Exercise 3: Retrieve on the Flat	20	Prey
Exercise 4: Retrieve Over the High Jump	30	Prey
Exercise 5: Broad Jump	20	Prey
Exercise 6: Long Sit	30	Pack
Exercise 7: Long Down	30	Pack
Maximum Total Score	200	

All the exercises for the Open class are done off leash, and the group exercises (the Long Sit and Long Down) are performed with the owners out of sight of the dogs for three and five minutes, respectively. For your dog, the Open class is the most exciting of the classes.

Note that some of the exercises require equipment. You can either buy the equipment or make it yourself. The specifications are contained in the AKC's Obedience Regulations, which you can get by contacting the AKC at 5580 Centerview Drive, Suite 200, Raleigh, NC 27606-3390 (919-233-9767; www. akc.org).

The Heel Free and Figure 8

You've no doubt discovered that heeling isn't as simple as it looks. You certainly need to keep practicing on a regular basis. Here's some food for thought: Heeling is the only exercise that you and your dog do as a team; all the other exercises the dog does on his own. But many handlers have a hard time with heeling.

You and your dog do the Heel Free exactly the same way as it's done in the Novice class and the only difference is the Figure 8, which is now done off leash (see Chapter 14).

The Drop on Recall

The Drop on Recall uses a combination of the "Come" and "Down" commands. As your dog is coming to you, you tell him to lie down, and then you call him again. The exercise starts as a recall, but after you've called your dog, the judge indicates for you to give the "Down" command or signal and then for you to call again. The command sequence goes like this: "Buddy, come," "Down," "Buddy, come." The dog has to remain in the Down position until called. The Front and Finish are also part of the exercise.

Being that Buddy's competing in the Open class, by now he certainly knows the "Down" and "Come" commands. The only really new concept he has to learn is to stop immediately when the command is given.

Getting Buddy to obey Down on command

Your Sequence 1 goal is to teach Buddy to obey Down on command.

You need to test Buddy's understanding of the command.

1. **With Buddy sitting at Heel and without giving him any visual cues, such as pointing to the ground, bobbing your head, leaning over, or bending your knees, quietly say "Down."**

   If he lies down, praise, count to five, and release.

2. **If Buddy doesn't respond to the command, or his response is unacceptable (not prompt enough, for example), *slowly* slide your left hand down the leash all the way to the snap and check straight down.**

   Keep your elbow locked and your arm at your side. Avoid checking across your body because that teaches Buddy to curl in front of you.

3. **Stand up, count to five, praise, and release.**

4. **Repeat until your dog lies down on command at your side.**

   This is the review progression for this exercise.

Use the following tips and tidbits to help:

✔ Many of you are blissfully unaware of your own body motions, and you may not be aware of the visual cues you're giving your dog. Always make sure that you aren't inadvertently moving some part of your body — even as much as a finger — and that you're facing straight forward. Note that because visual cues are so important to success in training, it helps to have someone else watch you and then tell you what you're doing. Better yet, occasionally videotape each other. Or stand in front of a mirror and watch yourself.

✔ The purpose of counting to five after a given response is so the dog focuses on what it is you want and doesn't immediately start doing something else.

✔ When you're trying to decide what's an unacceptable response, keep in mind that your dog's size and structure determine how he performs the Down exercise. Some dogs are structurally unable to lie down without first going into the sitting position. So long as they stop any forward progress when the command is given, your dog won't be penalized for first assuming the sitting position and then lying down.

Getting Buddy to Down while he's walking

Sequence 2's goal? Get Buddy to respond to the "Down" command while he's in motion. Buddy has to learn to respond promptly to the "Down" command even when he's moving.

1. **With Buddy sitting at Heel, say "Let's go" and start to walk.**

   Don't use the "Heel" command because this isn't a heeling exercise.

2. **After several steps, say "Down" as you come to a halt and not after you have stopped.**

   If you aren't careful about the timing of the command, Buddy may confuse the "Down" command with the Automatic Sit.

3. **Praise if he does it, count to five, and then release straight forward.**

   The release here is the beginning of teaching Buddy to move briskly forward from the Down position.

4. **If he doesn't drop, slowly slide your left hand down the leash to the snap and check straight down.**

5. **Praise, count to five, and release.**

Getting Buddy to Down while you're still walking

Sequence 3's goal is to get Buddy to go down at your side from motion, while both of you are in motion and while you continue walking. *Note:* Before you try Sequence 3, review Sequences 1 and 2 in the preceding two sections.

1. **Say "Let's go" and start walking.**

2. **After walking several steps, say "Down" and continue walking to the end of the leash.**

3. **Turn to face Buddy, praise, count to five, and release backward.**

   When you release him, remember that you're teaching him to come briskly to you after you've dropped him. (See Chapter 14 for info about releasing backward.)

4. **If Buddy doesn't drop, start again.**

5. **As you give the command, slowly slide your left hand down the leash to the snap and check straight down.**

6. **Go to the end of the leash, turn, praise, pause, and release.**

   When he responds reliably, go on to the next progression.

Getting Buddy to Down while he's running

Sequence 4's goal is to get Buddy to obey the "Down" command while he's moving fast — *and* while you continue moving.

Before you try Sequence 4, review Sequences 1 and 3. Then visualize how your dog comes to you on a recall. It's at *that* speed that he has to drop on command and without any unnecessary steps. Although you may not be able to run as quickly as he can, teach him to drop from a fast pace as you continue to the end of the leash.

Getting Buddy to stop and drop when coming toward you: The on-leash method

Sequence 5's goal is to teach Buddy to stop and drop from in front. The leash is on for this exercise. When Buddy has mastered the drop from a fast pace, you're ready to try the exercise with him coming toward you.

1. **Leave him in a Sit-Stay position and go to the end of the leash — facing him.**

2. **Call with "Buddy, come."**

3. **As he comes to you, take a step toward him on your right foot, keeping the left foot in place, and simultaneously signal by bringing your right arm straight up, and say "Down."**

   Keep the upper part of your body straight. Stepping toward Buddy will cause him to stop his forward progress. You can use either arm to signal Buddy.

4. **After he has dropped, bring your right foot back, lower your arm, praise, count to five, and release.**

   Use the release backward to teach him to come again quickly and enthusiastically after you've dropped him.

If Buddy doesn't drop, review Sequence 1 with a check and Sequence 4; then try it again.

After Buddy is coming toward you, don't check him into a Down position or do anything else that he may perceive as unpleasant — it will slow down his recall. What's important here is your dog's view of what is unpleasant — not your view. If he doesn't drop, or the drop is unacceptable, review Sequences 1 through 3.

Getting Buddy to stop and drop when coming toward you: The off-leash method

Sequence 6's goal is to teach Buddy to stop and drop from in front — off leash.

Go through Sequence 5, only do it off leash. You may want to review Sequence 1 with a little check before you try this exercise. As Buddy responds, gradually increase the distance between you and him.

Maintain the step-command-signal sequence until he's reliable. After that, first eliminate the step and then decide whether you prefer voice or signal. You'll probably want him to respond to either.

Getting Buddy to ignore distractions

Sequence 7's goal is to teach Buddy to ignore distractions.

Begin by having a distracter crouch about two feet from Buddy's line of travel and where you intend to drop him. Call and give him the command or signal to drop.

He may do one of several things:

- ✔ Anticipate the drop — that is, slow down or drop before you have given the command or signal

- ✔ Drop after he's gone past the distracter

- ✔ Not drop at all

- ✔ Avoid the distracter by arcing away from him or her

- ✔ Not respond to the "Come" command

- ✔ Actually do it correctly (not likely the first time you try this exercise)

Avoid having Buddy anticipate the drop by randomly alternating between Straight Recalls and Drop On Recalls.

Here's what you do if Buddy does one of those preceding things:

- ✔ **If Buddy anticipates the drop:** You need to show him exactly what you want him to do, that is, keep coming to you until you tell him to down. You show him as follows: Slowly go to him without saying anything, put the leash on the dead ring of the collar, and with a little tension on the collar, guide him to the spot where you were when you called him. (You go backward, Buddy goes forward.) Have Buddy sit in front, and then praise and release him backward. No extra command is given. Alternate on a random basis between Straight Recalls and Drop On Recalls to avoid anticipation.

- ✔ **If Buddy drops past the distracter or doesn't drop at all:** Slowly approach him without saying anything. Put two fingers of your left hand, palm facing you, through the collar, back to front, at the side of his neck. Take him to the spot where he should have dropped and reinforce the command from in front. Don't repeat the command. Praise your dog, count to five, and enthusiastically release backward.

What Buddy is telling you is that he lacks the confidence to drop near the distracter. Your job is to show him that he can do it. His confidence will increase with each successive correct repetition.

✔ **If Buddy arcs away from the distracter or doesn't respond to the "Come" command:** Use two distracters, facing each other about eight feet apart, and teach Buddy to drop between the distracters.

Note that Buddy may also start to anticipate the Come from the Down. If he does, slowly approach your dog without saying anything. Then put two fingers of your left hand, palm facing you, through the collar, back to front, at the side of his neck, and take him back to the spot where he should have stayed and reinforce the Down from in front. Don't repeat the command. Praise, count to five, and enthusiastically release backward.

As Buddy gains confidence and responds correctly, work your way through the different levels of distractions. Being that you're competing in the Open class, you've already trained him to ignore these distractions for the Novice recall, so it won't take him very long to figure out what you want.

At some point, you have to decide whether to use a signal or a command to drop your dog because you can't use both. Experiment with Buddy to decide whether you need to use a signal or a command when in the ring. Buddy's Personality Profile can help you with your decision (see Chapter 5). If he's weak in defense (fight) behaviors, you'll be better off using the command rather than the signal. If he's high in prey behaviors, you'll be more successful with a signal.

The Retrieve on Flat

For this exercise, the judge tells you to throw the dumbbell and then send your dog, who's expected to retrieve the dumbbell, present to front, give up the dumbbell on command, and then finish on command. Your command sequence is "Stay," "Take it," "Give," and "Buddy, heel." Buddy must do all the other parts of this exercise on his own.

Anytime you change the content or the complexity of an exercise, it becomes a new exercise for the dog, and you have to go back to the teaching progressions. If your dog was bred to do it, he should learn quickly. If he wasn't bred to do it, it'll take longer.

We cover the details of the "Retrieve" command in Chapter 15. ***Note:*** Many dogs retrieve without being formally taught, and this kind of retrieving is called a *play retrieve*. If you've done distraction training, your dog will have shown you whether you can rely on his cooperation. Ask yourself, "Is he retrieving for me or for himself?" For greater reliability, teach him to retrieve for you.

You also may need to review the teaching progressions for the Front while your dog is holding the dumbbell. For your dog, a Front with the dumbbell isn't the same exercise as a Front without a dumbbell. It becomes a new exercise. You need to review the Front progressions in Chapter 14 with Buddy carrying the dumbbell in his mouth.

How quickly Buddy will generalize the Front while carrying the dumbbell depends on the extent to which the exercise is in harmony with his instincts. Retrievers, for example, do it almost automatically, but other breeds may need a few repetitions.

The Retrieve Over the High Jump

The principal features of this exercise are that your dog jumps over the jump, picks up the dumbbell, and promptly returns with it over the jump. The judge's commands are "Throw the dumbbell," "Send your dog," "Take it," and "Finish." Your commands to Buddy are "Stay," "Jump," "Give," and "Buddy, heel."

For this exercise, we introduce *target training*. As the name implies, you teach the dog to go to a target. After your dog has learned that, you can then place a jump or other obstacle between your dog and the target. In order to get to the target, the dog has to jump the obstacle. Target training gives the appearance of being a game. Yet it's a highly effective way of teaching your dog a variety of complex exercises.

Target training

The principle is simple, and so is the execution. Place a target on the ground three feet in front of you and Buddy. We use the tops of 2-pound cottage cheese containers as targets. Put a treat on the target (see Figure 16-1) and send Buddy to the target.

Make the exercise fun and exciting for your dog by using several targets, with the objective that he goes where you tell him.

Figure 16-1:
Placing the
treat on the
target.

The progressions are as follows:

- ✔ **Progression 1:** Get your dog's attention on the treat, go to the target, say "Out," place the treat on the target, and let your dog pick up the treat. Repeat three times.

- ✔ **Progression 2:** Start three feet from the target, say "Stay," place the treat on the target, go back to your dog, and say "Out" as you motion with your left arm and hand in the direction of the target. Praise him when he gets there and call him back to you. Repeat three times.

- ✔ **Progression 3:** Over the course of several sessions, increase the distance from the target to 50 feet in increments of 2 feet.

- ✔ **Progression 4:** Have a helper place a treat and then send your dog.

This is an exciting exercise for your dog, especially if he's high in prey behaviors. How many repetitions your dog will perform depends on his Personality Profile and the number of prey behaviors he has (see Chapter 5).

Anytime you work with treats, make sure that your dog is hungry. Depending on the number of his prey behaviors, you may need to use something special, such as homemade liver treats. Experiment to find out what works best to keep your dog interested.

The sequences for teaching the Retrieve Over the High Jump

Most dogs have to jump an obstacle equal to the dog's height at the withers. A short definition of *withers* is the highest part of the dog behind the neck, where the shoulder blades meet. Some breeds have to jump only three-fourths of their height at the withers. The AKC Obedience Regulations specify which breeds jump three-fourths of their height and which ones jump once their height.

Not all dogs are natural jumpers and jumping is an athletic activity, no matter the breed. Like any other athletic activity, it requires conditioning. Just because Buddy jumps on the furniture doesn't mean he'll automatically jump over the High Jump. You have to teach him and, for his safety, teach him correctly as we explain in the following sequences.

Getting Buddy used to the jump

Your Sequence 1 goal is to get Buddy accustomed to the jump:

1. **Put your leash on the dead ring of Buddy's training collar and walk him up to the jump, which is set at *teaching height* (the dog's height at the elbows).**

2. **Touch the top board with your left hand and let him examine the jump.**

3. **Step over the jump and encourage him to follow.**

   You can use a treat to get him to go over. The command is "Buddy, jump."

4. **Repeat until he goes over the jump without hesitation.**

Teaching Buddy to jump on his own

Sequence 2's goal is to teach your dog to jump on his own:

1. **Sit Buddy three feet from the center of the jump.**

2. **Tell him to "Stay," step over the jump, and put his target three feet from the jump.**

3. **Facing your dog, place a treat on the target, stand up, and call him over the jump with "Buddy, jump."**

4. **Repeat until Buddy is comfortable going over the jump — five to ten times per session.**

Jumping repetitions aren't necessarily only to teach Buddy the exercise but also to condition him physically. You need to look at any jumping exercise as an athletic endeavor on the part of your dog, which requires the same kind of conditioning that applies to human athletic endeavors.

Getting Buddy to jump by himself — and from different angles

The goal of Sequence 3 is to get your dog to jump by himself and from different angles:

1. **Leave Buddy ten feet from the jump and go to the other side by stepping over the jump.**

2. **Focus his attention on the center of the top board, take three steps backward, pause, and say "Buddy, jump."**

   Don't tap the top board as you say "Jump" because it teaches your dog to jump on a visual cue rather than on the command.

   After you see that he has committed himself to jump, back up to give him enough room to land.

3. **Praise as he lands and release backward, giving him a treat.**

Few people can throw the dumbbell so that it always lands in the right spot, and some people never get it there. So you may as well teach your dog to jump from different angles. Leave Buddy facing the right upright of the jump, ten feet away. Go to the other side by stepping over the jump, focus his attention on the center of the top board, take three steps backward, pause, and say "Buddy, jump." Repeat the exercise by having Buddy face the left upright.

Getting Buddy to jump while holding the dumbbell

Sequence 4's goal is to get your dog to jump while holding the dumbbell:

Have Buddy hold the dumbbell and follow the progressions in Sequence 3. Here, you're teaching the Return Over the Jump part of the exercise.

Teaching Buddy the Motivational Retrieve

Sequence 5's goal is to teach your dog the Motivational Retrieve.

1. **With Buddy at heel, put two fingers of your left hand, palm facing you, through your dog's collar at the side of his neck, back to front.**

2. **Hold the dumbbell in your right hand and get him excited about retrieving the dumbbell.**

3. **From ten feet, say "Buddy, jump" and briskly approach the jump.**

4. **Two feet before you get to the jump, throw the dumbbell and let go of your dog.**

5. **Continue to approach the jump and, as he picks up the dumbbell and turns around to look at you, focus his attention on the center of the jump.**

   As he commits himself to jump, back up to give him enough room to land.

6. **Praise, take the dumbbell, and release.**

7. **Repeat until your dog jumps, retrieves, and returns reliably.**

Also practice this sequence with "bad" throws so your dog learns to come back over the jump from different angles. Picture a 45-degree line going away from you from each upright and condition Buddy to return over the jump from anywhere within that area.

Getting Buddy to wait

The Sequence 6 goal is to teach Buddy to wait:

1. **Position yourself facing the center of the jump, at least eight feet from the jump, and tell Buddy "Stay."**

2. **Put two fingers of your left hand through his collar and throw the dumbbell.**

3. **Very gingerly let go of the collar, count to five, and say "Buddy, jump."**

4. **After he jumps, quietly follow him, and after he picks up and turns to face you, focus his attention on the center of the jump.**

5. **As he commits himself to return, back up so he has enough room to land, take the dumbbell, and release.**

6. **Repeat until he stays without two fingers in the collar and returns without any help from you, and throw the dumbbell at least eight feet beyond the jump.**

For the Retrieve Over High Jump, you're required to stand at least eight feet from the jump and throw the dumbbell at least eight feet beyond the jump. And be sure to practice some "bad" throws, too (see Sequence 5).

Raising the jump

Sequence 7's goal is to raise the jump:

Begin raising the jump in two- or four-inch increments, depending on the size of your dog. If the height of the jump becomes an issue, condition your dog at a lower height.

How high is high enough?

How high your dog has to jump depends on his breed. Some breeds jump once their height at the withers and some three-fourths their height. The AKC Obedience Regulations specify the height each breed has to jump. The jump height is set at the nearest multiple of two inches. For example, Landseer Newfoundlands have to jump three-fourths of their height at the withers. Or a 27½-inch-tall dog has to jump 20 inches.

Difficulties with jumping are never disciplinary in nature — your dog is trying to tell you something. Your dog's structure may be such that he's unable to do what you ask, or he may experience pain for any number of reasons.

Getting Buddy to ignore distractions

The goal of Sequence 8 is to teach Buddy to ignore distractions:

Follow the distraction training progressions in Chapter 15. In addition, have a distracter stand close to an upright while the dog is jumping and, after he's successful, have the distracter try to get your dog to go around the jump on the return by talking to him or enticing him with food. Your helper doesn't, of course, use the dog's name.

Anytime your dog goes around the jump on the return, slowly approach him and put two fingers of your left hand (palm facing you) through the collar at the side of his neck, back to front. Take him back to where he picked up the dumbbell, say "Stay" (he can Stand, Sit, or Lie Down), go over the jump yourself to the other side, focus his attention on the top board, step back, and tell him "Jump." Praise as he lands and then release. Then try it again.

Buddy may also try to go around the jump on the way out. If so, slowly approach him. If he has already picked up the dumbbell, take it out of his mouth and put it back where he picked it up. Now return with Buddy to the starting point and send him again.

Don't say "No" under any circumstance or do anything else that may discourage your dog. You want to put Buddy in a position where he can figure out for himself the desired response. Instead of doing anything that might discourage him, you want to help him by literally showing him exactly what to do, which may include physical guidance. The hardest part for you will be to keep your mouth shut and remain patient.

You know how many repetitions it takes for your dog to learn, so don't get impatient. You want him to keep on trying until he has figured it out, which is called the "Aha" response. Translated, it means "Aha! Now I know what you want." It's a powerful response because the dog has figured it out by himself, albeit with your help, instead of being told what to do. As a result, he responds with great reliability and enthusiasm.

The Broad Jump

For the Broad Jump, your dog is required to jump a distance equal to twice the height of the High Jump. Depending on the distance, it can be two, three, or four boards. It starts with you lining your dog up in front of and at least eight feet from the jump. The judge then says, "Leave your dog." You say "Stay" and go to a position facing the right side of the jump, with your toes about two feet from the jump, anywhere between the first and last board.

The judge then says, "Send your dog." You say "Buddy, over." As your dog jumps, you execute a right-angle turn in place. The dog must sit and finish as in the Novice class's Recall (see Chapter 14).

Getting Buddy used to the jump

Sequence 1's goal is to get your dog used to the jump:

1. **Set up the jump at twice the height of your dog at the elbows.**

   With a small dog, this means only one board.

2. **Put a target eight feet from the center of the jump.**

3. **Walk Buddy up to the jump and let him examine it.**

4. **Position yourself and your dog eight feet from the center of the jump.**

5. **Show him a treat and use it to lure him over the jump with the command "Over."**

   At this point, it doesn't matter how he gets to the other side, just so he goes from one side to the other.

6. **Place the treat on the target and let him have it.**

7. **Praise and release.**

8. **Repeat this sequence several times.**

Getting Buddy to jump on command

Sequence 2's goal is to teach Buddy to jump on command:

1. **Put your dog in a Sit-Stay eight feet from the center of the jump.**
2. **Walk over the jump and place a treat on the target.**
3. **Face your dog and attract his attention to the treat by tapping the target.**
4. **Call him over the jump with "Buddy, over."**
5. **Repeat until he jumps without hesitation on your command.**

Getting Buddy to make the turn

The goal of Sequence 3 is to teach your dog to make the turn:

1. **Start as in Sequence 2, but now stand at a right angle to the jump one step away from the target and call your dog over the jump.**
2. **As you give the command, take a step with your right foot toward the target and with your right arm point to it.**
3. **When Buddy picks up the treat, bring your right foot back, praise, and release.**
4. **When Buddy responds reliably, take two steps backward from the target, and then three, and so on, until you can send him over the jump with you standing about five feet from the target.**

   Whenever you leave him, you're still stepping over the jump.

5. **Now that you can send him over the jump with you standing about five feet from the target, begin moving in the direction where you'll ultimately stand when you send him over the jump.**
6. **Stand about five feet from the target, take one step to your right, and then send Buddy over the jump.**

   Remember, the Step and Point toward the target.

7. **As soon as he picks up the treat, call him with "Come," turn to face him, and have him sit in front.**
8. **Set up again.**
9. **Take another step to right, send him over the jump, and so on.**
10. **Repeat this sequence, one step to the right at a time, until you're standing facing the board(s), with your toes about two feet from the jump.**

11. **Finally, with target and treat in place, go directly to your position facing the right side of the jump, with your toes about two feet from the jump, anywhere between the first and last board, and send him over the jump.**

    Keep using the Step and Point for the first few repetitions. When Buddy jumps reliably, stand still when you send him. For the final product, you can use either the command "Buddy, over," *or* give a signal with either your right or left arm.

As Buddy becomes proficient with this exercise, eliminate the "Come" command and introduce the Finish. For most of your repetitions, you want him to sit in front. For the Finish, you want to keep him guessing, so do it infrequently. When you don't want him to finish, release him backwards.

Dogs learn very quickly what the end product is supposed to look like, and they begin taking shortcuts. For example, to get to you more quickly, Buddy may start to jump at an angle in your direction. You can prevent this from happening by keeping the target and treat in place for most of your practices.

Getting Buddy to ignore distractions

Sequence 4's goal is to work on Buddy to ignore distractions:

Practice with a distracter about two feet from the target and work your way through first, second, and third degree distractions. Remember to stop the session after the first correct response. That's the one you want Buddy to remember. Resist the temptation to do the exercise just one more time. Your dog just may become creative, in which case you may be there for a *long* time until you get another correct response.

Out-of-Sight Stays

The last two exercises in the Open class are the three-minute Sit-Stay and the five-minute Down-Stay. Any of the Stay exercises are boring to practice, but are nerve-racking when you're in competition. So you do need to practice them and under various conditions, including in the rain.

As an introduction to Out-of-Sight Stays, follow these steps:

1. **Leave Buddy in a Sit-Stay and go six feet in front of him.**

2. **Pause for ten seconds, walk past him, and stand six feet behind him with your back to him.**

3. **Practice with distractions and have your helper tell you when Buddy moves and you have to reinforce the Stay.**

   At this stage, that scenario will be highly unlikely. When you're ready to go out of sight, gradually increase the length of time you leave Buddy.

4. **Begin with ten seconds and, over the course of several sessions work up to the three minutes for the Sit-Stay and five minutes for the Down-Stay.**

   If you experience difficulties, such as if Buddy's breaking the stays, shorten your time and rebuild the exercise. Nine out of ten times, the problem is your dog's lack of confidence, and *that's* what you need to work on.

Chapter 17

The Utility Dog Title

A fter your dog obtains the American Kennel Club's (AKC) Companion Dog Excellent title (see Chapter 16), you're eligible to enter the Utility class, which is intended to be the most difficult and challenging class. Curiously, what makes this class difficult isn't the exercises, but the order in which they're done. Each year the AKC awards approximately 10,000 Companion Dog titles, 3,000 Companion Dog Excellent titles, and 600 Utility Dog titles. This chapter fills you in on what to expect.

The Utility Class: What's Expected from You and Buddy

The Utility class consists of six exercises, each with a specific point value (see Table 17-1). For a qualifying score, you and Buddy have to earn more than 50 percent of the available points for each exercise and a final score of at least 170 out of a possible 200.

Table 17-1	The Utility Class
Required Exercises	*Available Points*
Exercise 1: Signal	40
Exercise 2: Scent Discrimination, Article No. 1	30
Exercise 3: Scent Discrimination, Article No. 2	30
Exercise 4: Directed Retrieve	30
Exercise 5: Moving Stand with Examination	30
Exercise 6: Directed Jumping	40
Maximum Total Score	200

Not All Exercises Are Created Equal

We characterize the exercises the dogs are required to do in two categories:

- ✓ Action
- ✓ Control

Action exercises tend to be motivational for the dog — something he enjoys. Examples of action exercises are Heeling, Retrieving, Jumping, and Coming. *Control exercises* are demotivational — not something that is fun and exciting. Examples of control exercises are the Sit and Down-Stay, the drop for the Drop on Recall, and the Stand for Examination. The Front and the Finish can be either, depending on the dog's perception.

With that in mind, take a look at Table 17-2, which lists each category that the various exercises for the Utility class fall into.

Table 17-2	Drives and Categories for the Utility Class Exercises	
Required Exercise	*Behavior/Drive*	*Category*
Signal:		
Dog heels	Pack	Action
Dog stands at heel	Pack	Control
Dog lies down on signal	Pack	Control
Dog sits on signal	Pack	Control

Required Exercise	Behavior/Drive	Category
Dog comes on signal	Pack	Action
Scent Discrimination:		
Dog selects by scent one article out of eight	Prey	Control (that is, more control than action because the article is placed rather than thrown, and the dog has to discriminate)
Dog retrieves and brings it back to handler	Pack	Action
Directed Retrieve:		
Dog is sent out	Prey	Action
Dog retrieves one of three articles	Pack	Action
Moving Stand with Examination:		
Dog heels	Pack	Action
Dog stands on command	Pack	Control
Judge examines dog	Pack	Control
Dog goes to heel	Pack	Action
Directed Jumping:		
Dog leaves handler	Prey	Action
Dog jumps	Prey	Action

You can see from Table 17-2 that the potentially most devastating impact on the dog's motivation comes from the Signal exercise, which is immediately followed by another control exercise. It's not until the Directed Retrieve that the dog starts to have any real fun.

To maintain your dog's enthusiasm in practice sessions, alternate as much as possible between action and control exercises.

Obviously, the dog can learn the Signal exercise and even do it with some degree of verve, provided that you don't turn him off in the teaching and practicing phases. When you see that an exercise has a dampening effect on your dog, immediately follow it with something he likes, such as a Retrieve. You may have to split up the Signal exercise into its component parts to keep your dog motivated and only once or twice a week practice it the way it's supposed to be done.

Your dog doesn't look at all exercises in the same light. Some he considers more fun than others. By observing the impact an exercise has on your dog's psyche, you can keep him enthusiastic and motivated.

The Signal Exercise

For the Signal exercise, you dog needs to respond to the "Heel," "Stand," "Stay," "Drop," "Sit," and "Come" signals. The exercise starts with a regular heeling pattern. Then the judge says, "Stand your dog." At that point, you come to a halt and signal your dog to stand at the Heel position. The position is the same as the Automatic Sit at Heel except the dog has to stand at heel. The judge then tells you, "Leave your dog," and you give the "Stay" signal and go to the other side of the ring and face your dog. The judge then signals you to Drop, Sit, Call, and Finish your dog. You're not allowed to use verbal commands. The entire sequence is done without any verbal commands.

Giving the hand signal to heel

You give the hand signal to heel with your left hand, which moves from left to right, palm down, in front of the dog's eyes (see Figure 17-1). First, give the signal together with the command. After several repetitions, eliminate the command.

Getting Buddy to stand at heel on signal

You give the signal with your left hand, from right to left. Your palm is down and parallel to the ground, above and ahead of the dog's eyes.

The Stand isn't a very exciting or motivating exercise for your dog, so we don't recommend practicing it more than five times during a session. And always follow it with something your dog likes.

Figure 17-1:
Signaling
your dog to
heel.

Introducing Buddy to the "Stand" signal

Your Sequence 1 goal is to introduce your dog to the "Stand" signal:

1. **Review standing your dog at heel (see Chapter 14).**

2. **Put the thumb of your right hand through the collar under the dog's chin.**

3. **Stand your dog with the command and signal.**

4. **Make sure that his front feet remain in place.**

5. **Praise and release.**

6. **Repeat this sequence ten times, not necessarily at one session.**

Getting Buddy to stand at heel from motion

Your Sequence 2 goal is to teach your dog to stand at heel from motion:

1. **With Buddy off leash, in Heel position, say "Let's go" and start walking.**

2. **As you come to a halt, and before you've brought your feet together, place your right hand against your dog's chest, give the signal with your left hand, and say "Stand."**

   Concentrate on putting your right hand against his chest so that Buddy can't advance past Heel position.

   Also, make sure that you stop him *standing* in Heel position. If necessary, prevent him from sitting by placing your left hand against his right thigh.

3. **Praise and release with a treat.**

4. **Repeat this sequence five times per session over the course of several sessions.**

   After each Stand, praise and release enthusiastically with a treat. The object is to have Buddy stand at heel without any tension on the leash.

Getting Buddy to stand out of turns

Sequence 3's goal? To teach the stand out of turns:

Repeat Sequence 2 after a right turn, an about-turn, and a left turn.

Getting Buddy to stand from a fast pace

Sequence 4's goal is to teach the Stand from a fast pace:

Teach Buddy Sequence 2 from a fast pace. Although not absolutely necessary, standing him from a fast pace is a good indicator of how well he knows the stand at heel from motion. It's also a fun way to practice.

Getting Buddy to drop from a Stand and Sit from a Down

Use the same signal that you use for the Drop on Recall (see Chapter 16) by bringing your right arm straight up above your shoulder as though you're reaching for the ceiling.

Getting Buddy to drop from a Stand

Sequence 1's goal is to teach your dog to drop from a Stand:

1. **Stand your dog at heel, on leash.**

2. **Neatly fold the leash into your left hand.**

3. **Say "Stay" and step in front of your dog.**

4. **Kneel down and place two fingers of your left hand, palm facing down, through his collar, under his chin.**

5. **Signal with the right hand and say "Down," at the same time lightly pushing against his chest with your left hand. (See Figure 17-2.)**

   If necessary, apply a little downward pressure on his collar. (You can use either arm. For the sake of simplicity, we assume it's the right.)

   The purpose of the pressure against his chest is to prevent Buddy from moving his feet forward as he drops — the natural tendency for most dogs. You want to teach him to collapse in *place* because that's what the Obedience Regulations require. Look at his feet as you drop him. With pressure against his chest, they don't move forward.

   The downward pressure on the collar reinforces the drop. Be careful that you don't inadvertently pull him toward you because that would make him move his feet forward. Practice until he lies down in place without any pressure on his collar — and with the signal only.

6. **Say "Stay," stand up, praise, and release with a treat.**

Figure 17-2: Using the "Down" signal.

Getting Buddy to sit from a Down

Sequence 2's goal? To teach your dog to sit from a Down.

With your right arm hanging naturally at your side, the back of the hand facing the dog, turn your hand so the palm faces your dog. Then bring your arm out and away from your body, no higher than your waist, keeping your elbow locked. The object is to train your dog to respond to the turning of your hand. In the teaching phase, the arm moves in front of your body so you can lure Buddy into a Sit with a treat:

1. **On leash, down your dog from a Stand as in Sequence 1.**

2. **Say "Stay" and stand up.**

3. **Put your left hand, which holds the leash, against your right hip.**

4. **Have a treat in your right hand, held naturally at your side, and make sure that the back of your hand is toward the dog.**

5. **Say "Sit," turn your right hand so that the palm faces your dog, and lure your dog into a Sit with the treat.**

   Bring the treat to a point directly above his head so that your dog sits straight up by bringing his front feet under him rather than moving forward. Practice this maneuver until the dog sits as soon as you turn your right hand. That's what you want, so be sure you reward that response with a treat.

6. **Praise and release backward.**

Play a game of Sit from a Down and Down from a Sit. Hold the treat in your signal hand and randomly reward correct responses. Be sure to count to five after every change in position so that your dog can focus on what you want. Play only as long as Buddy is an enthusiastic participant.

Reinforcing the Sit

Sequence 3's goal is to teach the reinforcement of the Sit:

1. **Start as in Sequence 2 but without a treat in your hand.**

2. **Give the command and signal and — at the same time — give a little check with your right hand on the leash straight up, palm up, to a point directly above your dog's head.**

3. **Bring your hand back to your side.**

4. **Praise and release with a treat.**

This is the review progression for this exercise. Alternate on a random basis between using a treat and a little check. Then eliminate the command and practice until your dog responds reliably to the signal.

Increasing your distance

Sequence 4's goal? To increase the distance:

1. **Down and Sit your dog from three feet in front — on leash.**

2. **As you give the signal, take a step toward Buddy with your right foot, keeping your left leg in place.**

   The step toward your dog reinforces the response by keeping your dog in place and stops him from moving forward. Note that as you increase the distance, you may need to reinforce the Sit with a little check.

3. **Bring your leg and arm back to their original positions.**

4. **Praise and give him a treat for every correct response.**

After Buddy masters this exercise from three feet, increase the distance to six feet. As you increase the distance, continuing with the step is important. Remember, Buddy's natural tendency is to come to you, and you want him to drop and sit in place.

Introducing distractions

At this point in the training, introduce distractions, beginning with first degree (see Chapter 13 for info on the degrees). The distracter stands ten feet from the dog at a 45-degree angle. After you leave Buddy in a Stand, the distracter approaches in a nonthreatening, benign manner to within two feet of him. Give the "Drop" signal, with the step toward your dog. If he does drop, praise and enthusiastically release. If he doesn't drop, slowly go to him and reinforce the Down by putting two fingers of your *left* hand (not the one that gave the signal) through his collar, under his chin, and placing him down. When he does it correctly, praise, release with a treat, stop, and go on to something else.

Carefully work your way through the three levels of distractions from six feet in front, on leash. After that, take the leash off and gradually increase the distance until Buddy does the exercise with you standing 40 feet in front of him.

Giving the "Come" and "Finish" signals

Time to wrap up this whole Signal exercise:

1. **Leave your dog in a Sit-Stay and go to the end of the leash.**

2. **With your left hand holding the leash at your left side, say "Come" and give the signal by bringing your right arm shoulder high and then to the center of your chest.**

3. **Praise and release.**

   Note that at this point — when you release your dog — there is no Front or Finish.

4. **Do five repetitions of Steps 1 through 3 — not necessarily in a row or during the same session.**

5. **Now go through it again but eliminate the command; then praise and release.**

   If Buddy doesn't respond to the signal, give him a little tug on the leash.

   Be sure to practice without the command until your dog responds reliably to the signal.

6. **Now try the exercise off leash from six feet in front; then praise and release (see Figure 17-2).**

   From six feet away you can't expect much speed. There's little motivation to come quickly for such a short distance. As soon as you increase the distance, though, Buddy will pick up speed. Keep making it exciting for him by using a treat and the Release.

7. **For the Finish, use the same signal that you use for the Novice class and Open class.**

   Remember, you don't want to front or finish the dog every time he comes to you. Use the Release as an alternative.

The Scent Discrimination

Maybe you've already taught your dog the Find Mine trick with dollar bills (see Chapter 24). If so, this exercise should go quickly. The only difference between the two is that you perform the Scent Discrimination exercise with metal and leather articles, usually dumbbells, five of each. Buddy is first required to retrieve one, either metal or leather, and then the other, which you have scented, from among the remaining four leather and four metal.

 When teaching your dog the Scent Discrimination exercise, avoid the "he should know better" pitfall if your dog brings back the wrong article. Under no circumstances do you want to second-guess your dog. He obviously thought he retrieved the right one.

Getting Buddy to retrieve leather and metal articles

Your Sequence 1 goal is to teach your dog to retrieve leather and metal articles:

You may have to review the teaching progressions for the "Retrieve" command (see Chapter 15), depending on how your dog responds. Leather items are rarely a problem, but metal items can be. Your dog must retrieve either kind reliably before you can go on.

Getting Buddy to use his nose

Sequence 2's goal is to teach Buddy to use his nose:

First, you need to introduce him to the game of Find. For example, when training outside, hide the article around a corner. Let him see you take the article and return. Send him with "Find it." When he brings it back, release backward with great enthusiasm and reward him with a treat. Note that the first time you try this game, you may have to show him where you put the article.

As Buddy catches on, increase the difficulty so that he has to use his nose to find the article.

Introducing Buddy to the articles

Your Sequence 3 goal is to introduce Buddy to the articles:

For this purpose, use a *scent board,* a piece of pegboard commensurate with the size of your dog and large enough to accommodate all eight articles placed six inches apart. Get Buddy accustomed to walking on the board by heeling him over it several times and having him sit on it. Then have him retrieve an article from the board — first by throwing it on the board and then by placing it on the board. Release backward and reward. ***Note:*** You want your dog to be comfortable retrieving from the board before you begin to add other articles.

Prepare the board for the next sequence by tying one of each article on the board, with the tie underneath. Let the board air out for 24 hours so it has little, if any, of your scent on it.

Tying an article to a board prevents the dog from picking up the incorrect article and encourages him to keep looking for the right one. You can also tie the articles to a piece of carpeting, although some of the larger dogs sometimes bring back the entire piece of carpeting. If that happens to you, use a board.

Teaching Buddy Scent Discrimination

Sequence 4's goal is to teach your dog Scent Discrimination:

1. **Make sure that your hands are clean and free from chemicals and perfumes.**

2. **With you and Buddy facing the board from ten feet away, scent a metal article by slowly rubbing the bar of the dumbbell for 20 seconds and briefly let him hold the article.**

3. **Take the article out of his mouth, say "Stay," and place the article on the board, letting him watch you place it on the board.**

4. **Go back to heel and send him with "Find it."**

5. **If Buddy tries to pick up an incorrect article, encourage him to keep looking by saying, "You can do it!" in an excited tone of voice — or anything other than the original command.**

6. **When he picks up the correct one, quietly say "That's it" with a big smile on your face.**

7. **Release backward and reward.**

Repeat the sequence by placing the scented leather article in a different location on the board until you're sure that Buddy is using his nose to find the correct article. At the same time, gradually increase the distance you stand from the board to 20 feet. During this sequence, stop the praise for picking up the correct article but continue to smile. You don't want Buddy to become dependent on praise and wait for it before he returns, so eliminate it as soon as you can. Release and reward Buddy after he has returned. Stop after two successive successful responses — one metal and one leather.

Tie two more articles on the board and let the board air out for about two hours before the next round. After each successful round, tie two more articles on the board until all eight articles are tied on the board, letting the board air out after each addition of articles.

Getting Buddy to discriminate between your scent and someone else's

Sequence 5's goal is to teach your dog discrimination between your scent and another person's. Up until now, Buddy has learned only to find your article among unscented ones. The object of this exercise is to teach him to find your article among those that someone else has touched.

Before you send your dog, have a helper briefly touch the articles on the board. Then place yours. You and Buddy are still facing the board.

Some handlers make an effort to give the dog their scent by briefly holding their hand in front of the dog's nose. We feel that by now your dog should know your scent and consider the effort superfluous. It also loads up the dog's nose with scent just when you want his nose to be clear.

Some dogs catch on quickly, and others need to go back to the beginning with two articles tied down. You'll have to experiment with Buddy to see how he does. Try it with all eight articles tied down. If he gets hopelessly confused, start at the beginning.

When your dog is reliable at this step, introduce distractions the same way that you do for the Retrieve.

Weaning Buddy off the board

Your Sequence 6 goal is to wean your dog off the board:

Reverse the procedure and untie two articles. After each successful round, stop. Over the course of several sessions, repeat until all the articles are loose on the board. If he comes back with the wrong article, slowly approach him, take the article out of his mouth, take him back to the starting position, and send him again. Don't do anything that might discourage your dog.

Teaching your dog the Scent Discrimination exercise mainly involves building his confidence. You want to encourage him and not discourage him.

Doing this exercise on the board and doing it on any other surface isn't the same. Begin to wean Buddy from the board by placing the scented article on the floor/ground in front of the board. When he is successful, using ordinary kitchen tongs, place two unscented articles on the floor/ground in front of the board, along with the scented one. When he's steady retrieving the correct article, place the remainder of the articles, two at a time, on the floor/ground in front of the board. After he is reliable with all the articles on the floor/ground, eliminate the board.

Right after it looks like Buddy has finally gotten the hang of it, he may go through one or more regressions, meaning that he may give the appearance of not having the foggiest idea of what this exercise is all about. You can recognize it by the number of successive incorrect responses: He brings back the wrong article, you send him again, and he brings back another incorrect article, and so on. This situation is *normal,* and you should expect it. The best advice we can give you is to put him back on the board for several days as a form of review.

Teaching Buddy the Turn and Send

Sequence 7's goal is to teach your dog the Turn and Send:

1. **For the finished product, you and Buddy will have your backs turned to the eight articles as the judge places the article that you scented among the unscented articles.**

   The judge then says, "Send your dog."

2. **You can then make a right about-turn in place, at the same time sending your dog, or you can have him Sit at Heel and then send him.**

3. **With Buddy in Heel position, show him the article, give the command "Find it," make an about-turn in place, and throw the article, letting him chase it.**

4. **Practice several times until Buddy catches on to the maneuver.**

5. **Put out your articles and repeat the procedure, only this time throwing the article into the pile.**

6. **Following a few repetitions of that maneuver, line up with Buddy in Heel position with your backs to the articles from about 20 feet away.**

7. **Tell him to stay, place your scented article in the pile, return to Buddy, and send him with "Find it" as you make an about-turn in place to the right.**

Unless there's a compelling reason to have your dog Sit at Heel, we suggest that you send him as you make the turn. It's more motivational.

The Directed Retrieve

This particular exercise requires Buddy to retrieve one of three predominantly white gloves, such as white cotton gardening variety, which are placed at the unobstructed end of the ring about 15 feet apart. You're required to give your dog the direction to the designated glove with a single motion of the left arm and hand and a verbal command.

The exercise starts with you and Buddy in the center of the ring with your backs to the gloves. The judge says something like "Glove number one," which designates the glove behind you on your right. Glove number two is the one directly behind you, and number three is the one to your left.

Other than teaching Buddy how to retrieve a glove, the only new maneuver you have to teach Buddy is the turns in place, with the emphasis on *place*. When working on the turns in place, keep in mind that the more accurate your dog is on Heel position, the less likely he is to make a mistake.

The turns in place are the make-or-break maneuvers for the Directed Retrieve exercise.

All turns in place start with Buddy sitting at heel, leash in Control Position.

Teaching a right turn in place

You can teach this turn in three progressions — first placing your right leg, and then taking a step on the right leg, and then making the turn in place by turning your right foot at a 90-degree angle to the left, heel to heel to the left:

- **Progression 1:** Place your right foot at a 90-degree angle one large step to the right. With "Buddy, heel," close with your left foot and guide your dog into Heel position. Praise and release. Repeat 25 times.

- **Progression 2:** Say "Buddy, heel," take a step to the right, close with the left, and guide your dog into Heel position. Praise and release. Repeat 25 times.

- **Progression 3:** Say "Buddy, heel" and turn in place to the right, closing with the left. Praise and release.

Teaching a right about-turn in place

Here's what you need to do:

- **Progression 1:** Say "Buddy, heel," take two steps forward, turn around to your right (keeping your feet together), take two steps forward, and guide your dog into Heel position. Praise and release. Repeat 25 times.

- **Progression 2:** Say "Buddy, heel," take one step forward, turn around, take one step forward, and guide your dog into Heel position. Praise and release. Repeat 25 times.

- **Progression 3**: Say "Buddy, heel," make two right turns in place, and guide your dog into Heel position. Praise and release.

Teaching a left turn in place

Here are your progressions:

- ✔ **Progression 1:** Place your left foot directly in front of your dog's front feet. Say "Buddy, heel," take a large step with your right foot (past the left), and close with the left, guiding your dog into Heel position with slight backward pressure on the leash. Praise and release. Repeat 25 times over the course of several sessions.

- ✔ **Progression 2:** Place your left foot directly in front of your dog's front feet. Say "Buddy, heel," take a small step with your right foot (past the left), and close with the left, guiding your dog into Heel position with slight backward pressure on the leash. Praise and release. Repeat 25 times over the course of several sessions.

- ✔ **Progression 3:** Say "Buddy, heel," put your right foot at a 90-degree angle directly in front of your left (in a T position), and guide your dog into Heel position with slight backward pressure on the leash. Praise and release. Repeat 25 times over the course of several sessions.

- ✔ **Progression 4:** Say "Buddy, heel" and make two left turns in place, guiding your dog into Heel position with slight backward pressure on the leash. Praise and release.

Teaching how to retrieve the gloves

Give the direction by holding your left arm at the side of the dog's head, and your fingers pointing straight to the glove. Immediately following, say "Take it." What you may not do is give your dog the direction and then pump your left arm as you send him for the glove.

Although the Obedience Regulations permit you to send your dog as you give the direction, the regulations also permit you to first point in the direction of the glove, called *marking,* immediately followed by the command "Take it."

For the center glove, your arm is stretched out so that your elbow is in line with the dog's nose, which gives him a better mark. You may bend your body and knees to the extent necessary in giving the direction to your dog. When giving the direction, make sure that your fingers are indeed pointing at the designated glove.

Before you start on this exercise, you may want to review the "Retrieve" command with a glove.

Here's what you do:

- ✔ **Progression 1:** With your dog sitting at heel and a glove in your left hand (held between your thumb and fingers), get your dog excited about the glove. Throw the glove, holding your arm as you would if you were to mark the glove, and say "Take it." After he picks it up, praise and release. If he doesn't retrieve, review teaching him to retrieve the glove (see Chapter 15 for retrieving).

- ✔ **Progression 2:** After your dog retrieves the glove and you've introduced him to the direction, place a glove 15 feet to your right, 15 feet to your left, and 15 feet in front of you. Say "Buddy, heel" and make a right turn in place. Buddy now faces the glove on your right. Mark the direction with your left arm. You may have to hold on to your dog by placing two fingers of your right hand through his collar. Send your dog with "Take it." Praise and release after he has picked up the glove.

  Repeat for the glove on the left and the center glove. After three successful repetitions, move the gloves on your right and left two feet straight ahead and start all over. After each set of three successful repetitions, move the gloves on your right and left two feet straight ahead until they're in line with the center glove. Send your dog to different gloves in a random pattern.

What if he goes to the wrong glove? Let him try to work it out for himself by maintaining the signal. For example, suppose that Buddy goes to number two rather than number one. Hold the signal facing number one. When Buddy returns to you, he immediately notices that something is wrong: You're not standing up straight but are still pointing to the glove. He may try to do one of several things, like

- ✔ Insist on giving you the glove, which you don't take.

- ✔ Give up and do nothing.

- ✔ Go for another glove, probably the correct one.

If he retrieves the correct glove, stand up, praise, and release. If he does nothing, approach the number one glove while still holding the signal and get him to pick it up — preferably just by pointing at it and without an extra command. When he does, praise and release. If he doesn't, reinforce the Retrieve.

Every time you help your dog, you're assuming the responsibility for his behavior. You want him to learn that it's *his* responsibility to make the right decision. To do that, you have to give him a chance to work things out for himself.

After Buddy has learned the direction portion of the exercise, you can introduce the Turn and Send. Remember that Buddy won't see the gloves being placed; he'll have his back to them in the ring. The Obedience Regulations permit you to turn either to the left or to the right when making the turn in place to face the designated glove. You need to experiment to discover which is best for you and your dog.

The Moving Stand with Examination

For this exercise, you're required to heel your dog for about ten feet when the judge tells you to "Stand your dog." Without pausing or breaking your stride, you give the command and/or signal to stand and continue walking 10 to 12 feet. Then you turn and face your dog. The judge examines your dog, a little more thoroughly than he does in the Novice class, and then he says, "Call your dog to heel." You then give the command and/or signal for Buddy to go *directly* to heel.

Here are the progressions:

✔ **Progression 1:** With your dog on leash and at heel, say "Let's go" and start walking. After several steps, give the signal to stand, say "Stay," and continue walking. When you get to the end of the leash, turn and face your dog. Tell him what a clever fellow he is, count to five, and release. Practice ten times over the course of several sessions.

For the Moving Stand, the dog must Stand and Stay on command without taking any steps forward while you keep walking.

If Buddy needs help, use the same technique you use to teach a Stand at Heel (see Chapter 14).

Now try it off leash.

✔ **Progression 2:** Start again with your dog on leash. Take several steps, stand your dog, go to the end of the leash, and face him. Count to five, signal, and say "Buddy, heel," guiding him into Heel position. Praise and release. The Obedience Regulations permit you to give both the signal to heel and the command for this exercise.

When Buddy correctly goes to Heel On Leash, try it off leash. Then gradually increase the distance you leave him in a Stand until you can go about 10 to 12 feet, as required by the regulations, before you turn and face him.

✔ **Progression 3:** Finally, you need to practice the examination part of the exercise with a helper.

The Directed Jumping

For this exercise, your dog has to go — on command — from one end of the ring to the other, between the bar and the high jump. The bar and the high jump are in the center of the ring about 18 feet apart. You then give your dog the command and/or signal for one of the jumps, after which he has to front and then finish. The entire procedure is then repeated for the other jump.

The "Go-Out" command takes a little time to teach because the dog can see absolutely no rhyme nor reason for this exercise.

We approach this exercise in three parts: the Go-Out, the jumps, and putting the two together. When Buddy has learned the Go-Out and the Directed Jumping parts, put them together.

Teaching Buddy the "Go-Out" command

For Progression 1 and to teach Buddy to leave, use food or an object, like a stick or a toy. To teach him where to go, use a box, made from PVC pipe, that's commensurate to the size of the dog. Then put the box in front of a barrier, such as a section of fencing or the side of a house.

1. **Get your dog used to the box by heeling him into the box and then calling him into it.**

2. **Put a target (see Chapter 16) inside the box.**

3. **With Buddy on leash, show him a treat and say "Out" as both of you go into the box.**

4. **Place the treat on the target and let him pick it up. Praise, encourage him to turn around in the box, and release backward.**

5. **Repeat until Buddy is comfortable with going into and turning in the box.**

6. **Leave Buddy in a Sit-Stay ten feet in front of the target, let him see you place a treat on the target, go back to Heel position, and send him with "Buddy, out."**

   You may signal him at the same time with your left hand in the direction you want him to go.

7. **When he gets to the target, let him take the treat, praise, and call him back.**

With each successive repetition, increase the distance to the target by two feet until you're 75 feet from the target. Repeat at that distance 50 times over the course of several sessions.

Teaching the Go-Out is pure target training with the addition of the box so that the dog knows where to sit.

Now you're ready for Progression 2:

1. **Remove the target.**

2. **Leave Buddy in a Sit-Stay ten feet from the barrier, go into the box, face your dog, point to the ground, and go back to Heel position.**

3. **Send your dog and, after he has left, quietly follow him so that when he gets to the spot you indicated, you're in front of the box.**

4. **Say "Buddy, sit," using the "Sit" hand signal and a step forward to make him sit in place.**

5. **Reward him with a treat, held in the hand that gave the signal.**

   From now on, Buddy is only rewarded for going to the designated spot, and he has to learn that the reward comes from you. If your dog has difficulty catching on, don't hesitate to reintroduce the target on a random basis.

With each successive repetition, increase the distance to the target by two feet until you're 75 feet from the target. Repeat at that distance 50 times over the course of several sessions.

The Obedience Regulations don't specify the commands you have to use, and the commands don't have to be in English. But excessively loud commands, as in yelling at the dog, aren't permitted.

During this progression, Buddy learns to turn and sit in the box. Continue to follow him and use the step and signal so he understands that you want him to turn and sit immediately. The step and signal prevent him from getting into the habit of taking several steps toward you, which you don't want.

So what do you do if Buddy doesn't leave or only goes part of the way? Without saying anything, slowly approach him, put two fingers of your left hand through the collar (back to front, palm facing you, at the side of his neck), and take him to the spot you indicated. Reinforce with "Sit," let go, give him a treat, and release. Send him again.

Now for Progression 3 — sending your dog two times in a row:

1. **Leave Buddy in a Sit-Stay, go into the box, point to the spot, and go back to Heel position.**

2. **Send him and, when he gets to the spot, say "Buddy, sit."**

3. **Praise, count to five, release, and call him back to you.**

4. **Line him up at Heel position and send him again.**

5. **When he gets there, have him sit; then go to him, praise, reward, and release.**

Repeat this sequence 50 times.

If he doesn't leave you or doesn't go to the designated spot, show him where you want him to go. To keep your dog motivated, frequently reintroduce the target with a treat.

Introduce distractions as you have for previous exercises by having the distracter first stand midway between you and the designated spot, two feet from Buddy's line of travel and then two feet from the designated spot. Work your way through first, second, and third degree distractions. If Buddy veers away from the distracter, use two distracters, starting at eight feet apart, and teach him to go straight through.

Teaching Buddy Directed Jumping

Progression 1 is to introduce your dog to the bar jump:

1. **Set the bar jump at *teaching height* (the height of your dog at the elbows).**

2. **Walk your dog up to the jump, on leash (dead ring), and touch the bar with your left hand.**

3. **Let him investigate the jump.**

4. **Start from ten feet away, say "Bar," and briskly walk toward the jump.**

5. **Let him jump as you go over with him or around the jump.**

Repeat until he jumps without any hesitation.

Progression 2 is to introduce your dog to direction:

1. **Set up the high and the bar jumps at teaching height, 18 feet apart.**

2. **Place your target ten feet from the center of the high jump.**

3. **Leave your dog in a Sit-Stay facing the high jump.**

4. **Go over the jump to the target and place a treat on the target.**

5. **Stand two feet behind the target facing your dog.**

6. **Say "Jump" and give the signal by bringing your arm up from your side, shoulder height, pointed toward the jump.**

   Buddy should go over the jump to reach the target and his treat.

7. **Praise and release.**

8. **Repeat the exercise for the bar jump, saying "Bar."**

You can now begin to work your way to the center position — 20 feet from the jumps and centered between them. Position Buddy facing the stanchion of the high/bar jump. Go over the jump and position yourself facing the same stanchion from the other side. Send Buddy to the target, praise, and release.

Gradually work your way back and to the center until both you and Buddy are 20 feet from the jumps, facing each other at opposite ends in the center. You always need to be in the mirror position to Buddy. Always step over the jump and place your treat. Then test Buddy's understanding by eliminating the target.

Begin raising the jumps in two- or four-inch increments, depending on your dog's size. Difficulties with jumping are never disciplinary. If your dog is having a problem with a jump, he's trying to tell you something. Listen to him.

Putting it all together

You're ready to combine the Go-Out with Directed Jumping:

1. **Put your box in front of the fence.**

2. **Leave Buddy midway between the two jumps.**

3. **Go to the box and point to the spot where you want him to go.**

4. **Return to Heel position, send him to the box, and tell him to sit and stay.**

   Buddy remains in the box for the Sit-Stay.

5. **Go back to the spot from which you are ultimately going to send him, that is, 20 feet from the centerline between the jumps.**

6. **Give the command and signal to jump.**

7. **Praise as he lands and release.**

Repeat the exercise for the other jump.

Now start with Buddy at Heel position, two feet back from the centerline between the jumps, and follow the same procedure. Repeat in two-foot increments until you stand at the appropriate spot for the exercise before sending your dog. This procedure is a precaution for the first few times you put the Go-Out together with the Directed Jumping. It should prevent Buddy from coming up with the idea (as he otherwise might) that he has to jump on the way out.

After every two Go-Outs, reinforce that exercise with five repetitions into the box. Reward the first, third, and fifth with a treat.

Give your dog a chance to work out on his own what it is you want. Before you jump in to help him, see what he does. He may surprise you. Be patient and keep your mouth shut.

What if Buddy makes a mistake and goes over the wrong jump? Try letting him work it out. Maintain your signal and wait. The response you want to see is Buddy going back into or near the box without any help or command from you. When he does, lower your arm, tell him to sit, and repeat the signal.

Suppose that Buddy does nothing and just sits in front of you not knowing what to do. Give him a chance until you're absolutely certain that he has stopped trying. Then take him back to where he started, leave him, return, and send him again.

Seeing a dog have the Aha! response — Buddy shows you that the penny has dropped and he's figured out what you want — is perhaps one of the most exciting aspects of dog training. To get there, you must never discourage your dog from trying, even if the response is incorrect. Permit and encourage your dog to solve these training problems, and you'll have a motivated student.

Part IV
Beyond Training: Addressing Your Dog's Needs

The 5th Wave · By Rich Tennant

"I don't think teaching the puppy how to help you cheat at cards was the training and bonding experience the Vet had in mind."

In this part . . .

Feeding your dog foods that keep him physically healthy contributes a great deal to his overall well-being and behavior — which ensures that training will be fun and rewarding for both of you. Because your dog's health is so important, this part talks about two issues that can affect how he behaves or misbehaves. Even the best-trained dogs can exhibit undesirable behaviors from time to time. If you understand the causes of the behavior, you can redirect Buddy and coax him back to being his polite old self. And meeting your dog's physical needs — with both preventive care and care for acute conditions — can help ensure that the two of you have a long and fulfilling life together. Finally, this part is where to look for professional help to train your dog.

Chapter 18

Feeding Your Dog

*Y*our dog's behavior, happiness, health, longevity, and overall well being are inextricably intertwined with what you feed him. Dogs, just like humans and all other animals, have specific nutritional requirements that need to be met. And to complicate matters, the needs of dogs vary. For example, even though your first dog may have done wonderfully well on Barfo Special Blend, the same food may be completely wrong for Buddy. Every dog has his own nutritional needs that may be quite dissimilar to those of your neighbor's dog. What your dog eats has a tremendous impact on his health and his trainability.

We aren't trying to turn you into an expert on canine nutrition, but you do need to know some basic concepts. If you do want to become an expert on feeding your dog, see *The Holistic Guide for a Healthy Dog,* 2nd Edition, by Wendy Volhard and Kerry Brown, DVM (Wiley).

You also need to know the most common and most visible symptoms of nutritional deficiencies. Recognizing these deficiencies saves you a great deal of money in veterinary bills because you can make the necessary adjustments to your dog's diet.

In this chapter, we discuss your dog's nutritional needs, finding the right food to maintain your dog's health, and how to interpret dog food labels. We also include a brief overview of your dog's digestive system functions. Finally, you can find our suggestions for several feeding options that meet both your lifestyle and your dog's needs.

Finding the Right Food for Your Dog

Not all dog foods are alike; there are enormous quality differences. The cliché "garbage in, garbage out" applies with terrifying validity. So many choices are available today that trying to make an informed decision can become an overwhelming task. In this section, we help you tackle the job by the process of elimination. Two commonly used criteria immediately come to mind: advertising and price.

In choosing a food for your dog, forget about advertising and price. They aren't valid criteria for selection. You need to make the decision based on what is in the food and on your dog's nutritional requirements.

- **Forget about advertising.** Disregard what the ad says about how good this food is for your dog. It may be okay for Buddy, but perhaps it isn't. You have to look at the food's ingredients.

- **Forget about price.** This works both ways. Just because one brand of food costs more doesn't necessarily mean it's better than a less expensive variety.

Following is a quick checklist to help you determine whether Buddy is getting what he needs. Note that for each item Buddy, not an advertisement, is the source of your information.

- ❑ He doesn't want to eat the food.
- ❑ He has large, voluminous stools that smell awful.
- ❑ He has gas.
- ❑ His teeth get dirty and brown.
- ❑ His breath smells.
- ❑ He burps a lot.
- ❑ He constantly sheds.
- ❑ He has a dull coat.
- ❑ He smells like a dog.
- ❑ He is prone to ear and skin infections.
- ❑ He has no energy or is hyperactive.
- ❑ He easily picks up fleas.
- ❑ He easily picks up worms and has to be wormed frequently.

All the items in the previous checklist happen occasionally with any dog — but only occasionally. When several of the items on the list occur frequently or continuously, you need to find out why.

Reading labels and making choices

On the back of every dog food package is information that helps you decide which food is right for your dog. The information lists the ingredients in order of weight, beginning with the heaviest item. The package contains the guaranteed analysis for crude protein, fat, fiber, moisture, ash, and often calcium, phosphorus, and magnesium ratios. The label may also state that the food is nutritionally complete or provides 100 percent nutrition for the dog. To make this claim, the food has to meet the nutrient requirements of the Association of American Feed Control Officers (AAFCO) — a guarantee that some form of testing, usually anywhere from two to six weeks, has been done on the product.

A dog food company must also list its name and address and give its telephone number, plus the date of manufacture, the weight of the product in the package, and usually the life stage for which the food is intended. The life stage can be puppy, maintenance, adult, performance, old age, or light food for overweight dogs.

If Buddy doesn't eat the amount recommended for his weight on the package, he's not getting the Minimum Daily Requirement of known nutrients.

The saying "You get what you pay for" isn't necessarily true with dog food. There is a surprisingly small difference between good and not-so-good food, and some not-so-good foods are higher priced than good foods!

The following types of dog food are available:

- **Performance:** A high-quality food, performance food lists two or three animal proteins in the first five ingredients — usually two kinds (chicken and lamb, chicken and fish, beef and chicken, and so on).

  Although these foods are marketed primarily for working or breeding animals, they're the best-quality foods on the market for all dogs. Performance foods also contain the correct quantity of fats and oils needed for energy, good coat, and skin. Performance foods don't contain soy, which dogs can't digest.

- **Super Premium 1:** These foods usually contain an animal protein first, followed by several grains. Although they provide energy for your dog from high fat levels, they're not as good as the performance foods because they contain less animal protein.

✔ **Premium:** These dog foods contain a high level of protein, but you need to look at the source because the protein can come from grains and not animal protein. These foods may also contain soy.

✔ **Regular, Econo, Low Protein, or Light (Lite):** Foods listed with these names are full of grains and are guaranteed to make your dog into a couch potato. They're animal protein deficient and, although marketed for the older dog, in our opinion they should be taken off the market. They produce voluminous smelly stools, caused by the inability of the dog to break down and digest this food. Dogs fed this diet for any length of time show classic signs of animal protein deficiencies (see the "Animal protein deficiencies" sidebar later in this chapter).

Giving meat to a carnivore

Your dog is a carnivore and not a vegetarian. He needs meat. His teeth are quite different from yours — they're made for ripping and tearing meat. They don't have flat surfaces for grinding up grains. His digestion starts in his stomach and not in his mouth. All the enzymes in his system are geared toward breaking down meat and raw foods. Buddy is a carnivore, and he needs to eat meat to stay healthy.

Your dog's body, as well as yours, consists of cells, a lot of them. Each cell needs 45 nutrients to function properly. The cells need the following:

✔ Protein, consisting of 9 to 12 essential amino acids

✔ Carbohydrates

✔ Fat

✔ Vitamins

✔ Minerals

✔ Water

All these nutrients need to be in the correct proportion for the necessary chemical reactions of digestion, absorption, transportation, and elimination to occur. If the cells are going to be able to continue to live, the exact composition of the body fluids that bathe the outside of the cells needs to be controlled from moment to moment, day by day, with no more than a few percentage points variation.

These nutrients are the fuel, which is converted into energy. Energy produces heat and how much heat is produced determines the ability of your dog to control his body temperature. Everything your dog does, from running and playing, to working and living a long and healthy life, is determined by the fuel you provide and the energy it produces.

The term *calorie* is used to measure energy in food. Optimally, every dog will eat the quantity of food he needs to meet his caloric needs. The food you feed must provide sufficient calories so your dog's body can achieve the following:

✔ Produce energy to grow correctly

✔ Maintain health during adulthood

✔ Reproduce

✔ Grow into a quality old age

Keeping your dog's diet rich in protein

The back of dog food packages tell you how much protein is in the food. How much protein is in dog food is important, but even more important is the source.

The manufacturer has choices as to what kind of protein to put into the food. The percentage of protein on the package generally is a combination of proteins found in plants or grains, such as corn, wheat, soy, and rice, plus an animal protein, such as chicken, beef, or lamb.

By law, the heaviest and largest amount of whatever ingredient contained in the food has to be listed first. By looking at the list of ingredients, you can easily discover the protein's origin. For example, if the first five ingredients listed come from four grains, the majority of the protein in that food comes from grains. The more grains in a dog food, the cheaper it is to produce. We wonder what Buddy thinks of such a food.

The activity level of your dog is likely to correspond with the amount of animal protein he needs in his diet. The majority of the Working breeds, Sporting breeds, Toys, and Terriers need extra animal protein in their diets. For instance, the busy little Jack Russell is apt to need more animal protein than a pooch that spends his time lying around the house.

Amino acid is the name given to the building blocks of protein, and when heated, they're partially destroyed. All dry and canned commercial dog food is heated in the manufacturing process. So commercial food contains protein that is chemically changed by heat and therefore deficient in amino acids. We show you how to compensate for that at in the "Feeding Buddy" section later in this chapter.

Animal protein deficiencies

When Buddy doesn't get enough animal protein or his diet is unbalanced in nutrients, one or more of the following may occur:

- ✓ Aggression
- ✓ Chronic skin and/or ear infections
- ✓ Compromised reproductive system, heart, kidney, liver, bladder, and thyroid and adrenal glands
- ✓ Excessive shedding
- ✓ Gastrointestinal upsets, vomiting, or diarrhea
- ✓ Impaired ability to heal from wounds or surgery, such as spaying and neutering

- ✓ Lack of pigmentation
- ✓ Poor appetite
- ✓ Some kind of epilepsy or cancers
- ✓ Spinning or tail chasing
- ✓ Timidity
- ✓ Weakened immune system that can't properly tolerate vaccines

This is only a short list of the more common symptoms associated with an animal protein deficiency.

Identifying Food for Growth at Critical Times

In contrast to humans, dogs grow *fast*. During the first 7 months of Buddy's life, his birth weight increases anywhere from 15 to 40 times, depending upon his breed. By 1 year of age, his birth weight increases 60 times and his skeletal development is almost complete. For strength and proper growth to occur, he needs the right food. He also needs twice the amount of food as an adult while he is growing, especially during growth spurts. Nutritional deficiencies at an early age, even for short periods, can cause problems later on.

The most critical period for a puppy is between 4 and 7 months, the time of maximum growth. His little body is being severely stressed as his baby teeth drop out and his adult teeth come in. He's growing like a weed, and at the same time his body is being assaulted with a huge number of vaccines. During this time of growth, Buddy needs the right food so that his immune system can cope with all these demands and onslaughts.

To find out how you can protect him as best as possible, you need to take a look at different dog foods to find the ones that best meet the criteria for young Buddy's growth. In the following sections we give you some ideas of which foods to choose and what to add to them to make up for the deficiencies caused in processing.

Deciphering puppy food labels

Puppy foods do contain more protein than adult or maintenance foods. Manufacturers know that puppies need more protein for growth. Nonetheless, you still need to know the source of the protein — that is, animal or plant.

Look for a puppy food that has two animal proteins in the first three ingredients — or better yet, one that lists animal protein as its first two ingredients.

After you have selected a food for young Buddy on the basis of its protein percentage, your job isn't quite done yet. You have to check a few of the other following items.

Going easy on the carbohydrates

Your dog also needs carbohydrates found in grains and some vegetables for proper digestion. The digestive process first breaks down carbohydrates into starch and then into simple sugars and glucose, necessary for energy and proper functioning of the brain. Buddy also needs carbohydrates for stool formation and correct functioning of the thyroid gland.

Dogs don't need many carbohydrates to be healthy, and a diet low in carbohydrates and high in protein is an ideal diet. Oats, barley, and brown rice are carbohydrates that contain a lot of vitamins and minerals. They also contain protein and fat. Corn is popular because of its low price. Other sources of carbohydrates are vegetables, especially root vegetables.

Soy is another carbohydrate found in some foods. Soy admittedly is high in protein, but it binds other nutrients and makes them unavailable for absorption. We recommend that you stay away from dog foods containing soy.

Carbohydrates have to be broken down for the dog to be able to digest them. Dog food companies use a heat process to do so, and therein lies a problem. The heat process destroys many of the vitamins and minerals contained in carbohydrates. The question that comes immediately to mind is, "Where do dogs in the wild get the grains and vegetables they need?" The answer is from the intestines of their prey, all neatly predigested.

Knowing the value of fats — in moderation

Fat is either *saturated* or *polyunsaturated,* and your dog needs both. Saturated fat comes from animal sources, and polyunsaturated fat comes from vegetable sources. Together they supply the essential fatty acids (EFA) necessary to maintain good health.

In the manufacturing of the majority of dog foods, fat is sprayed on as the last ingredient. Fat makes the dog food palatable, like potato chips and French fries.

Saturated fat comes from animal sources and is used for energy. For dogs that get a great deal of exercise or participate in competitive events, the food needs to contain 20 percent animal fat. Not enough animal fat in your dog's diet can create

- Cell damage
- Dry skin
- Heart problems
- Growth deficits
- Lack of energy

On the other hand, too much animal fat in the diet creates

- Cancer of the colon and rectum
- Mammary gland tumors
- Obesity

Polyunsaturated fat is found in vegetable sources, such as flax seed oil, safflower oil, wheat germ oil, olive oil, and corn oil. Your dog needs polyunsaturated fat for a healthy skin and coat. Too little of this fat can produce skin lesions on the belly, thighs, and between the shoulder blades. If your dog has a dry coat, you may need to add oil to his food.

Linoleic acid is one of the three essential fatty acids that have to be provided daily in your dog's food. Safflower and flax seed oil provide the best source of linoleic acid and are the least allergenic. These oils are better than corn oil, which contains only a tiny amount of linoleic acid.

Lack of polyunsaturated fat in your dog's diet can cause

- Coarse, dry coat
- Extreme itching and scratching
- Horny skin growths
- Improper growth
- Poor blood clotting
- Skin lesions on the belly, inside the back legs, and between the shoulder blades

   ✔ Skin ulcerations and infections

   ✔ Thickened areas of skin

Look for food that contains both animal and vegetable oils.

What else is in this food?

Dog food manufacturers have choices on how to preserve the fat in food to prevent it from becoming rancid, such as using the chemicals BHA, BHT, ethoxyquin, or propyl gallate. If a fat is preserved with these chemicals, it has a long shelf life and isn't significantly affected by heat and light. Even so, many dog owners prefer not to feed these chemicals to their dogs, especially ethoxyquin. (Check out the sidebar, "Common chemicals used in dog foods" in this chapter for more info on these chemicals.)

A manufacturer can also use natural preservatives, such as vitamins C and E and rosemary extract. Vitamin E is listed as *tocopherol*. The downside to natural preservatives is a shorter shelf life, no more than six months, *provided* the food is stored in a cool, dark place

Common chemicals used in dog foods

When you're reading dog food packages, distinguishing what a preservative is and isn't can be difficult. Following is a list of the more common chemicals seen on the packages:

✔ **Antioxidants:** Used to preserve the fats in the food. These are BHA, BHT, ethoxyquin, and propyl gallate. Ethoxyquin has been linked to birth defects and immune disorders, so you may want to stay away from products that contain it.

✔ **Humectants:** Used to prevent food from drying out or getting too moist. These are calcium silicate, propylene glycol, glycerine, and sorbitol.

✔ **Mold inhibitors:** Used to retard the growth of molds and yeast. These are potassium salts, sodium or calcium proprionate, sodium diacetate, sorbic acid, and acetic or lactic acid.

✔ **Sequestrants:** Used to prevent physical or chemical changes to the color, odor, flavor, or appearance of the food. These are sodium, potassium or calcium salts, and citric, tartaric, or pyrophosphoric acids.

✔ **Texturizers:** Not preservatives as such but used in meats to maintain their texture and color. The most common are sodium nitrite and sodium nitrate.

Note that natural preservatives are vitamins C and E and rosemary extract. Vitamin E is often listed as tocopherol.

What else isn't in this food?

Your dog needs vitamins in his food to release the nutrients and enzymes from the ingested food so that his body can absorb and use them. Without vitamins, your dog can't break down food and use it.

In researching our book *The Holistic Guide for a Healthy Dog,* (Wiley), we called dog food manufacturers to ask them their source of vitamins and how they protected them against destruction from the heat process. Their responses were astonishing. They acknowledged awareness of the problem, and, to overcome it, they added more vitamins to the food to make up the difference. Of course, doing so is nonsense. If vitamins are destroyed by heat, it doesn't make any difference how much you put in the food. They'll still be destroyed.

We also discovered that most of the finished products weren't tested. In other words, vitamins and minerals go into the food, but what actually reaches your dog seems as much a mystery to some of the manufacturers as it is to us.

Two types of vitamins exist — water-soluble and fat-soluble. Water-soluble vitamins are B and C. Any excess is filtered through the kidneys and urinated out between four to eight hours after ingestion. For this reason, these vitamins must be present in each meal. Vitamins A, D, E, and K are fat-soluble and stored in the fatty tissues of the body and the liver. Your dog needs both types.

Because of the heat used during processing, dog food lacks two important water-soluble vitamins that dogs need to maintain their health.

- **Vitamin C:** A fairly common misconception is that dogs don't need extra vitamin C because they produce their own. Although they do produce their own vitamin C, they don't produce enough, especially in today's polluted environment.

  Vitamin C strengthens the immune system, speeds wound healing, helps the function of the musculoskeletal system, and is needed whenever the dog gets wormed, is given drugs of any kind, or is put under any kind of stress. A lack of vitamin C in the diet commonly results in urinary tract infections, cystitis, and limps.

  Buddy needs vitamin C for healthy teeth and gums. In the old days, sailors often suffered from a vitamin C deficiency due to the lack of fresh fruits and vegetables while at sea. This malady is called *scurvy* and results in weakness, anemia, spongy and inflamed gums, and dirty teeth. The same thing happens to the vitamin C–deficient dog.

- **Vitamin B:** This vitamin, which comprises a number of individual parts, is called vitamin B-complex. Also water-soluble and fragile, vitamin B is needed for energy and to promote biochemical reactions in the body that work with enzymes to change the carbohydrates into glucose, as well as to break down protein.

Vitamin B-complex helps to maintain the health of the nervous system, skin, eyes, hair, mouth, and the liver. This vitamin is necessary for muscle tone in the digestive tract and proper brain function. Vitamin B also helps to alleviate anxiety and depression, and is important to the older dog to maintain his health.

 Because vitamins begin to break down when you open your dog food bag and expose the food to the elements, close the food up tightly and keep it away from light. Doing so helps to retain the quality of the contents. (Vitamins B and C are particularly sensitive to exposure.)

Because not enough of either vitamin B or C is contained in any processed dog food to meet your criteria for raising Buddy, you have to add these vitamins to his diet. We use the carefully tested vitamins from PHD Products with our own dogs.

Adding minerals

Minerals make up less than 2 percent of any formulated diet, and yet they're the most critical of nutrients. Although your dog can manufacture some vitamins on his own, he isn't able to make minerals. The minerals are needed

- ✔ To correctly compose body fluids
- ✔ To form blood and bones
- ✔ To promote a healthy nervous system
- ✔ To function as coenzymes together with vitamins

Because between 50 and 80 percent of minerals are lost in the manufacturing process, we recommend that you add extra minerals to your dog's food.

We recommend adding the product Wellness, manufactured by PHD Products, to your dogs' daily diet. Wellness provides an herbal vitamin/mineral mix from natural sources and contains all those vitamins and minerals that are lost in the processing of commercial food. It supplies Buddy with the necessary tools needed to absorb and break down his food and protects him from viruses and bacteria found in his environment.

Quenching his thirst — keeping fresh water around

Your dog needs access to fresh water in a clean, stainless steel bowl at all times. The exception is when the puppy is being housetrained, when you need to limit access to water after 8 p.m. so that the puppy can last through the night.

Water is the most necessary ingredient that dogs need on a daily basis. Without water, your dog will die. If a dog has adequate water, he can live for three weeks without food, but he can live only a few days without water. Your dog uses water for the digestive processes, breaking down and absorbing nutrients, as well as maintaining his body temperature. Water helps to detoxify the body and transport toxic substances out of the body through the eliminative organs. Water also keeps the acid levels of the blood constant.

The kind of food you feed your dog determines how much water your dog needs. For example, kibble contains about 10 percent moisture, and your dog needs about a quart of water for every pound of food he eats. A dog fed only canned food, which is around 78 percent moisture, needs considerably less water. If fed raw foods, a dog may drink less than a cup of water a day because the food contains sufficient water.

City water systems usually provide water free from parasites and bacteria by using chemicals such as chlorine, aluminum salts, soda, ash, phosphates, calcium hydroxides, and activated carbon. According to a study reported in *Consumer Reports* in 1990, the main contaminants remaining are lead, radon, and nitrates. Lead comes from water pipes in houses built early in the last century. Radon is a by-product of uranium found in the Earth's crust and is more prevalent in water from wells and ground water in the northeast, North Carolina, and Arizona. Water from lakes and rivers is less contaminated with radon. Nitrates come from ground water sources and contain agricultural contaminants.

Note also that the more grains in the food the more alkaline it is, and Buddy will drink more water to maintain his correct acid/alkaline balance. If Buddy is drinking too much water, a change in diet to a more acidic food (one containing more animal protein) may be in order. If Buddy still continues to drink a large amount of water, it could be the beginnings of a kidney or bladder infection. When in doubt, visit your vet for a checkup.

You can test to see if Buddy's pH is correct by going to the pharmacy and picking up some pH test strips. Place a strip into Buddy's urine when he goes out first thing in the morning to relieve himself. The pH should read between 6.5 and 6.7. If it's higher than 7.5 to 8 (7 is neutral), his diet is too alkaline.

Digesting information

Raw foods pass through a dog's stomach and into the intestinal tract in 4½ hours. So after that time span, the dog is already receiving energy from that food. Raw foods are the most easily digested by the dog.

Semimoist foods — the kind that you can find in boxes on the supermarket shelf and shaped like hamburgers or the kind that are in rolls like sausages — take almost nine hours to pass through the stomach. Dry foods take between 15 and 16 hours, so if you choose to feed Buddy any kind of dry processed dog food, it will be in his stomach from morning 'til night.

The following sections provide some insight into the food-processing issue.

Canned food

Ingredients in canned foods are measured in wet weight rather than dry weight (which is how kibble is measured). The ingredients listed on the label reflect the actual amount of raw ingredients that went into the can. Canned food lists protein as 8 to 10 percent, which is less than that found in kibble, but the protein is calculated differently. A simple and approximate way to compare the two is to double the amount of protein listed on the can to compare it with kibble. A listing of 10 percent protein on the canned food label equals around 20 percent on the kibble package.

Feeding canned food is much more expensive than feeding dry food because the moisture content in the can is around 78 percent, so you're paying for only 22 percent of dry ingredients. Canned food comes in different price ranges and in many qualities. Some canned foods contain only meat protein, and others contain primarily cereal grains. Some come in a stew form. In judging the quality of these foods, look for the AAFCO statement on the can. That statement assures you that the food has gone through some kind of testing.

Canned food is processed at a very high temperature that kills bacteria and viruses. Also, canned food contains fewer preservatives than kibble. Many dogs like their kibble pepped up with a bit of canned food, which contains little nutritive value because the heat processing effectively kills the vitamins and minerals in the food, as well as changes the amino acids in the protein.

Semimoist food

Although consumer friendly, semimoist food contains sweeteners or preservatives to give it a long shelf life. Coloring is added to make it look appetizing. As a sole diet for dogs, it may cause digestive upsets because of its ingredients and high preservative content. The moisture content ranges from 20 to 25 percent. Some natural semimoist foods are available on the market. One comes in the shape of a large sausage, and small pieces can be cut off for treats. Dogs fed these products exclusively on a regular basis may develop digestive problems.

Sugar is commonly listed as the fourth or fifth ingredient in these foods. The chemical name for sugar is *dextrose*. Sugar stimulates the pancreas to produce insulin, which is needed to break down carbohydrates and sugar in the food. The pancreas has to work overtime to produce enough insulin to break down this food, setting the stage for diseases of the pancreas, which can cause not only digestive upsets but also behavioral problems. Hyperactivity is the most common of the behavioral problems.

Raw food

Our years with dogs have made it abundantly clear that feeding a balanced raw diet — which emulates what Buddy would eat in the wild — is the best and most efficient way to feed a dog. A correctly formulated raw diet provides all the known nutrients in a form the dog can quickly digest and turn into energy. Dogs fed this way live longer and are much healthier than their counterparts who are fed commercial foods.

We have always felt that many disease states, including musculoskeletal disorders (such as hip dysplasia), are certainly exacerbated — if not actually caused by — poor nutrition. Our belief along these lines has since been confirmed by veterinarian Marc Torel and scientific journalist Klaus Dieter Kammerer in their book, *The Thirty Years War: 1966–1996* (Transanimal Publishing House).

Many raw diets are available for you to choose from, but making the correct choice is even more difficult than comparing commercial dog foods. We apply the same criteria to the examination of raw food diets as we do to commercial foods: Both need to be clinically tested and provide a balanced diet for a dog. Diets, especially homemade ones, raw or cooked, that don't meet these criteria can do more damage to your dog than commercial dog food.

Before changing Buddy's diet, we recommend that your vet conduct a blood test on Buddy to establish a baseline. After Buddy has been on his new raw diet program for six months, have another blood test done and compare it to the previous one. The follow-up blood test can tell whether or not his new diet is an improvement.

You need to keep other considerations in mind. Feeding raw meat or raw chicken to a dog can cause digestive upsets if the meat contains a high level of bacteria in the form of E. coli or salmonella. Although a dog that has been fed raw foods for a long time can easily deal with both of these bacteria, a sick dog or a dog just being transferred over to a raw diet may become sick.

The reason is that the dog's digestive system isn't the same as a human's. The dog's stomach acid is very strong, and in a healthy dog, this acid kills any bacteria that enter it. A sick dog, or a dog switching over to a raw diet, needs a transition diet to rebuild that stomach acid to the point where it can deal with either E. coli or salmonella. After the transition diet is followed, you need to use a simple method of killing bacteria the first time meat is used: Put the meat or chicken into a sieve in the sink, pour boiling water over it, and cool it before feeding. Doing so kills the bacteria. After taking this step for a couple of weeks, the stomach acid will be strong enough to deal with the bacteria without problems, and you can introduce the raw meat.

Enzymes and enzyme robbing

Enzymes make a body tick. Your dog's body already has enzymes; your dog also makes them through what you feed him.

When semimoist food or dry food sits in the dog's stomach, it does so because not enough enzymes are in the stomach to break it down. Remember, a dog's stomach is designed to deal with raw foods.

So the stomach sends a message to the brain: "Hey, brain, we need some more enzymes down here." The brain responds, "Okay, okay, but I need some time." It then gathers enzymes from the heart, the liver, the kidneys, and other parts of the body to be transported to the stomach. In the meantime, the food sits there until enough enzymes are collected for digestion. This process is called *enzyme robbing*.

A dog's vital internal organs — his heart, liver, and kidneys — need the enzymes that they contain to function at their best. When a dog consumes semimoist and dry foods, some of these enzymes must be diverted to the stomach to aid in digestion. Ultimately, the dog's vital organs lose out. Robbing various organs in the body of the enzymes that they themselves need to function correctly can have a detrimental effect on those organs. If a dog has a predisposition for problems in his heart, kidneys, or liver, such enzyme loss can hasten that disease and reduce the dog's life span.

Feeding Buddy

This section provides you with four options for feeding Buddy — from the easy way out, to using a beefed-up version of commercial dog food, to making your own. Only you can decide which option is best for your lifestyle and your comfort level.

More than 30 years of breeding, raising, working, and living with dogs of several breeds have had a profound effect on our way of thinking. Even so, we're realists. You're a busy person and may not even cook for yourself, much less be concerned about what goes into your dog. Fortunately, you can take some shortcuts to safeguard your dog's health.

Option 1: The easy way out

Option 1 consists of feeding commercial kibble enhanced by one supplement. This option is the simplest method of adding the nutrients lost in processing commercial kibble.

For people feeding their dogs commercial kibble, sprinkling a whole food additive onto the food and mixing it with a little water adds those nutrients lost in the manufacturing process. The product we suggest is called Endurance, which contains liver and natural vitamins and minerals. It aids digestion, reduces shedding, and increases vitality and longevity. Endurance is available from www.phdproducts.com.

Option 2: Beefed-up commercial food

Option 2 adds supplements and fresh foods to commercial kibble. The quantities of the respective ingredients listed in this section are for a 50-pound dog. You can adjust this recipe according to your dog's weight. When calculating the amount for the weight of your dog, err on the side of too little, rather than too much. Some dogs eat more than their weight indicates, and some dogs less. You dog's metabolism and the amount of daily exercise he gets determine the amount of food he needs. Use common sense and keep all ingredients in proportion.

Feed the following twice a day:

> 1½ cups Performance Food
>
> ¼ teaspoon of vitamin C
>
> 1 vitamin B-complex
>
> ⅛ teaspoon of vitamin/mineral mix (Wellness from PHD)
>
> ¼ cup of beef (hamburger, 80 percent), or ⅔ meat and ⅓ beef liver for a total of ¼ cup. You can also use chicken and chicken livers.
>
> 2 tablespoons fresh vegetables
>
> 2 tablespoons fresh or dried fruit

To the morning meal, add one Amino Acid Complex tablet (Nature Most), and, four times a week, one large egg cooked for five minutes, served with shell. Once a week substitute cottage cheese for the meat on one day, and unflavored yogurt containing acidophillus on another day.

For vegetables use carrots, parsnips, beets, sweet potato, broccoli, leek, zucchini, squash, or any vegetable your dog likes. Chop the vegetables in a food processor or parboil them to make it easier for your dog to digest the cellulose. Whenever you can, use vegetables that are in season.

For treats, try carrot sticks, dried liver, broccoli, parsnips, lettuce, bananas, prunes, cucumbers, or fruit or vegetable in season.

Making major changes in Buddy's diet without keeping track of how these changes affect him isn't a wise idea. We recommend that you have a blood test done before making a dietary change and again six months later.

Option 3: Natural Diet Foundation formula

Option 3 is the lazy man's way of feeding a balanced homemade diet. All the work is done for you. You need to add only two ingredients in the morning meal and one ingredient in the evening meal, mixed with a little water.

The National Diet Foundation (NDF) formula, available from PHD, is the same as our homemade diet in option 4, except that it's dehydrated. This carefully formulated diet meets the needs of dogs of different breeds, of different ages, and of those dogs that live in different climates. It was clinically tested prior to marketing. Because no heat is used in the processing of the food, all the vitamins and minerals are unaltered by the food processing. It uses only human-grade ingredients and is the next best thing to making your own.

For the morning meal, all you add is water, yogurt, and vegetables. For the evening meal, all you add is meat. Directions for amounts to feed are on the package.

Option 4: Wendy Volhard's Natural Diet recipe

Making your own dog food is becoming a popular option, although it's hardly a new one. Every dog alive today can trace its ancestry back to dogs that were raised on homemade diets. The dog food industry, in comparison to dogs themselves, is young — maybe 50 to 60 years — although canned meat for dogs was sold at the turn of the 20th century. Originally, the commercial foods were made to supplement homemade food.

Why make your own?

Many dogs don't thrive on commercially prepared rations. They exhibit disease states, often mistaken for allergies, which are deficiency diseases caused by feeding cereal-based foods. A dog in his natural state would eat meat. His prey would be that of a grass-eating animal — an herbivore. Along with the internal organs and the muscle meat, he would eat the predigested grasses and plants of the carcass. Those grasses and plants would consist of no more than 20 to 25 percent of his total diet. He would raid nests from ground-breeding birds and eat the eggs, and he would catch the occasional insect. He would maybe forage on certain weeds and grasses and eat berries and fruit.

In formulating the Wendy Volhard Natural Diet (ND) we stay within these boundaries — with the exception of the insects. Although domestication has changed the appearance of many dogs through selective breeding, the digestive tract of the dog remains substantially the same as it always was. You really do have a wolf in your living room.

The Natural Diet consists of two meals. One is a cereal meal plus supplements, which comprises 25 percent of the total diet. The other 75 percent is a raw meat meal plus supplements. In separating these meals — both of which are balanced — the digestive system uses enzymes present in the stomach and intestines to efficiently and quickly break down the food. It decreases the load on the digestive organs, which are maintained in a healthy state for a longer period of time.

For more information on how to make your own food, read *The Holistic Guide for a Healthy Dog,* 2nd Edition, by Wendy Volhard and Kerry Brown, DVM (Wiley).

Benefits of the Natural Diet

The advantages of feeding the Natural Diet are many:

- ✔ **The diet increases health and longevity.** Diabetes, skin, ear, and eye problems are rare, and so is hip dysplasia and bloat. Teeth rarely, if ever, have to be cleaned. Fleas, ticks, and worms are almost unheard of on the Natural Diet. Overall vitality and energy are unequaled.

- ✔ **You can tailor the diet to individual needs.** Doing so is beneficial for some breeds of dogs, especially imported dogs or relatives of imported dogs, who have difficulty in digesting corn contained in the majority of prepared commercial diets. You can also substitute individual ingredients as necessary. Dogs are able to digest and utilize the Natural Diet.

✔ **The diet contains a lot of moisture in the natural ingredients.** As a result, the dog drinks little water.

✔ **Young dogs raised on this diet grow more slowly than dogs raised on commercial food.** They also have fewer musculoskeletal problems.

✔ **Dogs love to eat it.** A happy dog is a healthy dog.

Transferring to the Natural Diet

Unless your dog is already used to a raw diet, you need to put him on the following short-term transitional meal plan to avoid digestive upsets that may come from the switch to the Natural Diet.

Note: This diet is for a 50-pound dog. Adjust it according to your dog's weight. And make sure that fresh water is always available to your dog.

Day 1: No food. At mealtime, feed 2 teaspoons of honey mixed with a cup of lukewarm water.

Day 2: In the morning, give honey and water as in Day 1. In the evening, give 1 cup of yogurt or kefir and 2 teaspoons of honey.

Day 3: In the morning, give 1 cup of yogurt or kefir and 2 teaspoons of honey. In the evening, give 1 cup of yogurt or kefir, 2 teaspoons of honey, and 1 teaspoon of dry or 2 tablespoons of fresh herbs.

In the fall and winter, rotate the following herbs: Parsley, nettles, corn silk, burdock root, ginger root, golden rod, watercress, rosemary, sage, dandelion root, and alfalfa.

In the spring and summer rotate dandelion leaves and flowers, borage, peppermint leaves, sorrel, goldenrod leaves, rosemary, watercress, comfrey leaves, alfalfa, and milk thistle.

Day 4: In the morning, give 2 cups of yogurt or kefir, 2 teaspoons of honey, 1 tablespoon dry or 2 tablespoons of fresh herbs, and ½ ounce (dry weight) of cooked oatmeal. In the evening, give 1 cup of yogurt or kefir, 2 teaspoons of honey, 1 tablespoon dry or 2 tablespoons of fresh herbs, 2 ounces of (dry weight) cooked oatmeal, and 1 garlic capsule.

Day 5: In the morning, give ½ normal ration of cereal and supplements as listed in the Natural Diet chart shown in Table 18-1. In the evening, give ½ normal ration of meat meal as listed in Table 18-1.

Day 6: In the morning, give the normal amount of food as listed for Days 1 through 6 in Table 18-1. In the evening, give the normal amount of food as listed on Days 1 through 6 in Table 18-1.

Now your dog is ready to follow the full Natural Diet listed in Table 18-1.

Table 18-1	Natural Diet — 50-Pound Dog
Breakfast (Days 1–6)	**Dinner (Days 1–6)**
3 oz. grain mix (dry)	12 oz. meat (days 1–5)
2 teaspoons of molasses	2½ oz. liver (days 1–5)
2 teaspoons of safflower oil	14 oz. cottage cheese (day 6)
200 IU vitamin E	200 mg vitamin C
200 mg vitamin C	1 teaspoon of cod liver oil
50 mg vitamin B complex	1 tablespoon of apple cider vinegar
1¼ egg, small (4 times per week)	½ teaspoon of kelp
½ cup of yogurt or kefir	1 teaspoon brewer's yeast
	1½ garlic capsule (325 mg)
	2½ bone meal
	2 tablespoons of wheat germ
	3 tablespoons of wheat bran
	2 teaspoons of dry herbs
	2 tablespoons of fruit (alternate days)
Breakfast (Day 7)	**Dinner (Day 7)**
2 ⅓ oz. grain mix (dry)	Fast
200 mg vitamin C	
50 mg vitamin B complex	
1 cup of yogurt or kefir	
4 teaspoons of honey	

Give your dog a bone

Once or twice a week, give your dog a bone as a special treat. They love large beef bones, raw chicken necks, and the tips off chicken wings. If you're not sure about how long these items have been in the supermarket case, douse them with boiling water to kill any bacteria before feeding. The side benefit of feeding bones is that your dog has beautiful, pearly white teeth that don't need to be cleaned.

What about table scraps?

There is nothing wrong with adding table scraps to Buddy's food, *provided* they don't exceed 10 to 15 percent of his total diet. Many dogs love leftover salad, meat scraps, and veggies. In fact, for the picky eater, table scraps are often the best way to get him to eat his rations.

You do need to avoid certain foods, particularly those with a high sugar count, such as chocolate and highly salted foods.

Feeding too many bones, however, can give him constipation and hard, chalky stools. Be careful, too, to give your dog only large bones that can't splinter.

When you give your dog a bone, leave him alone. Dogs get possessive about their bones. Bones are one of the few items that may cause Buddy to growl at you if you try to take one away from him. It's a very special treat, and he wants to be in a place to relax and enjoy it. Let him go to his crate, which is the perfect place for him to enjoy his bone in peace. Letting him go there gets him away from other dogs or cats in the family, the children, and you. Give him a few hours just to indulge himself. Let him be a dog. After a few days of chewing a fresh bone, it loses its magic, and most dogs will allow the kids, other dogs, or you to pick it up or handle it.

Chapter 19

Understanding Your Dog's Health

In This Chapter

▶ Knowing when *more* doesn't equal *better* (the overvaccinating problem)

▶ Identifying when you have to vaccinate

▶ Understanding hypothyroidism

▶ Going to a doggy chiropractor

▶ Looking at homeopathy — medicine or magic?

▶ Poking around with acupuncture

A dog that is fed correctly and given enough exercise and mental stimulation through training rarely exhibits behavior problems. He deals well with stress, hardly ever gets sick, and keeps his youthful characteristics into his teens.

In Chapter 18, we talk about the influence of nutrition on health and behavior. In this chapter, we cover some of the more common health concerns and how they can affect your dog's behavior. You can quickly figure out that when your dog doesn't feel quite right, he also doesn't act quite right.

Here Comes That Needle Again (The Overvaccination Issue)

During the past 20 years, we've seen a steady increase in the number of vaccinations that dogs receive. Sadly, instead of improving the dogs' health and longevity, the practice has had the opposite effect.

Overvaccinating has created unintended and undesirable reactions to vaccinations, which result in *vaccinosis,* the term used to describe those undesirable reactions. The reactions can range from none or barely detectable to death. And they may occur as a result of one vaccine, several vaccines given at the same time, or repeated vaccinations given in a relatively short timeframe.

Too many vaccinations too close together can cause a puppy's immune system to break down and can result in serious health problems (see the sidebar "Our sad song about Caesar," a pitiful case-in-point story about an overvaccinated puppy). We want to make it clear right here that we aren't against vaccinations. But what we are against is random, repetitive, routine, and completely unnecessary vaccinations.

And as for annual booster shots — where do they fit into this picture? Actually, they don't. According to Kirk's *Current Veterinary Therapy* XI-205 (W.B. Saunders Co.) the textbook used in veterinary schools, no scientific basis or immunological reason necessitates annual revaccinations. Immunity to viruses can last for many years — even for a dog's lifetime.

When your dog already carries the antibodies against a particular virus, a revaccination can wreak havoc with his immune system. The many adverse reactions to unnecessary vaccinations have caused breeders, dog owners, and vets to begin questioning the need for boosters and to become more cautious in the way vaccines are administered. By law, your dog only needs a rabies vaccination and the rabies booster only every three years. Don't ever give your dog a rabies shot before he is 6 months of age.

Some breeds of dogs have extreme — even fatal — reactions to vaccines that are tolerated by other breeds of dogs. Some develop odd behaviors such as

- Aggression
- Anxiety or fear
- Epilepsy and other seizure disorders
- Excessive licking
- Insomnia
- Snapping at imaginary flies

A rabies vaccine given in conjunction with other vaccines can be responsible for aggression, epilepsy, and other seizure disorders.

How do you know if your dog will have a reaction to a vaccine? You don't, and therein lies the problem. Fortunately, you don't have to take the chance. When you take Buddy in for his annual physical checkup, you can ask your vet to do a *titer test,* a blood test that tells you whether Buddy has *antibodies* (or resistance) to the diseases for which he's already been vaccinated. If he has a high *titer,* or level of antibodies, to the disease, you don't need to have him revaccinated. Titering is becoming a more acceptable alternative to revaccinations.

Immunologists are discovering a direct correlation between the increase in autoimmune and chronic disease states with the increased use of vaccines.

Many holistically trained vets now believe that the benefits of many vaccines are outweighed by the risks and that dogs are better off if you go with one of these options:

- ✔ Vaccinate lightly with vaccines spaced out by at least three to four weeks.

- ✔ Only vaccinate once for parvo and distemper when your dog is young with one booster four weeks later. Have your vet draw some blood and send it off to a laboratory to establish the level of antibodies your puppy carries. If the puppy is protected, you don't need any more vaccines. Titer again at one year and vaccinate only when the titers are low.

- ✔ Don't have your puppy vaccinated for rabies (which is mandatory) before 6 months of age. Make sure this vaccine is at least one month away from any other vaccines.

- ✔ Use a homeopathic alternative to vaccines.

If you're interested in the holistic approach, you can work out a vaccination schedule for your puppy by consulting *The Holistic Guide for a Healthy Dog,* 2nd Edition (Wiley). As vets learn more about vaccines and their side effects, the information supplied to them is continuously being reviewed and updated. Also check out "Homeopathy: Medicine or Magic" later in this chapter for more info.

The bottom line? Before vaccinating your dog, discuss the safety with your veterinarian if Buddy

- ✔ Is on any kind of medication
- ✔ Isn't perfectly healthy

    (*Note:* In the literature that vaccine manufacturers supply to vets, it specifically states that no dog should be vaccinated unless he's in perfect health. Remember that.)

- ✔ Has any skin, eye, or ear infections
- ✔ Has recently been treated for fleas, ticks, or worms
- ✔ Has had prior reactions to vaccines
- ✔ Hasn't received supplemental vitamins and minerals
- ✔ Is scheduled for teeth cleaning, spaying or neutering, or any other surgical procedure

Boarding, Schooling, and Vaccinating

Sometimes you have to vaccinate your dog. Many boarding kennels and obedience schools, for example, require proof of vaccination although titers are becoming more acceptable.

Our sad song about Caesar

We remember one consultation involving a 4-month old Great Dane puppy, Caesar. When he came to us, he was virtually paralyzed. The vet had told the owners that Caesar probably had contracted some spinal disease, not uncommon in giant breeds, and that nothing could be done. The owners came to us as a last resort. By that time, Caesar didn't want to eat, had become urine incontinent, and was constipated. Our first step was to take Caesar to our own vet. After a blood test and X-rays, our vet considered a number of diagnoses, but couldn't determine anything definitive.

In the meantime, we examined Caesar's history with the owners, and here's what we uncovered:

✔ The breeder gave Caesar distemper and parvo vaccines at 6 weeks of age.

✔ The new owners picked up Caesar at 7 weeks of age.

✔ Under the terms of the seller's guarantee, Caesar was taken to the owners'

veterinarian within 48 hours of purchase for a health evaluation.

✔ On that visit, Caesar was wormed and given a 5 in 1 vaccination.

✔ These vaccinations were repeated at 9, 11, and 13 weeks.

✔ During that time span, Caesar was wormed two more times as a so-called precautionary matter, even though no fecal sample was taken to see whether he actually had worms.

✔ At 15 weeks of age, Caesar received another set of shots, to which the rabies vaccine had been added.

✔ Two days later, Caesar collapsed, having received 23 vaccines in 9 weeks.

This sad story does have a happy ending. Through acupuncture, chiropractic, dietary, and homeopathic remedies, we managed to piece Caesar back together into a normal dog.

So you need to know this: If you vaccinate Buddy and then immediately take him to a boarding kennel, you may be exposing him to the risk of the very diseases that the vaccine is supposed to protect him against. Immunity to disease develops about 21 days *after* your dog has been vaccinated against the disease, so make sure that Buddy's vaccine has been given a minimum of three weeks before you board him.

Before you vaccinate, call the facility. Some boarding kennels are now recognizing titer tests (see the preceding section for details about titer tests).

Because not everything's cut and dried in this world, suppose that Buddy is one of those dogs who have adverse side effects from vaccinations, and as a result, you adamantly refuse to vaccinate him, and now you can't find a boarding kennel that will honor your wishes. What then? Well, you're going to have to find someone to come in and dog sit for you while you're away. And if the local obedience organization doesn't accept you either, then you may have to get a private trainer to come to your home (see Chapter 20).

Vaccinating even a healthy dog stresses his immune system, whether or not you see a reaction. And boarding a dog is stressful — even at the nicest boarding kennels. Under stress, Buddy is vulnerable to picking up disease.

Uncovering the Rise in Doggy Hypothyroidism

Providing poor nutrition, overvaccinating, and neutering or spaying a puppy too early can cause a disease called hypothyroidism. *Hypothyroidism* refers to an underactive thyroid gland, which causes physical as well as behavioral abnormalities. Rarely seen until the 1970s, this disease has become more prevalent as the way of managing dogs has changed in the last 30 years. More than 50 percent of all dogs today show some signs of this disease.

The thyroid gland is part of the endocrine gland system. This system not only controls many of the hormones in the body but also the brain's ability to deal with stress.

Hypothyroidism can be partially hereditary in nature. If your dog's parents had the disease, the chances of him getting it are quite high.

The physical manifestations of hypothyroidism can be

- Heart disorders
- Lack of control over body temperature — the dog is either too cold or too hot under otherwise normal conditions
- Oily, scaly skin and blackened skin on the belly
- Some kinds of paralysis
- Seizures
- Thinning of the hair on each side of the body, usually around the rib cage
- Weight gain

Behavioral manifestations may include

- Aggression to people or other dogs
- Being picked on by other dogs
- Difficulty learning
- Fear and anxiety, including separation anxiety and fear of thunderstorms

✔ *Lick granulomas,* where the dog licks constantly at one spot, usually on a leg, and goes down to the bone

✔ Obsessive-compulsive behavior, such as spinning and extreme hyperactivity

✔ Overreaction to stressful situations

✔ Self-mutilation

Note: The preceding behaviors were reported in a 1997 English study, and nearly all the abnormal behaviors disappeared when thyroid medication was administered.

How can you tell if Buddy has a thyroid-related problem? If he's exhibiting any of the behaviors listed in this section, make an appointment with your vet as soon as possible. If you want to reassure yourself that Buddy doesn't have hypothyroidism, have your vet do a blood test and ask for a *complete* thyroid panel. The results can tell you whether Buddy needs medication. All laboratory reports indicate a low and high normal reading for each test done. Many vets believe that when a dog shows a *low* normal reading, the dog needs to be on medication. High readings are uncommon in adult dogs.

The Bone Crusher: "Oh, My Aching Back"

Performance events, especially agility, are athletic activities for a dog. So are you really surprised that various parts of performing dogs' bodies might go out of whack? Because the dogs' performances are affected, many competitors routinely take their dogs in for chiropractic adjustments.

To keep your dog in tiptop shape, have a chiropractor examine him. Buddy may need an alignment. To find an animal chiropractor in your area, go to the American Veterinary Chiropractic Association's Web site at www.animal chiropractic.org. Dog chiropractors cost typically the same as a human chiropractor — about $45 a crack (no pun intended), depending on your location.

Misalignments of your dog's musculoskeletal system can affect not only his performance, but also his *behavior.* Our own introduction to a veterinary chiropractor came through our Briard, D.J. While he was growing up, D.J. was quite unpredictable when meeting new people or new dogs. His first reaction was to lunge and bark and show typical signs of aggression. We didn't take it too seriously, attributing it to his lack of maturity. We figured that with training and gaining confidence, he'd grow out of it.

Although the behavior diminished to a certain extent, it didn't disappear. At that point, we decided to have D.J. examined. We learned that one of the vertebrae in his neck was impinging on the optic nerve and that he had never been able to see properly. After he was adjusted, he was a different dog.

After that experience, we had all our dogs examined. These examinations disclosed a number of weaknesses that we had been aware of but didn't know how to address. For example, our Dachshund's jaw was out, which caused him discomfort and affected his behavior and performance. With treatment, he became a much happier dog.

Having a chiropractor look at your puppies to make sure that everything is in order is a good idea. Vigorous play, especially with other dogs, can cause all manner of misalignments, which then may interfere with proper growth.

Homeopathy: Medicine or Magic

Many dogs experience fear or anxiety under different conditions. For example, anxiety can occur

- ✔ When Buddy goes on a trip away from home
- ✔ Before and during thunderstorms
- ✔ When Buddy goes to the vet
- ✔ When Buddy encounters situations that he perceives as stressful

We've been quite successful in dealing with this sort of anxiety with homeopathic remedies. In fact, we carry a small homeopathic emergency kit with us wherever we go, just in case. You can find one at www.phdproducts.com.

Homeopathy relies on the energy of natural substances. These natural substances, which come from plants or minerals, are diluted to the extreme and then added to milk sugar pellets. This form of treatment, which was popular until the discovery of antibiotics, generally fell out of favor during the middle of the 20th century. Today, this form of treatment is enjoying an enormous resurgence all over the world, and many vets in Europe are trained both in traditional medicine and homeopathy.

Because the homeopathic remedies are so diluted, they're safe to use and don't cause side effects. They come in different strengths, called *potencies*. These potencies have numbers from 3X upwards. We use a diluted form at the 30C potency. You can find these remedies in the health food section of supermarkets, as well as in health food stores. Effective in dealing with many conditions, each dose consists of three pellets that you put into the back of your dog's mouth.

The following listing includes a few common homeopathic remedies we find useful and use frequently, along with what they treat. All are in the emergency kit we carry with us and that we mention earlier in this section.

- ✔ **Aconite:** fright, anxiety, and fear of thunderstorms
- ✔ **Apis:** Bee stings, any shiny swellings
- ✔ **Arnica:** Bruising from falls, dog bites, and recuperation from any operation
- ✔ **Belladonna:** Heat stroke and hot, red ears
- ✔ **Carbo Veg:** Bloating or gas
- ✔ **Chamomilla:** Vomiting of yellow bile and teething problems
- ✔ **Ferrum Phos:** Stops bleeding
- ✔ **Hydrophobinum:** (Sometimes called Lyssin), reaction to rabies vaccine
- ✔ **Hypericum:** Stops pain to nerve endings after injury or operations
- ✔ **Ignatia:** Grief, insecurity, stress, or sadness
- ✔ **Ledum:** Insect or spider bites
- ✔ **Nux Vomica:** Any kind of poisoning; recuperation after anesthesia
- ✔ **Phosphorus:** Sound sensitivity
- ✔ **Rhus Tox (poison ivy):** Rheumatism
- ✔ **Sulphur:** Good skin and mange remedy
- ✔ **Thuja:** Vaccine reaction

Many holistic vets are trained in homeopathy, and you probably can find one in your area without difficulty. To find a holistic vet in your area go to the American Holistic Veterinary Medical Association's Web site at www.ahvma.org.

Using More Needles: Acupuncture

Many vets today use acupuncture for a variety of chronic conditions. We've found that among its many applications, acupuncture is particularly effective with allergies, skin disorders, incontinence in old dogs, and the aches and pains that come with age.

The origin of acupuncture dates back to ancient China. The Chinese regularly practiced acupuncture on horses and then gradually tried it on other farm animals and finally dogs, cats, and birds. The practitioner punctures the skin with a fine needle at designated points on the body. Acupuncture serves to unblock energy and in so doing boosts the immune system, which aids in self-healing. Acupuncture causes the body to release endorphins and hormones while at the same time decreasing inflammation both internally and externally.

Where to go for other health-related concerns

Here are a few more resources available to you and your dog concerning his health:

✔ **Poison control:** As with your family, have a reliable poison control resource for your dog. We recommend the Animal Poison Control Center. You can call the center for 24-hour emergency information. The center has 20 full-time veterinary toxicologists on-call to work with you on an emergency with your dog, for a $45 per case fee. The number is 888-426-4435. For more information, check out the Web site at www.napcc.aspca.org.

✔ **Holistic health:** The Pet Health and Nutrition Center is a phone consultation service that offers a holistic approach to your dog's health. Since 1995, this dedicated group of nutritionists has provided care for more than 10,000 animals. These nutritionists offer alternative therapies, modestly priced consultations, and supplemental support for the treatment of numerous diseases through metabolic therapies. While working with vets, this group provides phone consultations and a support system by which pet owners are able to treat their dog or cat at home for most illnesses and diseases. If your dog needs help, these are the folks for you.

✔ **Nutritional and homeopathic products:** PHD (which stands for Perfect Health Diet) supplies one of the highest quality lines of dog foods and supplements on the market today. Used by professional dog trainers, behaviorists, holistic vets, and discriminating pet owners to bring dogs back to health, we also use PHD for our own dogs. The products are all natural, contain no preservatives, and the foods ship directly from the factory to you, getting to you within three weeks of manufacture. You'll find the homeopathic emergency kit referred to in "Homeopathy: Medicine or Magic" earlier in this chapter, as well as the Natural Diet Foundation discussed in Chapter 18. PHD does no advertising, selling only by word of mouth and reputation, and was set up by professional dog people for dog people. Check out its Web site at www.phdproducts.com.

Acupuncture specializes in putting the body back into balance, and is ideal for conditions commonly found in dogs. Limps, incontinence, skin problems, and chronic diseases of major organs, such as heart, kidney, liver, lungs, and stomach, respond well to this modality. We advise seeking the help of an acupuncture veterinarian for middle-aged to older dogs. Treatments can make an older dog feel like a puppy again.

To find out more about acupuncture, contact the International Veterinary Acupuncture Society (IVAS), one of the fastest growing veterinary organizations. More than 400 vets are trained yearly by this group, and have been for the last ten years, so you can find a trained vet in your area without too much difficulty. You can also check out the society's Web site at www.ivas.org for more information.

Chapter 20

Seeking Expert Outside Help

*Y*ou have a number of choices when it comes to Buddy's education.

You can

✔ Train out of a book, such as this one.

✔ Participate in group classes.

✔ Have someone else do the training.

Each choice has its own pros and cons, and your own personality and lifestyle determine your preference.

No matter what decision you make, you need to keep in mind that there are enormous quality differences, not only in terms of training effectiveness, but also in how the dogs are treated. Dog training is a completely unregulated area, and anyone, yes, anyone, can proclaim himself a trainer.

When you attempt to make a rational choice, remember that there are many ways to train a dog. Beware of anyone who says only their way is the right way. Successful dog training depends not so much on the "how," but on the "why." Dogs aren't a homogeneous commodity, and the approach to training has to take into account the dog's Personality Profile (see Chapter 5), as well as your own personality.

Teaching skills aren't the same as training skills. To teach people how to train their dogs, an instructor needs good communication and people skills, as well as a thorough knowledge of dog training.

Table 20-1 breaks down the three major categories of training resources available to you.

Table 20-1	Available Training Choices	
Choice	**Pros**	**Cons**
Training out of a book	Least expensive. You can train how you want, what you want, and when you want. You're not tied to a regular schedule. Location isn't a problem.	You need to be highly self-motivated or training will fall by the wayside. You have no one to critique you. Possibly not enough exposure to other dogs.
Group classes	Very economical. Someone tells you what you may doing wrong and can help you succeed. You get the opportunity to meet similar people. It keeps your training on track with weekly sessions. It provides continuous socialization with other dogs.	Schedule and location may be inconvenient. The instructor dictates how, what, and when. The training method may not be right for you or your dog.
Having someone else do the training	Little time commitment required of you.	Very expensive. Training method may not be how you want your dog trained.

Within these three major categories, you have additional options. The other choices include

   ✔ **An obedience class:** If you find you need outside help after trying the techniques in this book, we recommend an obedience class where you're instructed how to train your dog. Aside from the socialization with other dogs, the time you spend together will strengthen the bond between you and your dog. (See the next section, "Going to Class — Obedience and Training Schools" for more information.)

✔ **Lessons from a private dog trainer:** You can take private lessons from an instructor, either at your house or some other location. Under such an arrangement, the instructor teaches you what to do, and you're then expected to practice with your dog between sessions. In terms of time and effort, this is one of the most efficient arrangements. (For more info, see "Finding a Private Trainer" later in this chapter.)

✔ **Boarding school:** We typically don't recommend sending your dog away to a boarding school, but we do include it because it is an option for some people, especially when dealing with extreme aggression. You send your dog away for three to six weeks during which time an instructor trains your dog. (See "Heading to Boarding School" later in this chapter for more tidbits.)

Another related option is a doggie daycare center, many of which offer training, but again, you'll have to learn how to get Buddy to respond to your commands.

✔ **Doggie camp:** These camps are perfect if you and your dog want to head away for a short vacation. On the vacation you spend time with an instructor who helps you train your dog. (Check out "Enjoying The Great Dog Camp Adventure" later in this chapter.)

Going to Class — Obedience and Training Schools

Having taught obedience classes for 30 years, we're naturally biased in favor of this choice. A basic class usually addresses your most immediate concerns, such as not pulling on the leash, the Sit and Down-Stay, and Come.

The purpose of the class is to show you what to do, have you try it a few times to make sure you've got it right, and then send you home to practice. Be prepared to practice at least five times a week. Most classes are sequential in nature. If you miss a class, you'll fall behind and may have a hard time catching up. Falling behind is discouraging and may cause you to drop out. When you go to a class, don't expect the instructor to train your dog. That isn't her job.

We think taking Buddy to school is perhaps one of the best things you can do for you both. It gets you out of the house into an atmosphere where you can spend quality time together. Both of you have fun while learning useful things that make living together that much easier. Obedience classes are conducted in almost every community and are an excellent way for you and Buddy to learn together.

Until quite recently, obedience or kennel clubs conducted the majority of classes. Today, however, schools or private individuals teach many classes. The difference has nothing to do with the quality of the training, but relates solely to profit motive. Clubs are nonprofit organizations and the instructors, usually members who have trained and shown their own dog, generally volunteer their services. Training schools and individuals who hang out their shingles are for-profit organizations.

To train for participating in performance events, join an organization that offers training for that goal. The organization's instructors can coach you and your dog in the intricacies of the various requirements.

Choosing a good training class

To locate a class, look in the phonebook under a heading such as "Pet & Dog Training" to find out what your community offers. Chances are you'll have several choices.

Call one of the organizations listed to find out where and when the class meets. Ask whether you can observe a beginner class. If you aren't allowed to observe a class, which would be highly unusual, forget that organization. When you find one where you can observe a class, do so, but leave Buddy at home so that he doesn't interfere with the class and you aren't distracted.

Here are a few questions you need to ask yourself about the class you're observing:

- **What is your first impression of the class?** You're looking for a friendly, pleasant, and positive atmosphere.

- **Do the dogs seem to have a good time?** You can quickly tell if the dogs are enjoying themselves or if they'd rather be at home biting their favorite bone.

- **How does the instructor deal with the class participants?** You want the instructor to be encouraging and helpful, especially to those who seem to be struggling.

- **How does the instructor deal with the dogs?** You want the instructor to be nice to the dogs, not yell at them or create anxiety or fear.

- **Does the instructor appear knowledgeable?** As a student, you aren't likely to be able to tell whether or not the instructor actually is knowledgeable, but at least he needs to give the appearance of being so.

- **What is the ratio of instructors to students?** We always aim for a one to five ratio, with a limit of 15 students for one instructor with two assistants.

- **Is the space adequate for the number of dogs?** Insufficient space can be a cause for aggression in a class situation.

If you don't like what you see, find another organization. If you like what you see and hear, then it may be the right class for you and Buddy. But while you're visiting, you need to find out a few more bits of information:

- ✔ **The cost of the class and what is included:** For example, our basic training course, or Level 1 as we call it, consists of eight 50-minute sessions and includes a training collar and leash, weekly homework sheets, and a copy of our book, *What All Good Dogs Should Know* (available from amazon.com), as part of the fee.

- ✔ **The schedule of classes, the level of classes, the fee, and the length of the program:** The conditions vary from class to class. A beginner class can run anywhere from four to ten weeks, at a cost $50 to $200, depending on who teaches it and where you live. Price isn't necessarily an indicator of quality, nor is the length necessarily an indication of how much you learn. The majority of beginner classes last from six to eight weeks and cost about $100.

- ✔ **The goal of the program:** What can you expect from your dog upon completion of the class? This is pretty much under your control, because you're the one who is going to train Buddy. To be successful, you need to be prepared to practice with him five times a week. Two short sessions a day are preferable to one longer session, but for most people that isn't realistic. How long each session lasts depends entirely on your aptitude and Buddy's Personality Profile (see Chapter 5).

Puppy training classes

Taking Buddy to an obedience class as a puppy is the best investment in his future you can make. The joy of taking a puppy to class is that he can socialize with other young dogs and have fun, yet be taught manners and learn how to interact with his own kind. Buddy's brain at this point in his young life is just like a sponge, and he'll remember nearly everything you teach him now for the rest of his life. He'll learn all those lessons that will make him an ideal pet.

Look for an organization that offers puppy classes, preferably one that teaches basic control to puppies, rather than just socialization and games. Nothing is wrong with socialization and games; both are necessary, but at the right time and in the right context. Look for a class where the people are having fun with their dogs and where the instructor is pleasant and professional to the students. Above all, you want to see happy dogs.

You want Buddy to associate meeting other dogs as a pleasant but controlled experience, not one of playing and being rowdy. As he grows older, playing and being rowdy is no longer cute and will make him hard to manage around other dogs.

The ideal puppy class allows the puppies to interact with each other for up to three minutes before the class starts for the first two classes only. After that, the puppies are allowed to play for three minutes after class. This way Buddy learns that he must be obedient to you first, and the reward is playing after he has worked, a lifetime habit you want to instill while he is young.

Stay away from the classes where you're told that Buddy is too young to learn obedience exercises. This type of organization shows a lack of knowledge of dog behavior.

You can expect that your puppy will learn to Sit, Down, and Stand on command, Come when called, Stay when told, and Walk on a Loose Leash. An excellent program, with well-trained instructors, will also have Buddy doing the same exercises off leash, as well as on signal. For Buddy, these exercises are easy stuff.

Advanced training classes

The majority of people who go on to advanced training start training their dogs in a beginner class. They then discover that the organization offers more advanced training as well as different activities. You may find, for example, that in addition to obedience training, the organization also trains agility, perhaps even tracking, and that some of the members have therapy dogs, and so on. You might get bitten by the training bug, and if you and Buddy enjoy what you're doing, go for it.

Finding a Private Trainer

You may have serious time constraints, and so you may want to consider a private trainer. Private trainers aren't cheap, but it's better than not training at all. In selecting a private trainer, ask for references and call them. You also want to inquire into the trainer's experience.

After you've found a trainer, he usually does the training at your residence, which is an advantage because the trainer gets to see where and how Buddy lives, and can tailor a program to meet your special needs. But before you sign on the dotted line, watch how he interacts with Buddy and especially how he works him.

At some point you'll have to become involved and learn the various commands Buddy has learned and how to reinforce these commands. After all, the object is for Buddy to obey you, not just the trainer. You'll be expected to work Buddy under the trainer's direction so that you can learn what and how he was taught.

In selecting a private trainer, be choosy. This individual has a great impact on shaping your dog's skills. Don't be afraid to ask for references and to grill the trainer on his experience. Remember, anyone can declare himself a dog trainer!

Heading to Boarding School

When you outsource the job by sending your dog to a boarding school, Buddy will typically be boarded at the training facility for a specified period, such as three to six weeks.

Sending Buddy to boarding school isn't an option that we can strongly advocate. Why get a dog that you don't want to spend time? We view this option as one of last resort, when you absolutely can't make any other arrangements. For us, at least, it seems a contradiction of having a dog in the first place.

If boarding school is the only option for you, here are some things you need to look for. Before you take this step, inspect the facility.

- How are the dogs housed?
- Is it clean?
- How do the other dogs look?
- Ask for a demonstration.
- Trust your instincts — Buddy is your dog!

After your dog has completed the program, the trainer will then work with you for several sessions to show you how to get Buddy to respond to you. It's then your responsibility to keep up the training.

As an alternative to sending Buddy off for three to six weeks, you may want to consider a doggie daycare facility that also offers training. That way at least you can pick Buddy up in the evening and monitor his progress.

Enjoying The Great Dog Camp Adventure

All camps combine a vacation element, where you and Buddy can enjoy each other. If you feel you want to take a week's vacation with Buddy, where you can go have fun and learn more about dogs, training, or a particular activity, then dog camp is the place for you.

Dog camps have been around ever since we can remember. When we became serious about training and competing with our dogs, dog camps are where we went. They were great fun and invaluable learning experiences. In 1977, we started our own camps, and since then have conducted almost 100, in the United States, Canada, and England.

Most dog camps last from four to five days, and the number of participants can range from 20 to more than 100. A few of the distinguishing features are

- ✔ Some are highly structured, with each hour of the day filled with specific activities, while others are more loosely organized.

- ✔ Some camps are program driven, where you learn a particular approach to training, and others are activity driven, where you're exposed to a variety of things you and Buddy can do together.

- ✔ Some are designed for a particular activity, such as agility or obedience competition, and others are more general.

- ✔ Some require prior training experience, and others don't.

- ✔ Some include room and board in the tuition; others include only the camp itself.

- ✔ Some are held in full-fledged conference centers offering every conceivable amenity, others in more Spartan settings.

A good starting point for more information about dog camps is the Internet.

Part V
The Part of Tens

The 5th Wave   By Rich Tennant

@RICHTENNANT

Peterson's
PUMPKIN PATCH

CLOSED

DANGER
GOURD DOG
ON DUTY

In this part . . .

This part is packed with quick lists that you can read in a flash. Here you can find ten (okay, eleven) sporting activities that you and Buddy can share together, ten commands every dog needs to know, ten reasons why dogs do some of the things that they do, and ten or so tricks that will amaze and astound. Have fun!

Chapter 21

Ten (Okay, Eleven) Fun and Exciting Sporting Activities

● ●

In This Chapter

▶ Sharing sporting activities

▶ Trying some activities for fun and games

● ●

*I*n addition to obedience competition, you and your dog can participate in numerous other competitions and events. Some are for specific breeds, such as herding trials, and others are for all dogs, such as agility. Many are conducted under the auspices of the American Kennel Club (AKC), and some aren't, such as Schutzhund trials. Still others are for one breed, such as the Portuguese Water Dog rescue trials and the Newfoundland Club of America's Water Rescue and Draft Dog events.

The AKC awards more than 50 different performance titles in eight different categories. And other organizations have an almost equal number of titles.

- ✔ Obedience titles — 6, plus 5 Versatility titles, each consisting of an agility, obedience, and tracking title, Rally titles, and more
- ✔ Hunting Test titles — 4
- ✔ Field Trial titles — 2
- ✔ Herding titles — 6
- ✔ Tracking titles — 4
- ✔ Agility titles — 17
- ✔ Earthdog titles — 3
- ✔ Lure Coursing — 3

Obedience Competitions

Obedience competitions are one of the oldest performance events in which any breed registered with the AKC can participate. The AKC awards six obedience titles: Companion Dog (CD), Companion Dog Excellent (CDX), Utility Dog (UD), Utility Dog Excellent (UDX), Obedience Trial Champion (OTCh), and National Obedience Champion (NOC). (See Chapters 14 through 17 for requirements.)

In addition, the AKC has five Versatility titles. A Versatility title requires that the dog has earned an agility, obedience, and tracking title.

Agility Events

Agility is one of the AKC's newest events. It has experienced phenomenal growth over the last ten years, and with good reason: Dogs love it, competitors love it, and it has enormous spectator appeal. Agility competitions began in England and were then introduced in the United States by Charles ("Bud") Kramer in the early 1980s. Kramer was instrumental in its success as an activity in which all dogs could participate. He also developed the increasingly popular Rally Obedience (see Chapter 13).

After a slow start, the popularity of agility competitions exploded. It's an exciting and exhilarating sport for both handler and dog (see Figure 21-1). You may have already seen it on one of the cable television channels that specializes in televising dog events.

The AKC isn't the only organization that sponsors agility trials, but it now has the largest number of trials. Other organizations sponsoring agility trials are the United States Dog Agility Association (USDAA), which started it all, the Australian Shepherd Club of America (ASCA), and the North American Dog Agility Council (NADAC). There are also international agility competitions.

The dogs, under the direction of their handlers, negotiate a complex obstacle course that includes walking over a three- or four-foot-high plank, weaving in and out of a series of poles, jumping over and through objects, and going through tunnels. To compensate for the size differences among dogs and to make the competition fair, four height divisions exist. You and Buddy can earn nine AKC agility titles, as well as titles awarded by other organizations. The original four titles are shown in Table 21-1.

Figure 21-1:
Admiring
a dog in
action
during an
agility trial.

Table 21-1	The Original AKC Agility Titles
Title	*Requirements*
Novice Agility (NA)	Three qualifying scores under two different judges
Open Agility (OA)	Same
Agility Excellent (AX)	Same
Master Agility (MX)	Must have earned the AX title and then qualify ten more times

Other than the exercises themselves, there are some significant differences between agility trials and obedience trials. We outline the differences in Table 21-2.

Table 21-2   Differences between Agility and Obedience Trials

Agility	Obedience
Your dog has to be able to work on both your right and left side.	Your dog always works on your left side.
You have minimum time limits during which you and your dog have to complete the course.	There is no time limit (within reason).
The order in which the obstacles are to be negotiated varies, as do the obstacles.	The exercises and the order of the exercises are always the same.
Continuous communication with your dog is encouraged.	During your dog's performance of an exercise, you can't talk to your dog and can give only one command.

As with obedience, the level of difficulty increases with each higher class, as does the number of obstacles.

No doubt, part of the appeal of agility competition is its seeming simplicity. Almost any dog in reasonably good physical condition quickly learns the rudiments of the various obstacles. And, almost any handler who is also in reasonably good physical condition can compete in agility. But few things are ever as simple as they appear.

Beginning agility is deceptively simple, but it's not as easy as it looks. Because the courses you and your dog have to negotiate are never quite the same, there is a premium on your ability to communicate with your dog. Any lapses in communication invariably result in Buddy's failure to complete the course correctly. You're also competing against the clock and have to make split-second decisions. In addition, you need to memorize the course before you and your dog compete.

You can see what makes agility so exciting. The two of you really have to work as a team and keep your wits about you. We highly recommend that you try it. You'll be amazed how your dog will take to it. We aren't suggesting that you try to set up an agility course in your backyard — few of us have the wherewithal to do that. Find out from your local dog organizations where agility trials are being held and then take a look. Most communities have a group or an individual who has classes that meet on a regular basis where you and Buddy can get started. Even if you aren't interested in competing, agility courses are a good mental stimulation for Buddy, as well as good exercise for both of you.

Tracking Titles

The dog's fabled ability to use his nose and follow a scent is the basis for this activity. Any dog can participate, and if you enjoy tromping through the great outdoors in solitude with your dog, tracking is for you. Tracking is also the potentially most useful activity you can teach your dog. Many a tracking dog has found a lost person or lost article, not to mention the dogs that work in law enforcement.

Your dog's sense of smell is almost infallible. Local law enforcement often uses dogs to sniff out bombs, drugs, and other contraband. Researchers are even using them in cancer research to detect cancer in a person.

Buddy can earn three titles:

- ✔ **Tracking Dog (TD):** The track has to be at least 440 yards, but not more than 500 yards in length. A person lays the track 30 minutes to 2 hours before the event, and it has three to five turns. It doesn't have any cross tracks or obstacles.

- ✔ **Tracking Dog Excellent (TDX):** The track has to be at least 800 yards, but not more than 1,000 yards in length. The track has to be not less than three hours and not more than five hours old. It has to have five to seven turns. It has two cross tracks and two obstacles, such as a different surface or a stream.

- ✔ **Variable Surface Tracking (VST):** The track has to be at least 600 yards, but not more than 800 yards in length. Age of track is the same as for the TDX. It has to have four to eight turns. It has to have a minimum of three different surfaces, such as concrete, asphalt, gravel or sand, in addition to vegetation.

The principal differences between the classes are the age of the track and the surface.

Your dog has to complete only one track successfully to earn its title, unlike obedience or agility titles, for which three qualifying performances are required. You can also continue to compete at any level, even if you have earned your VST.

The basic idea of successful tracking is the dog's ability to follow the track layer's footsteps from beginning to end. A dog that veers too far away from the track and has obviously lost the scent is whistled off and doesn't qualify on that particular occasion.

Field Trials and Hunting Tests

Hunting tests and field trials are popular and test your dog's ability to demonstrate the function for which he was bred. They rival obedience and agility competitions in popularity. These events are for the pointing breeds, retrievers, spaniels, Beagles, Basset Hounds, and, you would never guess, Dachshunds. The tests are divided by type of dog and sometimes by specific breeds. Some of them, such as Beagles, work in groups of two, three, and seven or more.

The performance requirements vary, depending on the specific breed and the particular event. If Buddy is a Labrador Retriever, you and he can participate in both field trials and hunting tests, and the sky is the limit.

Earthdog Trials

These tests are for dogs bred to retrieve critters that live in tunnels or dens. The Dachshund, which translated means "badger hound," and the smaller terriers are eligible to participate in these competitions.

The object is to locate the quarry in a tunnel or a den. In the tests, rats, caged for their protection, or a mechanical, scented device, are used.

Tests are conducted at four different levels:

- First the dog takes an introductory test to see if he has any aptitude. There is no title for this test, but it's a prerequisite for a title.
- After the dog has passed the introductory test, he's eligible to compete for the Junior Earthdog (JE) title.
- Next is the Senior Earthdog (SE) title.
- Last is the Master Earthdog (ME) title.

Naturally, the level of difficulty increases with each title. As the levels progress, the distance from which the dog has to locate the den is increased and the tunnels that the dog has to encounter become more complex.

Earthdog trials are quite a specialized activity and explain the penchant these dogs have for redesigning the backyard. The instinct of terriers is to discover and root out the critters that live underground. This can lead to monumental "landscaping." Our Dachshunds are forever digging for moles or anything else that might be under the ground. Of course, anything recently planted must be immediately dug up just to make sure nothing edible has been buried.

Lure Coursing

An equally specialized activity is lure coursing, which is for the sight hounds. These dogs were bred to run down game over great distances. If you have ever seen a sight hound running flat out, you can appreciate how fast-paced and exciting lure coursing is.

In an AKC test an artificial lure is used, which the dogs follow around a course in an open field. Scoring is based on speed, which is blazing, enthusiasm, and endurance. Of course, it helps if the dog is actually chasing the lure and isn't off on a frolic of his own.

Again, the dog can earn three titles:

- Junior Courser (JC)
- Senior Courser (SC)
- Field Champion (FC)

Schutzhund Training

The word *Schutzhund* means "protection dog." After field trials, Schutzhund training is probably the oldest organized competition. It originated in Germany and is the progenitor of obedience exercises, tracking, and, to some extent, agility. It's hugely popular in Europe, but competitions are held worldwide. Although Schutzhund isn't an AKC performance event, it enjoys an avid following in the United States.

Schutzhund training is the progenitor of many of today's training activities. It dates back to the early 20th century, and many of its exercises have been incorporated into today's performance events.

It all began when the German Shepherd came to be used as a police dog. Billed as the only true multipurpose dog, he was expected to guard and protect, herd, track, be a guide dog for the blind and, of course, be good with children. Rigorous breeding programs were designed to cement these traits into the breed. Behavior was bred to behavior so that only those dogs with demonstrated abilities procreated. Looks weren't considered as important as ability.

As a police dog, a dog's main responsibility is to protect his handler. He also has to be able to pursue, capture, or track down suspects. Building searches require great agility, perhaps jumping into windows and negotiating stairs, even ladders. Naturally, he has to know all the obedience exercises.

It wasn't long before competitions began among and between police units to see who had the most talented and best-trained dog. Dog owners became interested and the sport of Schutzhund was born.

Schutzhund training consists of three parts:

- ✔ Protection
- ✔ Obedience
- ✔ Tracking

To qualify for a title, the dog must pass all three parts. When obedience and tracking were introduced in this country, they were patterned on the requirements for the Schutzhund dog. Agility competitions derived in part from the Schutzhund obedience exercises, which include walking over the A-frame as well as different jumps.

Schutzhund training, which is a rigorous and highly athletic sport and one of the most time consuming of all dog sports, isn't limited to German Shepherds. Other dogs of the guarding breeds that have the aptitude can participate. Even some of the nonguarding breeds can do it, although you won't see them at the upper levels of competition.

Flyball Competitions

Flyball is a relay race, with four dogs on a team, over four hurdles spaced ten feet apart to a box that holds a tennis ball. The dogs, each in turn, jump the hurdles, retrieve the tennis ball, and return over the hurdles. When the dog crosses the finish line, the next dog starts. The team with the fastest time wins, provided there were no errors, such as a dog going around one or more of the hurdles, either coming or going.

Flyball was invented in the 1980s and is a popular, extremely fast-paced competition. For information, click on the North American Flyball Association's Web site at www.flyball.org.

Freestyle Performances

Canine Freestyle is a choreographed musical program performed by a dog/handler team, sort of like figure skating for pairs. The object is to display the team in a creative, innovative, and original dance. In Freestyle, the performance of every team is different, although the various performances often share basic obedience maneuvers.

Started in the early 1990s as a way to bring some levity to obedience training, Freestyle has caught on like a house afire. Chances are you have seen it on one of the cable shows featuring dog activities. Freestyle is fun to watch and fun to train. For more information, see The World Canine Freestyle Organization's Web site at www.worldcaninefreestyle.org.

Skijoring

One way to describe *skijoring* would be cross-country skiing supplemented by dog power. Skijoring is an exhilarating winter sport in which a person wearing skis is drawn over snow by one or more dogs. The sport originated in Scandinavia and translated means "ski-driving." The dog is harnessed and a line is attached to the harness. The skier in turn attaches the line to a skijoring belt, which she wears around her waist. And off they go with the dog propelling the skier along. Any medium-sized dog (30 pounds or more) can participate — finally he has an outlet for his desire to pull. Of course, the skier can't expect the dog to do all the work and she has to actively contribute.

Skijoring can be divided into two general categories:

- **Recreational:** For owners who just enjoy being out with their dog
- **Competitive:** Such as Sprint Racing and Long Distance Racing

Would it surprise you that top sprint skijorers can reach speeds close to 30 miles per hour and that long distance races are sometimes as long as 320 miles? And here you thought your dog had a lot of energy. For more information, click on the North American Skijoring and Ski Pulk Association's Web site at www.nasspa.com.

Important Jobs that are Fun for Dogs

Okay, one more thing to add: We can't forget important tasks that well-trained dogs can perform! Earlier in this chapter, we describe a variety of recreational activities for you and your dog. But in this section, we take training and sporting a bit farther. Here we give you a brief overview of the many tasks that dogs perform for people who are unable to perform these tasks themselves. Listing such important tasks with dog sports and recreation may be a bit odd, but many dogs and their owners greatly enjoy performing these deeds and have the added satisfaction of providing a valuable service. You may want to look into them!

Service dogs

The term "service dog" was used to describe police dogs and dates back to the beginning of the 20th century. Training for this job started in Germany and the dog was, you guessed it, the German Shepherd. Dogs used in the military for various duties, such as guarding, reconnaissance, surveillance, mine detecting, and peace keeping, are called service dogs.

Detection dogs

After man discovered dog's incredible scenting ability, the detection dog was born. Humans have approximately 10 million olfactory cells, compared to a Labrador Retriever's 220 million and the German Shepherd's 200 million.

Dogs are now routinely used to detect drugs and explosives and search for victims buried in rubble and avalanches. The dog has even replaced the pig to hunt for truffles, probably because he isn't as inclined to eat the truffles he finds, as is the pig. Current experiments involve the use of dogs to detect cancer, giving new meaning to a "Lab" test.

Assistance dogs

Assistance dogs are used to help individuals in need. (See Figure 21-2.) The following include the main types of assistance dogs:

- **Guide dogs for the blind:** The use of dogs to assist blind individuals dates back to 1930, when the first training centers were started in England. Seeing-eye organizations tend to have their own breeding programs in order to cement the physical and behavioral traits necessary to become a reliable guide dog. Guide dogs undergo the most extensive training of any of the assistance dogs. The predominant breeds are German Shepherds, Golden Retrievers, and Labradors.

- **Dogs for the deaf and hearing impaired:** These dogs are trained to react to certain noises and to alert their masters. For example, jumping on the bed when the alarm clock goes on, tugging at his owner's leg when someone is at the door, or taking his owner's hand to alert him to the presence of an unexpected guest.

- **Dogs to assist the physically handicapped:** A good assistance dog for the handicapped can respond to about 50 different commands, such as retrieving objects that are out of reach or have been dropped, opening and closing doors, pulling wheelchairs, or turning light switches on and off. Excellent retrieving skills are a must (see Chapter 15 for how to teach your dog to become a reliable retriever). The majority of these dogs are Golden Retrievers and Labradors.

✔ **Therapy dogs:** The main purpose of the therapy dog and his handler is to provide comfort and companionship to patients in hospitals, nursing homes, and other institutions. The training is based on the Canine Good Citizen program (see Chapter 12), with some added requirements. Any well-trained dog with good social behavior skills can become a therapy dog.

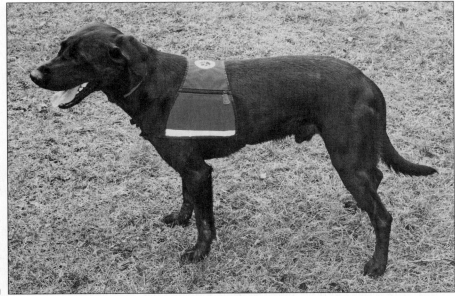

Figure 21-2:
You can recognize assistance dogs by their jackets.

In addition to their specialized skills, all assistance dogs play an important therapeutic role for their owners, especially children who have impairments that can cause them to become physically or emotionally withdrawn from society.

Companions

Most of you reading this book have a dog that serves as a pet and companion, a living being that is devoted to you, is always happy to see you, and doesn't argue or complain. What more could you ask for?

Chapter 22

Ten Basic Commands Every Dog Needs to Know

In This Chapter
▶ Figuring out commands for your dog's safety (and the safety of others)
▶ Mastering commands for your convenience (and the convenience of others)
▶ Remembering to *never* say no with your dog

*Y*our lifestyle dictates the commands most important for you and your dog, and you may not need all of them we include in this chapter. Nor does the order in which we list them necessarily reflect their relative importance to you. Chapter 7 contains the information you need to train Buddy to respond to these commands.

Sit — The Safety Command

Permitting Buddy to barge uncontrollably through doorways isn't a good idea — you may get mowed down in the process. Get into the habit of making Buddy sit before you open a door. After he sits, it doesn't matter whether you release him to go through first, or whether you go first and then release him, so long as he sits until you tell him it's okay to move.

Similarly, make him wait before you go up or down stairs, or get in and out of the car.

Sit — The Convenience Command

The "Sit" command lets you control Buddy during periods of excitement, such as the happy greeting when you return home, when visitors arrive, and when you're about to take him for a walk and want to put his collar and leash on. "Sit" is also the easiest way to stop Buddy from jumping on people.

One question we frequently are asked is, "He doesn't jump on me anymore, but how do I get him to stop jumping up on visitors?" Our advice is to enlist the help of friends and neighbors to train Buddy. Show the visitor how to induce Buddy into a Sit with a treat and the command, and then reward him with a treat. Ask as many people as you can to help you. It won't take Buddy long before he'll sit on his own in front of a visitor in expectation of his treat. At that point, you no longer need to give him a treat every time he responds correctly. A "good dog" with a scratch under the chin will suffice.

Stay

You use the "Stay" command when you want Buddy to remain in one position — Sit, Stand, or Down — until you tell him he can move again. Generally, the length of time you want him to stay in position is relatively short, no more than five to ten minutes. The key to its value is that he has to learn to stay until you release him. After he gets into the habit of releasing himself, the command has lost its usefulness. One example of when to use this command is when you feed your dog. Before putting his bowl down, tell him to "Sit" and "Stay." Put his bowl down, count to five, and then release him with "Okay."

Go Lie Down

Telling your dog to "Go Lie Down" is another command of convenience. During mealtimes, you don't want Buddy hanging out by the table. The "Go Lie Down" command tells him to chill out in his favorite spot until you're done, or when you have guests and he insists on making a nuisance of himself.

Come

"Come" is as much a command of convenience as of safety. You need this command any time you want Buddy to come to you for whatever reason — after he has enjoyed a nice romp in the park or when he is chasing a cat. Unless he responds reliably to the "Come" command, you need to keep him on leash in situations where he might be a danger to others or himself.

Easy

We use the "Easy" command when we don't want Buddy to pull on the leash. This command is useful for anyone who walks, jogs, or bicycles with his dog as a form of exercise. Use the same technique for pulling on the leash described in Chapter 8. Say "Easy" before you make your turn and continue walking. We also use "Easy" to teach our dogs to take treats from our hand without the alligator imitation.

Give

The "Give" command is useful for taking something out of Buddy's mouth that you don't want him to have and that he doesn't want to give up. The object can be anything, from one of your favorite possessions to the piece of meat he has just stolen off the counter.

Our favorite way of getting Buddy to give up whatever he has in his mouth is to trade — we offer him a treat in exchange for what he has in his mouth. If he has food, you may have to offer him something of equal value, such as a frozen chicken wing. We keep these in our freezer at all times because we use them as special treats. Of course, sometimes you don't have a treat handy, in which case you just have to open his mouth and remove the object.

Off

"Off" is a commonly used command for getting the dog off the furniture. The command is also frequently used to stop dogs from jumping on people, although "Sit" is a better choice because it's more specific.

Whether you allow your dog on the furniture is a matter of personal preference. You can certainly train him to stay on the floor, at least as long as you're in his presence. Chances are, however, that when you're gone, he'll settle on his favorite couch only to quietly slide off when he hears you coming home.

For those individuals who are adamant about keeping the dog off the furniture, there are several options:

✔ Don't give him the run of the house.

✔ Place a broomstick on Buddy's favorite chair or couch while you're gone. The broomstick works well with most dogs, although we know of instances where the dog simply removed the stick.

✔ Invest in one or more *Scat Mats*. Scat Mats come in different sizes and are designed to keep dogs and cats off the furniture by giving the animal a slight electric shock when it steps on it. The intensity of the shock can be regulated.

Scat Mats are also used to restrict access to a room or part of the house. Again, the device isn't foolproof, because some dogs figure out that they can jump over the mat.

The latest entry into pet containment approaches is the Innotek Instant Pet Barrier (www.innoteck.net). This device uses the same principle as the outdoor electronic fence to confine the dog within a certain room or area within the house.

Leave It

"Leave It" is another common command that tells the dog to ignore whatever interests him at the time. The object of his interest can be a cat, another dog, a person, or something on the ground.

No "No" Command

Our least favorite command is "No." We prefer to tell the dog exactly what it is we want him to do with an action command, such "Come," "Sit," or "Down." When the dog responds, we can then praise him by telling him how good he is.

"No" is nebulous, negative, and overused, and most of the time doesn't give the dog any specific instruction or directive. Worse yet, "No" doesn't generally lend itself to being followed by praise. For example, Buddy wants to jump on you, you yell "No," and he stops. Can you now praise him? No, because he may still be thinking about jumping on you and praising him encourages him to try again, not the message you want to give.

All in all, eliminate the word from your communications with Buddy. Of course, in an emergency, you do what you have to.

Chapter 23

Ten Reasons Why Dogs Do What They Do

In This Chapter

▶ Explaining some of your dog's curious behaviors

▶ Looking at a few behaviors you may wish they didn't have

....

*W*ho knows why your dog does some of the things that he does? Or more important, who *wants* to know why your dog does some of the things that he does? Well, if you're curious, this chapter offers answers to a few of these critical questions.

Why Do Dogs Insist on Jumping on People?

The behavior goes back to the weaning process. As puppies grow, the mother dog begins to feed them standing up, so puppies have to stand on their hind legs to feed. Then, as her milk decreases, the puppies jump up to lick at the corner of her mouth, trying to get her to regurgitate her semidigested meal. When she does, it's the puppies' first introduction to solid food.

As dogs grow, jumping becomes more of a greeting behavior, as in, "Hi, good to see you," much like people shake hands when they meet someone. Because the behavior is so instinctive, modifying it is sometimes difficult. Although you're probably pleased that your dog is happy to see you, you'd also probably prefer a more sedate greeting, especially if Buddy is a large dog. And, because jumping up on people is a friendly gesture, we suggest modifying the behavior in a positive way (see Chapter 7).

Why Do Dogs Sniff Parts of Your Anatomy That You'd Prefer They Didn't?

When two dogs meet each other for the first time, they often go through what looks like a choreographed ritual. After some preliminaries, they sniff each other's respective rear ends and genitals. Dogs "see" with their noses and gather important information in this way. They can identify the dog's gender, age, and rank order, information that dictates how they interact with each other.

When meeting a new person, a dog wants to know that same information. Some are confirmed "crotch sniffers," while others are more subtle. Although embarrassing for the owner and the "sniffee," the behavior is harmless enough and easily remedied with the "Sit" command.

Why Do Male Dogs Lift Their Leg So Often?

All dogs *mark* their territory by leaving small amounts of urine, the male more so than the female. You can liken it to putting up a fence; it lets other dogs in the neighborhood know he has been there. The scent enables dogs to identify the age, gender, and rank order of every dog that has marked that spot.

When you take Buddy for a walk, he intently investigates various spots and then lifts his leg to deposit a few drops of urine to cover the area, thereby reclaiming his territory. Male dogs also have a special fondness for vertical surfaces, such as a tree or the side of a building. Corners of buildings are a special treat. Height is important because it establishes rank. Comical contortions can be the result, such as when a Yorkshire Terrier tries to cover the mark of a Great Dane. Females don't seem to have that need, which explains why they can do their business in a fraction of the time it takes a male.

Both males and females may also scratch at the ground and kick the dirt after urinating to spread their scent, thereby claiming a larger amount of territory.

Why Do Dogs Mount Each Other?

Both female and male dogs can display mounting behavior. More normally associated with males trying to flirt or breed a female, this behavior can be seen male to male, female to female, and female to male. Most people think it has to do only with sex, but it can be a dominance display with dogs of the same gender — the one on top reminding the other who is in charge — or it can be a behavior that is displayed when dogs that know each other well have been separated for some time. The behavior is then a form of bonding, like a hug, meaning, "I missed you." Instead of discouraging this behavior, we have found it better to leave the dogs alone; they work things out well between themselves. They have to, because they're pack animals and know exactly the message they're trying to convey, usually to bring harmony back into the household.

The only time this mounting behavior can be construed as abnormal is if a female has some vaginal discharge indicating some sort of infection, which smells as if she is in season. In that case, other dogs won't leave her alone, and a visit to the vet is the appropriate remedy.

Why Do Dogs Like to Chase Things?

Dogs chase things for a variety of different reasons:

- ✔ To chase intruders, be it people or other animals, off their property
- ✔ To chase a potential meal, such as a rabbit, squirrel, or chipmunk
- ✔ To chase just because the object is moving, such as cars, bicycles, or joggers
- ✔ To chase because it's fun

Whatever the reason, chasing usually isn't a good idea because it can endanger the safety of people and the dog. Unless you're prepared to keep Buddy on leash under circumstances where he is likely to chase, you need to train him to come when called (see Chapter 8).

Why Do Dogs Roll in Disgusting Things?

Dogs delight in rolling in the most disgusting stuff, such as dead fish, deer droppings, and similar decaying debris. To make matters worse, the urge to roll seems strongest just after Buddy has had a bath. Do dogs like to smell putrid?

Behaviorists believe that because the dog is a pack animal, he is merely bringing back to the pack the scent of possible food sources. The pack can then track down a meal. The behavior is instinctive. Most dogs roll at one point or another, some to a greater extent than others. It's just part of being a dog.

Why Do Dogs Eat Weeds or Grass?

Dogs come with many instinctive behaviors. One of those behaviors is the incredible knowledge of what weeds to eat and when. One reason a dog eats grass is to induce vomiting. He may have eaten something that disagrees with him, and the grass goes into the stomach and binds whatever it contains, which is then expelled. It's an adaptive behavior that protects the dog against indigestion and food poisoning. As a result, dogs that have access to the right kind of grasses, those with wide, serrated edges, rarely get food poisoning. Another reason dogs eat grass, wheat grass, for example, is as a digestive aid.

Dogs have an infallible knowledge of which weeds to eat. These weeds are often the very same that are found in capsules in the health food store to boost immune systems or any other body system. Should you stop your dog from eating weeds? Absolutely not! He knows much better what he needs than you do. Just make sure you don't expose your dog to areas that have been sprayed with chemicals.

Dogs also seem to have a sense of the medicinal value of various plants. When one of our Newfoundlands became arthritic, he would seek out the large patch of poison ivy we have on our property. During our daily walks, he would make it a point to stand in that patch for a few minutes, eat the grass that grew there, and then move on. At first we couldn't understand his behavior. We subsequently discovered that *Rhus Tox,* a homeopathic remedy for achy joints and rheumatism, is made from poison ivy.

Why Do Dogs Eat Disgusting Things?

Good question.

Why Do Some Dogs Scoot on Their Rear Ends?

Once in a while, your dog may appear to be sitting and then suddenly drag himself around on his front paws, with his rear end on the floor. It looks as if he is trying to clean his rear. This can mean that his anal glands — small scent sacks just inside the rectum — are full and need emptying. When they need emptied, you need to take him to your vet so she can express the glands. With some breeds, these small glands have to be emptied a couple of times a month. With other breeds, you never see this behavior.

Another reason for this behavior is tapeworms. The segments of worm are pushed out through the rectum and irritate the dog. To rid himself of the segment, he'll scrape his rectum on the carpet or on the grass outside. If you think your dog has worms, visit your vet and let her make a diagnosis.

Why Do Dogs Show Nesting Behavior?

Around eight or nine weeks after a female has come out of season, you may see her digging around her bed, turning in circles, collecting toys and putting them in her bed, and guarding the area from other animals and maybe even yourself. She's preparing a nest for her puppies. Sometimes even spayed females exhibit this behavior, and it's often accompanied by swelling of the mammary glands that may actually fill with milk.

In the wild, female dogs in a pack, even if they weren't pregnant or didn't have puppies, developed milk. This phenomenon ensures the survival of the litter in case something happens to the mother dog.

Chapter 24

Ten (or So) Tricks
for Fun and Gains

*E*very well-trained dog knows a trick or two that can impress friends and family alike. Tricks you can teach your dog can be simple or complex, depending on your dog's drives and your interest.

One of the more astonishing tricks, at least until you know how it works, requires a reliable retrieve on command. Others require no more than a simple "Stay," but to the uninitiated, they're equally astonishing. This chapter offers just a few to get you started.

For this chapter, we're indebted to Mary Ann Rombold Zeigenfuse, one of the lead instructors at our annual training camps and the trainer of President George H. W. and Barbara Bush's dog Millie. She wrote *Dog Tricks: Step by Step* (Howell Book House, Inc.), thereby keeping alive the tradition of anyone who has ever had anything to do with the White House, no matter how remote, becoming an author.

The Trick to Successful Tricks

The trick to teaching tricks is sequencing. *Sequencing* means breaking down what you want to teach your dog into components small enough for the dog to master, which lead up to the final product. For example, if you want to teach your dog to shake hands, also known as High Five, start by taking Buddy's paw in your hand with the command you want to use and then praise and reward him. Next, offer your palm, and so on.

When you decide on the kind of tricks to teach Buddy, keep in mind his Personality Profile (see Chapter 5). Tricks like High Five or Roll Over are easiest with dogs low in fight behaviors and not so easy with those high in fight behaviors. A dog high in fight behaviors wouldn't stoop so low — it's beneath his dignity.

Tricks learned quickly by dogs low in fight behaviors include

- ✔ High Five
- ✔ Roll Over
- ✔ Play Dead

Tricks learned quickly by dogs high in prey behaviors are

- ✔ Find Mine, such as keys, wallet, or whatever (dog must know how to retrieve)
- ✔ Jump through Arms or Hoop

Tricks learned quickly by dogs high in pack behaviors include

- ✔ Don't Cross This Line or Stay until I Tell You
- ✔ You Have Food on Your Nose

When you see Buddy do something that could turn into a trick, such as Sit Up and Beg, reward it and work on getting him to do it on command.

High Five

The object is to teach Buddy to raise one front paw as high as he can on command. This exercise has four sequences.

Your goal for Sequence 1 is to introduce your dog to the concept of the exercise: Shake hands.

1. **Sit your dog in front of you.**

2. **Reduce your body posture by kneeling or squatting in front of your dog so that you're not leaning or hovering over him.**

3. **Offer him your palm at mid-chest level and say, "Shake" or "Gimme Five," or whatever command you want to use.**

4. **Take the elbow of his dominant front leg and lift it off the ground about two inches.**

   (If you don't know your dog's dominant side, he'll quickly show you.)

5. **Slide your hand down to the paw and gently shake.**

6. **Praise enthusiastically as you're shaking his paw.**

7. **Reward with a treat and release him with "OK."**

8. **Repeat this sequence five times over the course of three sessions to get your dog used to this exercise and to hearing the command.**

When teaching your dog to shake and when you offer him your palm, reduce your body posture by either kneeling or squatting so that you don't lean or hover over him.

Your goal for Sequence 2 is for your dog to lift his paw.

1. **Sit your dog in front of you and reduce your body posture.**

2. **Offer your palm with the command "Shake."**

   Pause. You're looking for some sort of response. If nothing happens, touch his elbow and offer your palm again. Give him the chance to lift his paw.

3. **When he lifts the paw on his own, take the paw, enthusiastically praise, reward, and release.**

4. **If *nothing* happens, take his paw, praise, reward, and release.**

You'll find that as soon as you offer your palm, your dog will put his paw in it without waiting for the command. When this starts to happen, teach him to give you the other paw by saying "The Other One." (See the next section for more info on "The Other One.")

Stay with this sequence until your dog is lifting his paw off the ground on command so that you can shake it.

Your goal for Sequence 3 is to put his paw into your palm.

1. **Sit your dog in front of you and reduce your body posture.**

2. **Offer your palm at mid-chest level and say "Shake."**

   At this point, he should put his paw on your palm. Praise enthusiastically, reward, and release.

3. **If nothing happens, go back to Sequence 2.**

Stay with this sequence until your dog readily and without hesitation puts his paw on your palm.

Finally, your goal with Sequence 4 is to raise his paw as high as he can.

1. **Sit your dog in front of you and reduce your body posture.**

2. **Offer your palm at his chin level and say "Shake."**

   By now your dog should readily and without hesitation put his paw into your hand. When he does, praise, reward, and release. If not, go back to Sequence 3.

3. **Raise your palm, in two-inch increments, until you have reached your dog's limit. (If you have a Yorkie, you're done.)**

   After several repetitions, your dog will stretch his paw as high as he can. Praise, reward, and release.

The Other One

This trick is an extension of Shake, which is part of the High Five exercise in the preceding section. It follows the same sequences, except you want your dog to give you the other paw. What you'll see happening is that as soon as you offer your palm, your dog will give you his paw without waiting for the command.

You're going to use the same sequences as in the High Five exercise except that you'll point directly at the leg you want the dog to lift, that is, the other one, and you'll use a new command, such as "The Other One," or whatever. Buddy will soon figure out the difference, because he won't get the treat unless he gives you the correct paw.

You can now impress your friends and neighbors with how clever Buddy is.

Roll Over

Roll Over is always a great favorite. It requires the dog to lie on the floor and completely roll over sideways. As a prerequisite, the dog must know how to lie down on command (see Chapter 7).

Roll Over is always a crowd pleaser. You can easily teach most dogs that know the "Down" command and respond to a treat.

Your goal with Sequence 1, the first of three sequences, is to get your dog to roll over with a little help from you.

1. **Place your dog into the Down position, either with a command or a treat.**

2. **Reduce your body posture by kneeling or squatting in front of your dog so that you're not leaning or hovering over him.**

3. **Hold the treat in such a way that your dog has to look over his shoulder while lying on the ground.**

4. **Say "Roll Over" and slowly make a small circle around his head, keeping the treat close to his nose.**

5. **With your other hand gently help your dog roll over in the direction you want him to go.**

   When the dog has completely rolled over, enthusiastically praise, reward, and release.

6. **Repeat until your dog is completely relaxed with you helping him roll over.**

Your goal for Sequence 2 is for your dog to roll over on his own.

1. **Place your dog into the Down position, either with a command or a treat.**

2. **Reduce your body posture.**

3. **Say "Roll Over" and get him to follow the treat without any help from you.**

   When he does it, praise, reward, and release. If not, go back to Sequence 1.

4. **Repeat until your dog rolls over with a minimum of guidance on your part.**

Your goal in Sequence 3 is to get your dog to roll over on command.

1. **You don't have a treat in your hand, but be prepared to reward immediately when you get the correct response.**

2. **Say "Down" and then "Roll Over."**

   The first few times you do this, you may have to use the same hand motion as though you had a treat in it. Praise, reward, and release when your dog does it.

3. **Reduce the hand motion until he does it on command alone.**

4. **Praise, reward, and release.**

After your dog has mastered the trick, he'll offer this behavior anytime he wants a treat. Unfortunately, you can't reward him for that — he's now training you to give him a treat on demand. Instead, go to random rewards when he does the trick on command.

Play Dead

This trick is an old favorite and a logical extension of Roll Over. You can easily teach it to dogs low in fight behaviors. If your dog is high in fight behaviors, don't waste your time.

It consists of aiming your index finger and "firing" at your dog with a command such as "Bang," and your dog falls on his side or back and plays dead.

The goal of Sequence 1 is to get your dog to lie down on his side or back.

1. **With a treat in your "gun" hand, down your dog.**

2. **Lean over your dog and in a deep tone of voice say "Bang" as you point your index finger at him.**

   If he is high in flight behaviors, he'll roll on his side or back.

3. **Praise and give him a treat while he is in that position and then release him with "OK."**

   If he doesn't roll on his side or back, use the treat as you did for the "Roll Over." Then praise, reward, and release.

4. **Repeat this sequence until your dog responds to the "Bang" command.**

Your goal in Sequence 2 is for your dog to play dead from the sitting or standing position.

1. **Get your dog's attention by calling his name.**

2. **Lean over your dog and in a deep tone of voice say "Bang" as you point your index finger at him.**

   If he lies down and plays dead, praise, reward, and release. If not, show him what you want by placing him in the "dead" position. Praise, reward, and release.

Practice this sequence until he responds to the "Bang" command from the sitting or standing position.

Sequence 3 is when your dog plays dead at a distance.

1. **With your dog about two feet from you, get his attention by using his name and give the "Bang" command as you point your finger at him.**

   If he responds, praise, go to him, reward him, and then release. If not, show him what you want and start all over.

2. **Gradually increase the distance to about six feet.**

This last sequence goes quickly because your dog has learned to respond to the "Bang" command and signal. You can then gradually increase the time between his response and the praise, reward, and release to 30 seconds. After that, start giving the reward on a random basis.

Teaching Buddy tricks that use his natural tendencies is generally easier. If your dog has a quirky habit, you may find that you can turn it into a fun trick. When you see a behavior you want to turn into a trick, tell your dog how clever he is and give him a treat. For example, when you see Buddy do a play bow (front legs down and stretched out in front of him, rear leg standing up), and you want to turn the behavior into a trick, praise him when you see him do it and give him a treat. Next, give the behavior a command, such as "Take a bow," and when you see him do it, give the command, praise, and reward. It won't take long before Buddy responds to the command. Another example is "Sit up and beg," which is a favorite of one of our Dachshunds who sits up and begs any time she wants a treat. She is now rewarded only rarely for the behavior, but that doesn't stop her from trying.

Find Mine

The Find Mine trick is one of the most impressive tricks you can teach Buddy. It combines the Retrieve with the dog's use of his nose to discriminate between different articles. It's a terrific parlor trick that will astound and amaze your friends.

The goal of Sequence 1 is for your dog to retrieve something of yours, such as your keys.

1. **Get a leather or plastic key fob and put some keys on it.**

   Using something leather or plastic makes it easier for the dog to pick up and carry it.

2. **Get your dog excited about the keys and throw them a few feet in front of you with the command, "Find Mine."**

   When he brings them back, praise, reward, and release. If he doesn't, review the first few sequences of teaching the retrieve (see Chapter 12).

3. **Repeat until your dog readily brings back your keys.**

A dog's ability to differentiate between scents is far more acute than yours. Dogs can be taught to identify any number of objects by scent, including underground gas leaks.

Your goal in Sequence 2 is for your dog to find your keys.

1. **Tell your dog to "Stay" and with him watching you, place the keys in the corner of an armchair or couch.**

2. **Go back to your dog and send him with the "Find Mine" command.**

   Praise, reward, and release.

3. **Repeat several times, each time changing the location slightly, so Buddy gets used to looking for the keys.**

Your goal in Sequence 3 is for Buddy to find your keys by using his nose. This sequence is the heart of the trick and the real fun part.

1. **Tell your dog to stay and without him watching, place the keys on the floor, just inside the doorframe of another room.**

2. **Go back to your dog and send him with the "Find Mine" command.**

   What you want him to do is to find your keys by retracing your steps and then using his nose to locate the keys.

Over the course of several sessions, make the Find Mine game increasingly difficult. For example, a fairly advanced search would involve you going into one room, coming out again, and going into another room and putting the keys behind a wastebasket. Anytime he gets stuck, help him by showing him where you placed the keys. Remember to praise and reward correct responses, although you no longer have to do it every time.

The goal in Sequence 4 is for your dog to discriminate between objects (see Chapter 17).

For many years, this has been our favorite trick. Like any good trick, it's baffling if you don't understand how it's done, yet childishly simple for the dog.

It starts with the knowledge that a dog's nose is far more powerful than a human's, and that he's able to discriminate between different scents. He can certainly tell the difference between you and anybody else. Armed with this knowledge, you're ready to fleece anyone gullible enough to take on Buddy.

1. **Crumple up a dollar bill, place it on the ground and have your dog retrieve it with the "Find Mine" command.**

2. **Have a helper, such as a family member, also crumple up a dollar bill.**

3. **Place the bills on the floor about six inches apart and send your dog with the "Find Mine" command.**

   At this point the odds are better than 50 percent that he'll bring back your dollar bill. If he does, praise and reward. If he brings back the wrong one, just take it from him and send him again to get the correct one.

4. **Repeat until you're sure he's using his nose to identify your dollar bill.**

5. Have your helper add another bill.

Each time your dog is successful, have your helper add another bill, until there are a total of ten bills from which to choose. While Buddy is learning this trick, he will occasionally make a mistake and bring back a wrong bill. Take it from him and send him again with "Find Mine." Reward every correct response. You'll need to replace the wrong bill that the dog brought back — it now has his saliva on it.

The fun part comes when you change the denomination and get other people involved. Say you have a half-dozen visitors. During a lull in the conversation you say, "Did you know that our dog can tell a twenty dollar bill from a single?" Of course, nobody is going to believe you. So, you take out a twenty and ask if "anybody has any ones?" Crumple up your twenty and have the others crumple up their singles. Then have Buddy do his number.

A variation is to ask for someone else's twenty with the understanding that if your dog retrieves it, you get to keep it. Naturally, you can only handle that twenty and the person who gave it to you can't contribute any singles. Good luck!

Jumping through Arms or Hoop

A hula hoop makes a wonderful prop for this trick, in which you first teach your dog to jump through the hoop and then your arms. Start by getting a hoop commensurate with your dog's size.

The goal of Sequence 1 is that your dog jumps through the hoop on leash.

1. **Lay the hoop on the ground and take your dog over to examine it.**

2. **Put your dog on leash and walk him over the hoop.**

3. **Pick up the hoop and let the bottom edge rest on the ground.**

4. **Thread the leash through the hoop and encourage your dog to jump through with "Jump."**

   You can use a treat to get him to walk through the hoop. Repeat until your dog readily goes through the hoop with the "Jump" command. Praise, reward, and release for successful tries.

5. **Thread the leash through the hoop and raise it a few inches off the floor.**

   If necessary, use a treat to get him through and then enthusiastically praise. As your dog gains confidence, begin raising the hoop in two-inch increments until the bottom is eye level in front of him.

The goal of Sequence 2 is to get your dog to jump through hoop off leash.

1. **Take the leash off and present the hoop in front of your dog with the bottom no higher than the dog's knees.**

2. **Say "Jump" and let the dog jump through.**

   Praise and reward with a treat. Repeat but change the position of the hoop so that the bottom is level with the dog's elbows, and then his shoulder. How high you can raise it depends the athletic ability of your dog.

   Keep in mind that as soon as you get to about shoulder level (the dog's, not yours), you need a surface with good traction on which the dog can take off and land. Wet grass and slippery floors aren't good surfaces for this trick, unless you want your dog featured on a funniest home video show.

3. **Teach your dog to jump as you pivot in a circle with the hoop.**

   Pivot slowly at first and then increase speed, but never so fast that the dog loses interest or can't keep up.

Finally, Sequence 3's goal is achieved when your dog jumps through your arms.

1. **Review having your dog jump through the hoop at his shoulder level several times and then put the hoop away.**

2. **Squat down and let your dog see you put a treat at the spot where he is going to land.**

3. **Make a circle with your arms out to the side.**

   Keep the upper part of your body upright.

4. **Tell your dog to jump and when he does, tell him how clever he is.**

   Going around you to the treat is considered bad form, and you need to pick up the treat before he gets it. Then try again. It won't take him long to figure out the only way to the treat is through your arms. Stop after he has been successful.

Keep working on this trick until your dog jumps through your arms every time you make the circle.

Don't Cross This Line

This trick is an extension of door and stair manners (see Chapter 7). Its most useful application is to keep the dog out of one or several rooms in the house, either temporarily or permanently.

Because Don't Cross This Line is a good review of door and stair manners, remember that you have to release your dog to go through doors or up and down stairs. If you get lax about it, your dog will start releasing himself, thereby defeating the object of the training.

The goal of Sequence 1 is to review door manners on leash.

1. **Use the "Stay" or "Wait Until I Tell You" command.**

   Put your dog on leash.

2. **Walk toward the front door, say "Stay," and open it.**

   Make sure the leash is loose and that you aren't holding Buddy back. If he starts to cross the threshold, check on the leash to bring him back in.

3. **Close the door and start all over.**

   Because you may have already taught him to sit at the door before you release him, this review on leash will go quickly.

4. **Repeat until he begins to hesitate crossing the threshold.**

The goal of Sequence 2 is that your dog learns to cross the threshold with your permission.

1. **Walk toward the front door, say "Stay," and open the door.**

2. **Briefly hesitate and then say, "OK" and cross over the threshold with your dog.**

With Sequence 3, your goal is for you to go through the doorway and your dog not.

1. **Approach the door and open it.**

2. **Say "Stay" and go through the doorway.**

   If he tries to follow, pull him back by extending your arm through the door and then close the door on the leash.

3. **Open the door, but don't let him come out yet until you say "OK," and then praise.**

Your goal in Sequence 4 is to review Sequences 1 through 3 coming back into the house.

You have to release your dog to go through doors or up and down stairs. If you get lax about it, your dog will start releasing himself, thereby defeating the object of the training.

You can now apply the same principle to one or more rooms in the house. As a trick, you can teach it to your dog by drawing a line on the ground and using the line as a threshold. After your dog understands the basic principle, he'll catch on to anything you don't want him to cross.

You Have Food on Your Nose

This one is a cute trick. It involves balancing a piece of food on Buddy's nose until you say "OK." Some dogs even toss it in the air and catch it on the way down.

Your goal in Sequence 1 is to be able to cup your hand over your dog's muzzle. If you have taught your dog to retrieve, he already knows this.

1. **Sit your dog and pet him for a few seconds.**

2. **Cup your hand over his muzzle from the top, just as you do for the Retrieve (see Chapter 15).**

3. **Kneel or squat in front of your dog and keep your upper body straight.**

   With your other hand hold a treat near your dog's nose and get him to focus on the treat.

4. **Release with "OK" and give him the treat.**

   You need to be able to hold his muzzle so that you can put a piece of food on his nose.

5. **Repeat until you can cup his muzzle and he focuses on the treat.**

The goal in Sequence 2 is to put the treat on his nose.

1. **Gently hold his muzzle and put the treat on the dog's nose in front of your thumb.**

2. **Tell him to "Stay" or "Wait," and then release him.**

   The treat will either fall off or get bounced into the air.

Sequence 3's goal is to increase the time he balances the treat.

1. **Start by holding his muzzle and placing the treat on his nose.**

2. **Say, "Stay" and have your dog balance the treat for ten seconds, and then release him.**

3. **Repeat and increase the time to 20 seconds.**

With Sequence 4, your dog should balance the treat without help from you.

1. **Put the treat on his muzzle and then slowly let go of his muzzle, reminding him to "Stay."**

2. **Get him to focus on your index finger by holding it in front of his nose.**

3. **Wait a few seconds and release your dog.**

You can now gradually increase the time he holds the treat before you release your dog, as well as gradually increase the distance of your finger from the dog's nose.

What if he drops or tosses the treat before you said "OK"? Well, if you can't get to the treat before he does, reduce the time and distance until he is reliable again and then you can increase them.

Take a Bow

Performers customarily take a bow after a performance to accept the applause of the audience. This trick teaches your dog to take a bow after he has performed the tricks you've taught him.

For this trick your dog has to know the "Down" and the "Stand" commands. (Review the progressions for teaching the "Down" command in Chapter 7, and the progressions for teaching the "Stand" command in Chapter 14.)

The goal of Sequence 1 is to show Buddy what you want him to do.

1. **Stand your dog at Heel position.**

   With a small dog, you can teach this trick on a table. (Check out Chapter 8 for more info).

2. **Place your left hand, palm facing down, under your dog's belly with a little backwards pressure against his hind legs.**

3. **Place your right hand through the collar under his chin.**

4. **Say, "Take a bow" and apply a little downward pressure on the collar.**

You want Buddy to lower the front end and remain standing with the rear end. If he can't grasp the concept, use a treat to get him to lower his front end, keeping your left hand in place to keep the rear end standing. When you're successful, praise and release.

Practice until he lowers his front end on command with minimal downward pressure on his collar. Praise enthusiastically after each successful repetition.

Sequence 2's goal is for Buddy to lower his front end without your hand through the collar.

1. **Stand your dog, keeping your left hand under his belly.**

2. **Say, "Take a bow" and pat the ground in front of him with your right hand.**

When he lowers his front end, praise and release. Practice several times until he responds to the command without you patting the ground.

The goal of Sequence 3 is for Buddy to take a bow on command.

1. **Stand your dog, point to the ground in front of him with your left hand, and say, "Take a bow."**

   When he does, praise and release. If he tries to lie down, prop up his rear end with your left hand. Practice until you no longer have to prop up his rear.

2. **Finally, when he takes a bow on command, say, "Stay" and release him after several seconds.**

   Be prepared for your audience's applause.

Index

• E •

• S •